# Critical Thinking
## A Functional Approach

JAMES D. THORNTON
P.O. BOX 4454
BURLINGTON, VT 05406

# Critical Thinking
## A Functional Approach

**Eugene B. Zechmeister**
Loyola University of Chicago

**James E. Johnson**
Loyola University of Chicago

 Brooks/Cole Publishing Company
Pacific Grove, California

**Brooks/Cole Publishing Company**
A Division of Wadsworth, Inc.

© 1992 by Wadsworth, Inc., Belmont, California 94002.

Printed in the United States of America
10   9   8   7   6   5   4   3   2   1

**Library of Congress Cataloging-in-Publication Data**

Zechmeister, Eugene B.
    Critical thinking : a functional approach / Eugene B. Zechmeister,
James E. Johnson.
        p.     cm.
    Includes bibliographical references and index.
    ISBN 0-534-16596-6
    1. Critical thinking.    2. Decision-making.    3. Causation.
    I. Johnson, James E.        . II. Title.
    BF441.Z43    1991
    153.4′3—dc20                                        91-18045
                                                        CIP

Sponsoring Editor: *Vicki Knight*
Editorial Assistant: *Heather Riedl*
Production Editor: *Penelope Sky*
Manuscript Editor: *Barbara Salazar*
Permissions Editor: *Marie DuBois*
Interior and Cover Design: *Sharon L. Kinghan*
Art Coordinator: *Cloyce J. Wall*
Interior Illustration: *Fran Hughes (illustrations) and Roger Knox (figures)*
Typesetting: *Bookends Typesetting*
Printing and Binding: *Malloy Lithographing, Inc.*

To John, Dan, Liz, Peter, Katie, and Kathy

**E. B. Z.**

To Betty, Jim, Amy, Eric, and Shannon

**J. E. J.**

# Preface

Many people are likely to agree that an ability to think critically is worth developing. We would even predict a consensus on the idea that critical thinking can be taught, that it is more than the product of inborn dispositions and talents or the result of maturation. Yet, when questions are raised about what critical thinking really is, and about the ways one might go about teaching it, disagreements emerge. Plans to encourage critical thinking often sputter for lack of clear direction or because they become entangled in a mesh of abstract concepts. A goal that most people would agree is worth pursuing, the development of critical thinking skills, thus may not be attempted because of confusion surrounding definition and disagreement over methodology. By taking a practical, some might say operational, approach to the development of critical thinking, we have tried to cut through these abstract issues and to give students practical and effective tools they can use to enhance their ability to think critically in everyday situations.

At a practical level, critical thinking is effective, adaptive thinking. It is functional in that it *works* to help resolve the many everyday problems and dilemmas we encounter. Critical thinking generally is about problem solving and decision making. When the American educator and philosopher John Dewey referred to this process as reflective thinking, he meant the evaluation of evidence, and the formation of a plan to solve a problem or an explanation to remove a perplexity. As Dewey also emphasized, however, the development of critical thinking depends first on an attitude (a disposition) to gather and evaluate evidence carefully. A critical thinker must exhibit a *readiness* to be reflective. One way to develop this readiness, or willingness, to respond in a thoughtful and careful manner is to demonstrate the need for critical thinking. We can show that people frequently are biased in their evaluation, interpretation, and communication of evidence. They must be alert, in other words, to the possible illusions, distortions, and misconceptions they entertain because of limited cognitive processing abilities and the biases and attitudes that they bring to a situation. Once alerted, people can look for ways to guide their thinking. Thinking can be guided by principles (rules, frames, strategies) that are both salient and relevant to one's everyday experiences. We have operationalized critical thinking by presenting such principles and showing how they may be applied effectively in everyday thinking.

## • • • • • • • • •
## To the Instructor

Our emphasis is on everyday problems and experiences that are part and parcel of everyday living, and from which examples may be drawn to teach effective principles of reasoning and problem solving. Thus our approach is both practical and functional. A functional approach to everyday critical thinking is seen in the arrangement of topics. Many everyday problems involve questions of causality. In fact, we all tend to seek causal explanations for things. Relevant causal issues include those having to do with the reasons for our own and others' behavior, because most of our everyday problems concern ourselves and significant others. After the introductory Chapter 1, therefore, our starting point for developing critical thinking is this natural concern with causal attribution (Chapter 2). We proceed to discuss causal attributions about others' behavior (Chapter 3) as well as our own (Chapter 4).

The formation of plans and theories, which is a primary characteristic of the process of critical thinking, depends on searching for and finding relevant information. Critical thinking, in other words, proceeds from a good knowledge base. Thus we must be willing to examine what it is that we know, how we came to know it, and how our biases and frequently applied heuristics effect what we know (or think we know). In Chapters 5 and 6 we deal with ways to think more critically about what we believe and what it is that we know (and don't know). Students will learn in Chapter 6 how to evaluate critically what they know, and also will find many practical suggestions for improving learning and retention.

Finally, our plans and theories must be put to the test. We must be able to find out whether they work to resolve a dilemma or solve a problem. In Chapters 7 and 8 we emphasize the ubiquitous processes of problem solving and decision making, which are typically the objectives of critical thought. However, having an effective plan or theory often is not enough. We frequently have to convince others of the value of our plan and resist attempts to dissuade us from our approach. Even the best plans must be sold to others and defended against opposing arguments. In Chapter 9, we discuss effective principles of reasoning and argumentation. Finally, in Chapter 10 we integrate the student's experience and provide a framework for continuing to apply what has been learned.

Practice in applying thinking skills is necessary. It should include evaluation and feedback regarding the successful application of skills in many exercises emphasizing real issues. In keeping with a practical approach to the development of critical thinking, real-life problems with outcomes that matter should be emphasized. We believe that abstract brain teasers are of little use unless the problem solver is led to see the relevance of this kind of analysis to everyday situations. Examples and exercises should be chosen with attention to their applicability in the real world. Consequently, each chapter contains many opportunities to respond to problems and ideas discussed in the text. The exercises headed "Think about It" (TAI) require active reflection, and feedback is available at the end of each chapter. By emphasizing familiar topics and experiences, these sections begin the important process of transferring thinking skills to everyday domains.

## How to Use This Book

Although the book is directed to anyone who wishes to enhance his or her critical thinking skills, it is most appropriate for first- or second-year college students. It will be valuable to instructors who wish to introduce students to the practical value of scientific research on human cognition. We show how ideas derived from psychological research can be used to enhance everyday thinking. This approach is helpful to students in a variety of courses that emphasize the development of thinking skills: freshman seminars, and courses in educational and cognitive psychology, critical thinking, and management and leadership among others.

Students should need little guidance in using this book. The many "Think about It" sections require students to respond actively to the ideas and problems we have presented. By conscientiously working on these exercises and seeking feedback at the end of each chapter, students not only can practice applying critical principles or concepts but also will be in a position to evaluate their progress toward understanding these ideas and concepts. At the end of the major chapters are suggestions for additional reading about the topics we have discussed. As we emphasize in the final chapter (Chapter 10), the acquisition of critical thinking skills is a lifelong process. Students who have been encouraged to take their first steps toward developing their thinking skills systematically will, we hope, want to enhance them further by reading more about the ideas and topics we have introduced.

## Acknowledgments

Our first words of gratitude go to those students who have patiently listened as we tried out our ideas about critical thinking in our classes. It is because of their critical feedback that we have been able to develop our ideas about critical thinking. We also owe thanks to many colleagues who listened as we talked informally about the ideas expressed in these pages and who kindly read and commented on earlier versions of the book. We are particularly grateful to Dan O'Connell, S. J., Georgetown University; Ruth Maki, North Dakota State University; John Shaughnessy and David Myers, Hope College; Homer Johnson, Emil Posavac, and Tricia Tenpenney, Loyola University of Chicago; and Stanley Nyberg (where are you, Stanley?).

Special thanks are due to Fran Hughes, whose artwork enlivens the pages of this book. Through her drawings she was able to make clear what we often had trouble conveying in words. Elizabeth Zechmeister did admirable work on the indexes.

Our approach to critical thinking has been shaped by the many insightful comments of reviewers at all stages of this effort. We thank the following people for giving their time and attention to this project: Dr. Arthur Hendrickson, University of Minnesota at Duluth; Dr. Michael Bergmire, Jefferson College; Dr. Ann Dirkes, Indiana University; Dr. Ann Wilke, University of Missouri at Saint Louis; Dr. Michael Bradley, Motlow State Community College, Tennessee; Dr. Gordon Pitz, Southern Illinois University at Carbondale; Dr. Diane Van Blerkom and Dr. Malcolm Van Blerkom, University of Pittsburgh at Johnstown; Dr. Harvey Switzky, Northern Illinois University; Dr. Scott Tindale, Loyola University of Chicago; Dr. John Ruch, Mills College, California; Dr. Gretchen Chapman, The Wharton School of the University of Pennsylvania; and Dr. James Bell, Howard Community College, Maryland.

Finally, although books are written by the authors, they find a place on a bookshelf only because of the combined efforts of various editors who get the project and the authors together. Deborah Laughton started us running, and Phil Curson helped keep us moving, but the finish line was reached mainly because of the talents and interest of Vicki Knight. We also value the contributions of Penelope Sky, Barbara Salazar, Sharon Kinghan, and Marie DuBois. Vicki, the only regret we have is that you did not liberate us from a midwest winter to caucus at your office near the Pacific Ocean in California.

*Eugene B. Zechmeister*
*James E. Johnson*

# Contents

# Critical Thinking
## A Functional Approach

PART

1

# INTRODUCTION

# Critical Thinking:
# What Is It?
# Can It Be Learned?

Humans "are but reeds, the most feeble things in nature; but they are thinking reeds."

Blaise Pascal
(17th-century French mathematician and philosopher)

## • • • • • • • • •
# Introduction

*MacGyver,* a network television show introduced in the 1980s, centers on the adventures of a hero by that name. We admit to being fans of MacGyver, though we're not sure what he does for a living. Is he a private investigator, a secret agent, a retired physics professor? Either we never were told or we missed that episode. It doesn't really matter; MacGyver always shows up when people are in trouble. He catches crooks, finds missing persons, and saves the world from the plotting of evil types. All rather standard fare. Occasionally, however, he judges a science fair or steps in to coach a college hockey team on its way to a championship. Not so standard fare.

If you're acquainted with MacGyver, you'll probably know why he is one of our favorite people. For MacGyver is one of those people who survive by their wits. As far as we know, he doesn't own a gun; we've never seen him use one. He does own a Swiss Army pocket knife, which he uses in ingenious fashion to save his own neck and the necks of others. Consider one episode we saw.

MacGyver is held prisoner in a French winecellar after he had been captured by international jewel thieves. He is certain to be killed because he knows the whereabouts of millions of dollars' worth of missing jewels, and of course by this time he knows the identities of the bad guys. The main door to the cellar is guarded, but as the thieves prepare to kill his close friend, he devises a plan to use cylinders of compressed nitrogen to turn a wine barrel into a jet-propelled missile. He lashes the cylinders to the cart that holds the wine barrel. When he releases the compressed nitrogen, he thinks, the wine cart may move fast enough to break through a brick wall. It's a "basic law of physics," says MacGyver. The audience's reaction at this point, as judged by the preteens we observed, is "Good thinking!" Perhaps we should have mentioned that MacGyver knows a lot about electricity, physics, and science in general; viewers of an earlier generation no doubt see him as something of a youthful Tom Edison on the road.

The producers of *MacGyver* are trying to get across the idea that "good thinking," rather than fighting, stealing, and other less socially desirable approaches, is the answer to life's problems. Not a bad premise, in our view. By the way, the jet-propelled cart works and MacGyver gets free to catch the thieves and recover the jewels. Did you ever doubt?

## • • • • • • • • •
# What Is Critical Thinking?

We often have no trouble recognizing good thinking, perhaps because it stands out from the usual kind. Good thinking, or what we will term critical thinking, is, as one observer wryly commented, different from the kind of thinking that most of us habitually do (Nickerson, 1987). And what is it that most of us don't habitually do? Critical thinking has been said to involve three principal elements (Glaser, 1985, p. 25):

1. An *attitude* of being disposed to consider in a thoughtful, perceptive manner the problems and subjects that come within the range of one's experience.
2. *Knowledge* of the methods of logical inquiry and reasoning.
3. *Skill* in applying those methods.

You see now why we like MacGyver!

Having a proper attitude cannot be emphasized enough. The well-known early-twentieth-century philosopher and educator John Dewey once wrote that if he were compelled to choose between a proper attitude toward reasoning and the knowledge of the principles of reasoning, he would choose a proper attitude (Glaser, 1985, p. 27; Dewey, 1933). Dewey also emphasized that attitudes and knowledge go together in a good thinker, and that we need to work to weave them into "unity." In order to be a critical thinker we must be aware of the right principles, but this knowledge will be for naught unless we are disposed (inclined) to be thoughtful and perceptive.

Developing the proper mental attitude isn't necessarily easy. Like many things in life that are good for us, and that we may even be disposed to do—exercising, dieting, reading—becoming a critical thinker may require us to make changes in our customary ways of doing things. We have to cultivate good thinking just as we might cultivate a healthy body. And, like a good physical fitness program or a serious regimen of study in a major discipline, a program to improve thinking requires discipline. The American automaker Henry Ford supposedly once quipped that "thinking [and we assume he meant the critical variety] is the hardest work there is, which is why so few people engage in it." Two writers closely associated with the topics of critical thinking and educational reform put it this way:

"Thinking is natural, but unfortunately, critical thinking is not." However, they continued: "It is a skill capable of being perfected. It is also a matter of degree. No one is without any critical skills whatsoever and no one has them so fully that there are no areas for improvement" (Walsh & Paul, 1986, p. 13).

The need for critical thinking, according to the astronomer Carl Sagan, is linked to

nothing less than our survival—because baloney, bamboozles, bunk, careless thinking, flimflam and wishes disguised as facts are not restricted to parlor magic and ambiguous advice on matters of the heart. Unfortunately, they ripple through mainstream political, social, religious and economic issues in every nation. Finding the occasional straw of truth awash in a great ocean of confusion and bamboozle requires intelligence, dedication and courage. But if we don't practice these tough habits of thought, we cannot hope to solve the truly serious problems that face us—and we risk becoming a nation of suckers, up for grabs by the next charlatan who comes along. (Sagan, 1987, p. 13)

## Developing a Disposition to Think Critically

If we accept the idea that we should be inclined to be thoughtful or perceptive about the problems that confront us, exactly how do we go about it? How does a critical thinker behave? You might take your cue from people you know who are "good thinkers"—that is, people whom you respect for their ideas, reasoning, and insight. We've already mentioned one of our favorites. Consider someone who in your eyes is a good thinker. You might think about a friend, a teacher, a parent, or a government leader.

How would you rate that person on the following characteristics? Consider carefully the description of each trait and the examples of this kind of behavior before doing your rating. You might want to rate your critical thinker on a scale from 1 (poor) to 5 (excellent).

1. *Intellectual curiosity:* seeking answers to various kinds of questions and problems.

    Does this person ask interesting questions? have a "need to know"? delight in new experiences? like to read up on things?

2. *Objectivity:* using objective factors when one makes decisions and avoiding being influenced by emotional or subjective factors.

    Does this person remain cool when making decisions? look at the evidence and not the person? refrain from getting caught up in the emotional aspects of an issue?

3. *Open-mindedness:* being willing to consider a wide variety of beliefs.

    Does this person look at both sides of an issue? consider all views and not just the views of a few? seek an unbiased judgment?

4. *Flexibility:* exhibiting a willingness to change one's beliefs or methods of inquiry.

    Does this person avoid a dogmatic or rigid stance? remain open to compromise? try different approaches to a problem?

5. *Intellectual skepticism:* not accepting a conclusion as being true until adequate evidence is provided.

    Does this person avoid accepting "the obvious"? exhibit a show-me quality? challenge views for which the evidence is weak?

6. *Intellectual honesty:* accepting statements as true even when they don't agree with one's own position.

    Does this person seek all the evidence, both pro and con? really try to understand another person's viewpoint? support the truth even when it goes against his or her own position?

7. *Being systematic:* following a line of reasoning consistently to a conclusion.

    Does this person avoid irrelevant issues? arrange an argument in a logical fashion? look for a conclusion that follows directly from the evidence?

8. *Persistence:* being persistent in seeking to resolve disputes.

    Does this person stick to it? exhaust all possible lines of evidence? continue looking for an answer when others have given up?

9. *Decisiveness:* reaching a conclusion when the evidence warrants it.

    Does this person come to a conclusion? act on the evidence? follow through on a decision to act?

10. *Respect for other viewpoints:* willingness to admit that you are wrong and that others may be right.

    Does this person respect others' ideas? accept good arguments or solutions presented by others? identify his or her own viewpoint as one of several possible viewpoints?

These are the attitudes necessary for the development of a critical thinker (D'Angelo, 1971, pp. 7–8). As you can see, a disposition to approach problems in a thoughtful way is really multifaceted; we must cultivate a variety of behavioral traits if we are to be critical thinkers. An examination of this list of important dispositions, which is by no means exhaustive (see, for example, Ennis, 1987), reveals that we have our work cut out for us.

---

**THINK about It**

**1.1**   Now that you have characterized that friend or teacher in terms of these personal traits, it is time to analyze yourself. How do you rate in terms of Edward D'Angelo's (1971) characteristics of a good thinker?

Answer the following questions about *your* approach to problems and subjects that come within the range of your experience. You may need to refer back to the text in order to remind yourself about the specific behaviors that each of these traits represents. To answer each question, we suggest that you use a 5-point scale, where 1 = not at all or weak; definitely needs improvement, and 5 = yes, very much so; needs no improvement.

|  | **Circle one** | | | | |
|---|---|---|---|---|---|
| 1. Do I exhibit intellectual curiosity? | 1 | 2 | 3 | 4 | 5 |
| 2. Am I objective? | 1 | 2 | 3 | 4 | 5 |
| 3. Am I open-minded? | 1 | 2 | 3 | 4 | 5 |
| 4. Is my thinking flexible? | 1 | 2 | 3 | 4 | 5 |
| 5. Do I show intellectual skepticism? | 1 | 2 | 3 | 4 | 5 |
| 6. Am I intellectually honest? | 1 | 2 | 3 | 4 | 5 |
| 7. Am I generally systematic? | 1 | 2 | 3 | 4 | 5 |
| 8. Am I persistent? | 1 | 2 | 3 | 4 | 5 |
| 9. Do I exhibit decisiveness? | 1 | 2 | 3 | 4 | 5 |
| 10. Do I show respect for others' views? | 1 | 2 | 3 | 4 | 5 |

We suggest how you may use your answers to work on becoming a better thinker at the end of the chapter.

The doctrine of formal discipline stated that studying math and classical languages developed critical thinking.

## Critical Thinking: Can It Be Learned?

The philosopher Plato is credited with stating the doctrine of formal discipline, which holds that the study of difficult subjects, such as mathematics and Latin, will train the mind for effective thinking and problem solving (Nisbett, Fong, Lehman, & Cheng, 1987). As this idea progressed through the nineteenth century, curricula of many schools came to consist mainly of courses in languages (Latin and Greek) and mathematics; courses thought to emphasize only content were excluded. Thus, in this view, someone who learned to conjugate Latin verbs in their many complex forms (*amo, amas, amat,...*) was thought to have developed a shrewder mind than someone who escaped such mental exercise.

As others have pointed out (for example, Nisbett et al., 1987), modern psychology provided evidence that tended to discredit the doctrine of formal discipline, and contemporary theories of training critical thinking shy away from the idea that the brain is a "mental muscle" that one can strengthen merely by engaging in rigorous mental activity (for example, Bransford, Sherwood, Vye, & Rieser, 1986).

We believe that critical thinking can be developed by means of principles (rules, frames, strategies) that are both salient and relevant to "the problems and subjects that come within the range of one's experience" (Glaser, 1985, p. 25). The emphasis is on strategies or tactics of thinking (see also Perkins, 1986, 1987). These principles guide thinking; that is, they give thinking direction (Zechmeister, 1989). Of particular importance are those principles and rules that are called upon in the course of solving everyday problems (Nisbett et al., 1987). Thus we advocate an experiential approach to critical thinking, one that seeks to develop effective thinking by identifying principles that are helpful in everyday affairs. This approach permits us to talk about thinking strategies in the context of situations and problems with which most people are familiar. The relevance of these principles should then be readily apparent. Also, by drawing on common everyday experiences, we are able to build upon the natural repertoire of thinking strategies we all possess—that is, principles that we already know and that typically help us in everyday situations.

## Guided Thinking

Some of the important thinking principles with which you are already familiar are ones you have learned through trial and error or by modeling the actions of others. Consider the strategy you are likely to follow when you lose something—say, your wallet or purse. Most people work on the principle of "retrace your steps." In your mind, and perhaps even overtly, you retrace your activities after the last point at which you remember having the missing object in your possession. This principle no doubt has served you, we hope successfully, more than once.

Other familiar principles are peculiar to specific domains and probably were learned through direct instruction. A domain is simply an area or field of thought. We might talk, for example, about domains of mathematics, of science, of baseball, or of dating. You are acquainted with a myriad of domains, and whether you realize it or not, you already know many principles of effective thinking in these domains. For instance, think about the rules of good paragraph organization. Somewhere along the educational road someone taught you that an effective principle for writing a good paragraph is to write a topic sentence and then elaborate on the topic. This principle, which may be somewhat more detailed than we have described it, is no doubt one that you have used on numerous occasions when you were called upon to compose your thoughts about a subject and express them on paper. It guides the mental activity associated with composition.

You may have been introduced in junior high to the *FOIL* principle of expanding binomials. To illustrate this principle, consider how you might perform the following operation:

$$(a + b) \times (a - b) = ?$$

We were taught to multiply First positions (*a* times *a*), then Outside positions (*a* times negative *b*), then Inside positions (*b* times *a*), and, finally, Last positions (*b* times negative *b*), to get $a^2 - ab + ab - b^2$, which reduces to $a^2 - b^2$. Even

Behavior can be guided by keeping certain key principles in mind.

if you were not exposed to *FOIL*, perhaps you can still see our point. *FOIL* is a principle that effectively guides behavior and makes thinking easier and more efficient in the domain of algebra.

You probably have found yourself searching for effective thinking strategies whenever you have attempted to teach a new activity to someone. It is not an easy task to make difficult concepts clear, especially those that come naturally to you because you have practiced or rehearsed them so often. Consider, for instance, something that you do very well. It might be an athletic endeavor (volleyball?), a hobby (crocheting?), an academic subject (understanding biology?), or something as simple as getting along with your family dog. Now assume you have the job of teaching this activity to someone else. What are some of the things that you might say to orient that person to this task? Chances are, you will attempt to guide her by identifying some important principles to keep in mind as she does the task, principles that you once had to concentrate on but that now are probably second nature to you.

Because we are proficient in none of the activities we have mentioned (although one of us does own an ornery dog), let us illustrate our point by referring to the domain of golf. Not that we are proficient at golf, either, but we would like to be. We recently came across a book that aims to help improve your golf game. Co-authored by Jack Nicklaus, one of the world's most successful professional golfers, this book takes an "effective thinking principles" approach to golf, although it isn't actually identified as such. The book introduces the struggling golfer to "ten basics" of a good golf swing. These are principles that the golfer is asked to think about as he grasps the club and swings it with the goal of hitting that little ball in the direction of a hole. The first principle is "swing the same with every club." Even if you aren't very familiar with the game of golf, you are probably aware that it's played with a wide assortment of clubs—drivers, short irons, long irons, wedges, and so on. A novice seeing this display of clubs might try a different swing with each type of club, swinging through with some and holding up on others. Knowing this first principle allows one to pick up each club and practice the same swing. We're looking to see the effect on the golf course.

Whether the game is golf or life in general, once the right disposition is in place, effective thinking can be aided by the application of important thinking principles or strategies. For example, a major part of our everyday thinking involves reasoning about the causes of physical events as well as of people's behavior, a process that is called *causal attribution.* It is natural for people to strive to achieve a coherent interpretation of the events that surround them, and they do so by organizing events in such a way that one event is seen as the cause of another (Tversky & Kahneman, 1980). Thinking about the causes of things, in other words, helps to make the world meaningful and predictable. For this reason, in order to think critically about people and events, we need to be aware of important principles of causal attribution—that is, principles to help us decide what events are relevant to a particular behavior or other event.

To illustrate one such principle, consider the following fact. When we observe other people's behavior, we tend to underestimate the situational influences on their behavior and to overestimate the influence of personal dispositions. We tend, in other words, to blame the person and not the circumstances. This type of thinking is called the *fundamental attribution error.* It is often the basis for the hasty conclusions we sometimes draw about the people around us (Ross, 1977). The fundamental attribution error is discussed more fully in Chapter 3, when we deal at length with principles of effective thinking about the causes of behavior. We discuss it briefly here in order to demonstrate how knowledge of certain principles can guide your thinking about everyday problems of human behavior.

A student in one of our classes fell victim to this causal attribution error. She was upset that her young son was sometimes unresponsive to her and on occasion, for what seemed no apparent reason, was angry toward her. She felt that something must be wrong with him and was worried that he didn't like her. Initially, then, she attributed the problem to her son. After learning about attribution processes and thinking about the fundamental attribution error, she began to think more critically about the environmental events surrounding her child's anger. She discovered that her son's moodiness and anger usually surfaced after he had been watching television for a while. Unfortunately, mild depression is not unusual in some children after they watch TV for lengthy periods or when their favorite TV shows are interrupted. Circumstances, not a personal trait, were to blame. The fundamental attribution error also may lead us to explain the behavior of political leaders in terms of their "enormous power"—more power than they may in fact possess (for example, Tedeschi, Lindskold, & Rosenfeld, 1985). Note that we are not saying that personal dispositions are never causal; rather, what is important to recognize when we think about the reasons for people's actions, whether those people are our children or our leaders, is that we often lean toward personal as opposed to environmental attributions. To think critically about behavior, it helps to be aware of this bias. The principle we want to keep in mind as we observe others' behavior is: Be careful not to underestimate the situational influences on a person's behavior and to overestimate personal dispositions.

**THINK about It**

**1.2**   Look over the following list of activities. Select one or more with which you have had enough experience so that you consider yourself more than a beginner at the activity. Write down one or more critical principles that someone should keep in mind while performing this activity. To help you get started, at the end of the chapter we share an important principle that we learned about the first activity, shopping for bargains. You might want to look at this example before beginning the exercise.

Select from:
    shopping for bargains
    dating
    shooting free throws
    lighting a fire
    flying a plane
    driving a car on an expressway
    stopping blood flow from a wound
    fixing a leaky faucet
    riding a skateboard
    memorizing a list of facts
    writing a poem
    playing a video game

Activity: _____

Suggested critical principles: _____

_____

_____

Do you think your critical principles will be similar to those of another "expert"? You might consider comparing your suggestions with those of someone else who is proficient in your activity.

• • • • • • • • •
# A Functional Approach to Developing Critical Thinking

At this point, we hope that you have found our argument about the nature of critical thinking at least mildly convincing. We are not alone in saying that a disposition or inclination to approach problems and issues in a thoughtful and perceptive way must be established first. With this disposition in place, we must seek to learn and apply effective principles or tactics that are relevant to those problems and issues. In this way, our thinking will have direction; it will be guided and not aimless or wandering, as it sometimes is when we day-dream or associate freely about ideas or events. But what principles and tactics should we learn? And how do we learn them?

In our view, the principles or strategies that should be emphasized are those that permit us to think critically about the problems and issues that we typically encounter. The most important principles are those that work for us in our everyday experiences; they must, in other words, be functional. An assumption we make is that although the *specific* problems or subjects we encounter each day are numerous and varied, effective solutions or resolutions often depend on the knowledge and use of a few basic principles of critical thinking. For example, you already have been introduced to the fundamental attribution error, a kind of *mis*thinking that arises when we consider the causes of a person's behavior. Knowledge of this principle is relevant to thinking critically about the many different activities and behaviors of people we meet each day. Why is our roommate mad at us? Why does our employer change our work schedule at the last minute? When we think about the answers to these different kinds of problems, we want to consider both situational and personal influences, and to be careful not to exaggerate personal influences over those that are specific to the situation. When President Bush ordered U.S. troops to the Middle East in 1990, was he attempting to demonstrate his personal power as the president or was he caught up in a whole system of attitudes and economic policies associated with this situation? Knowledge of the fundamental attribution error should function to guide our thinking about the answers to such questions (although it may not deliver a definite answer).

The same everyday thinking that we typically use to make causal attributions about human behavior is called upon when we have to solve problems and make decisions. Consider the problem of choosing a career. The cognitive act of choosing whether or not to go to college in order to prepare for law school, or to attend vocational school to become an electrician, or to follow some other occupational path, are examples. Making a decision about one's future career is something that we can assume everyone does at least once, and very likely more than once in the course of a lifetime. An appropriate decision should take into account the limits and potential of a particular situation, as well as one's aptitudes, interests, and resources. There is an infinite list of such decisions—what television set to buy, what car to drive, whom to marry, what religion (if any) to belong to, and so forth. Every one of these questions requires the ability to consider in a thoughtful and perceptive manner those elements that impinge on this decision; all require an ability to think critically. When you have learned the principles of effective problem solving and decision making, you will be in a position to make the many everyday decisions as well as the once-in-a-lifetime choices. Some of these principles are discussed in Chapters 7 and 8.

Our approach, therefore, is to develop critical thinking in the context of the kinds of problems and subjects that everyone is likely to experience. Critical thinking skills are necessary in every domain, of course, whether it be math, automotive repair, science, history, language learning, plumbing, fashion design, or English composition. Should you be interested in any of these particular subjects, we hope you will have the opportunity to learn specific principles, such as *FOIL* in the domain of math, to guide your thinking in these particular areas. In this book we emphasize principles and tactics that are more broadly relevant, that apply in general to these many domains as well as to common everyday problems. The need to think critically about the causes of someone's behavior, to find a good solution to a problem, to make a good decision in the face of conflicting evidence—such experiences are familiar both to the plumber and to the scientist. These are experiences you have had as well.

## The Organization of This Book

Principles of critical thinking are organized in accordance with the cognitive activities associated with understanding, knowing, and deciding about everyday experiences. We understand something when we can identify its causes. As we indicated earlier, forming causal attributions about events, about the behavior of people, and even about our own behavior is a large part of our everyday thinking. In Part One of the book we examine some of the problems and biases associated with causal attribution. This section will also introduce you to some effective principles to guide your thinking when you make causal inferences.

In Part Two we discuss the bases for many of our beliefs and provide effective principles for acquiring new knowledge. What, for instance, contributes to superstitious behavior? to belief in astrology? Do we really know what we think we know? or do we often believe we know more than we do? What are effective principles of learning and remembering new information?

In Part Three we consider how to use information effectively to solve problems and to make decisions about the proper course of action in situations of uncertainty. Deciding what is "best" in a situation is often a difficult task. Knowledge of appropriate tactics for solving problems and for making good decisions is necessary if you are to be a critical thinker. It is also important to know how to construct a good argument and to detect flaws in the arguments presented to you. In Chapter 9, we introduce effective principles of argumentation. These principles will guide your thinking when you are called on to convince others of the appropriateness of a solution to a problem or a course

of action to take, as well as when others are trying to convi
ticular course of action.

## How to Use This Book

Understanding people and events, assessing what it is that we know and don't
know, solving problems and making decisions, and convincing others are complex tasks. It's no wonder that evidence of *un*critical thinking is so easy to obtain. In the following pages you will find principles and strategies to help you
with the difficult job of everyday thinking. To use them effectively you must
be willing to participate actively in this process. As you read the material in
the following chapters, try to do so in the thoughtful and perceptive manner
that, as you have seen, is characteristic of a critical thinker.

The text is frequently interrupted by questions and exercises calling on you
to "think about it" (TAI). You have already met two of these exercises. At the
end of each chapter, we provide answers or analyses appropriate to each exercise.

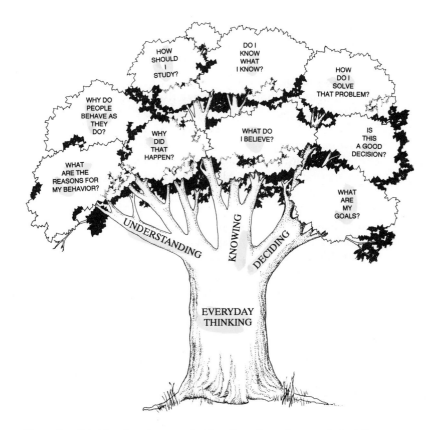

Everyday thinking involves understanding, knowing, and deciding.

Thinking about answers to these exercises is hard work, and it takes time. But so do most activities aimed at self-improvement, such as developing a healthy body or becoming proficient in an academic discipline. Moreover, the consequences of *not* working to develop an ability to think critically can be costly, just as costly as the consequences of *not* working hard to stay healthy or to succeed in a course of studies. How many times have you paid a price for an incorrect decision, for the inability to solve a problem, or, generally, for a mistake in thinking? Although working to become a good thinker is often difficult and takes time, it may not be as hard or as time-consuming as continually dealing with the consequences of not working to be a better thinker.

Did you take the time to become actively involved in the exercises in this chapter? If you did tackle these exercises, we hope you found that thinking about them can be interesting, even fun. You will find many opportunities to "think about it" as you progress through this book. By being disposed to consider these problems and exercises in a thoughtful and perceptive manner, you will be taking an important step toward becoming a better thinker. Should you wish to explore further the topics discussed in this book, suggestions for additional reading follow the discussion of the exercises at the end of each chapter.

## • • • • • • • • •
## Think about It: Discussion of Answers

**1.1**   To paraphrase an observation made earlier: Thinking skills, including the dispositions that characterize the mental posture of a critical thinker, are a matter of degree. No one is without any critical skills whatsoever and no one has them so fully developed that there are no areas for improvement.

Thus, if you answered 5 to more than a few (some people might say any) of these questions, you missed an important point about those traits that characterize a critical thinker. Although all of us show these traits to some degree, all of us can stand improvement. The goal of this exercise is to help you begin to think critically about your critical thinking. By examining those areas where you indicated a 1 or 2, or perhaps even 3, you should begin to see where you might begin to make an effort to develop your critical thinking posture.

At the risk of starting an argument, we urge you to consider asking someone who knows you well (and who exhibits the trait of objectivity) to rate you on each of these dimensions. Unfortunately, we don't always see ourselves the way others do (a topic, incidentally, of Chapter 4). Perhaps the truth is somewhere in between the objective person's view and your own.

**2.2**   A principle to keep in mind when you shop for bargains is this: If it sounds too good to be true, it probably is. We have tried to teach this principle to our preteens, who sometimes get over-excited about a "bargain" they have seen advertised on TV or in the newspaper. Thinking about this principle should lead them to look carefully at the supposed bargain and ask important questions about the quality and actual price of the product or offer. No doubt there are many other effective principles that are relevant to thinking critically when one shops for bargains; this illustration should get you started thinking about them. Now it's your turn.

## •••••••••
## Recommended Readings

Several good overviews on the development of critical thinking are available. A concise yet exceptionally good introduction is a monograph by Albert Benderson (1984) titled simply *Critical Thinking*. A somewhat longer monograph prepared by Joanne G. Kurfiss (1988), and also called *Critical Thinking*, examines the "theory, research, practice, and possibilities" of critical thinking in higher education. We are especially sympathetic to the "frames" approach to developing critical thinking outlined by D. N. Perkins (1986) in "Thinking Frames." At a somewhat more sophisticated level, we recommend Joan Bogkoff Baron and Robert J. Sternberg's (1987) edited volume, *Teaching Thinking Skills: Theory and Practice*. A particularly good way to stay current with trends and problems in the field of critical thinking is to subscribe to the periodical *Teaching Thinking and Problem Solving* (Hillsdale, N.J.: Erlbaum). This publication also contains announcements of regional and national conferences related to the development of critical thinking.

The works cited throughout Chapter 1 (and other chapters) may also, of course, be consulted for additional information. Complete references to these works and to the recommended readings are listed at the end of the book.

# UNDERSTANDING EVENTS, PEOPLE, AND OURSELVES

# Thinking about the Causes of Things

Happy are they "who have been able to perceive the causes of things."

Virgil
(Roman poet)

● ● ● ● ● ● ● ● ● ● ● ● ● ● ● ● ● ● ● ● ● ● ● ● ● ● ● ● ● ● ● ● ● ● ● ● ● ● ● ● ● ● ● ● ● ● ● ● ● ● ● ● ● ● ● ● ● ● ● ● ● ● ● ● ● ● ●

Much of our everyday thinking is about cause-and-effect relationships. Few of us have not asked about the causes of an illness, such as depression, about the reasons why so many young people drop out of school, about the causes of our own happiness. Causal reasoning helps us to make sense of the world and is the basis for many of our important decisions. We learned as children about the causes of things, and as a consequence we felt safer. As adults we also find that knowing the causes of things can reduce anxiety by allowing us to navigate safely in a world strewn with problems. In this chapter we examine the criteria for making appropriate decisions about the causes of things, and also look at ways we sometimes go wrong when we make causal inferences.

• • • • • • • • •
## Introduction

Child:      Look! There's a fly on the potatoes.

Parent:     Yes, I see it. It's flying away. Now, please eat your dinner.

Child:      What makes airplanes fly?

Parent:     Well, uh, they have engines, and propellers. That is, some have propellers; others use jet propulsion. You see, they move very fast and the wind lifts them up. I think. That's why they can get as high as the clouds.

Child:      Why are there clouds in the sky?

Parent:     Clouds are made of water. But the water isn't really water; I mean it isn't like in a swimming pool. It's more like mist, little pieces of water. You know, like fog, the kind we saw when we went to Grandma's house last night.

Child:      Why does Grandma brush her teeth in the sink?

Parent:     Be quiet and finish your dinner.

There appears to be a fundamental human motive to make sense of the world. And in order to make sense of something, we often seek to discover what caused it (Einhorn & Hogarth, 1986). Reasoning about the causes of things is a basic organizing feature of everyday thinking throughout the life span (Kuhn, Pennington, & Leadbeater, 1983). Our comprehension and memory for stories that we read, for example, are based on the network of causal connections that we construct among the events in the story (Bower & Morrow, 1990). Typically we understand a simple story by inferring and then following a succession of causally related events: rustlers steal cattle—sheriff chases them— rustlers shoot at sheriff—sheriff captures rustlers. We come to understand real life in much the same way.

A basic human motive to know the causes of something may be the reason for our early interest in why things occur, in what makes them happen as they do. One need only follow an active 3- or 4-year-old around (if you can keep up!) to see how this natural curiosity leads the child to investigate and question the world. Parents find that at about this age children have an almost endless supply of "why" questions (Why *are* there clouds in the sky?) as well as a penchant for getting into things. Because nature loses much of its mystery when we discover the causes of events, we often feel safer than we did before we knew the causes. You may remember being frightened as a child by the sounds and flashes of light that accompanied a thunderstorm. Learning what caused these events probably reduced your fear. As adults, most of us feel uneasy when we hear that a plane crashed for "unknown causes" or when we learn about a disease in our community "the cause of which is not yet known." As the Roman writer said, happy the person who perceives the causes of things.

We seek the causes of things not just to feel safe but also to guide our actions and to provide a basis for the decisions we make (Kelley, 1973). People look for the causes of things, in other words, in order to know what to do, as well as when and how to do it (Pittman & Heller, 1987). As we noted in Chapter 1, many everyday decisions are based on these causal attributions. Some are clearly trivial—for instance, when we try to make someone laugh by repeating a joke that caused us to laugh, or when we walk around a mud puddle that we judge would cause our shoes to get dirty. Other decisions based on a causal analysis are more important but still commonplace—for instance, when we cross a busy street assuming that a red light will cause cars to stop before hitting us, or when we set our alarm to cause us to awaken at a designated time.

Some decisions based on causal reasoning have very significant and long-term consequences, as when someone judges that the cause of her depression is her job and she quits, or when someone decides that a particular person is the cause of his happiness and he decides to live with that person. The results of our causal analysis also may have life-and-death consequences, as when people smoke cigarettes after deciding that smoking does not cause them harm, or when people advocate stricter handgun laws because they decide that the availability of guns causes unnecessary deaths.

In this chapter you are asked to consider carefully this process of causal analysis, and to look for ways to improve your thinking about the causes of things. An ability to think critically about causation helps us to bring about desirable outcomes, effects, ends, and to avoid undesirable ones. Although people are often correct when they infer causation, they are sometimes, as we all know, quite wrong. The consequences of an incorrect causal inference can be serious, perhaps even dangerous to our health.

## The Language of Causal Inference

The everyday language we use to discuss causation serves us fairly well. Most people would agree that when someone asks why something happened, or what produced an event, or what events led up to something, or what were the reasons for a particular incident, he or she is asking what caused it. Yet a little thought will tell you that the subject of cause and effect is a complex one. What exactly does it mean to say that something caused something else? For instance, which of the many events that surround an effect should we designate as causal? The success of our favorite baseball team may be attributed to its good pitching staff, but are there not other causes as well? When we discuss causation our everyday language often leaves many questions unanswered.

When we talk about the causes of things we are usually referring to what the Greek philosopher Aristotle called efficient causation. An *efficient cause* is one that brings about a change; it is one that produces another event (Taylor, 1967). An important distinction here is that between necessary and sufficient causes. A brief discussion of these aspects of causal reasoning should help to sharpen your thinking about causation.

A *necessary cause* is one without which the effect cannot occur. When we speak of event $X$ being a necessary cause of event $Y$, we are indicating that $Y$ will not occur unless $X$ is present. An example of a necessary cause is the act of drinking water. If we don't drink water, we will die. Thus the act of drinking water is a necessary cause of our being alive. Is a good pitching staff a necessary cause of our team's winning? If it is possible that an event could take place in the absence of a particular cause, then that cause is not necessary. We might suggest that pitchers of some kind are necessary because without pitchers we would not be able to field a team and thus could not play (and win) the game. If our hitters were so good that they never struck out, then the team might win without good pitchers. It is also possible (conceivable) that we might win by forfeit if the other team failed to show up. We need to think some more about causality.

A causal analysis must consider the concept of sufficiency. We agree, for example, that water is necessary for survival. But is drinking water sufficient for survival? Does a winning baseball team need *only* good pitching? Obviously there are other things that are important to life or to a winning team, such as air to breathe and batters to get base hits to allow a team to score runs. Thus water and pitching (if we are not including winning by forfeit) are necessary causes, but they are not sufficient. We won't live just because we drink water and our team won't win if it has only pitchers. A *sufficient cause* is one that is able to bring about the effect. For example, a runner on third base can score if he or she crosses home plate before the last out is made. In the right situation, the runner can steal home, tag up after a batter hits a fly ball, or advance when the batter hits a fair ball. Any of these events can be said to cause a run to score; each is sufficient to get the job done.

When any event occurs, many conditions might be considered causal. Some of these conditions, as we have suggested, are necessary for the event to occur. If any one *necessary* condition is missing, the effect will not happen. In a manner of speaking, all of these conditions taken together—the totality of necessary causes—are the cause of an event (Taylor, 1967). When all these necessary conditions are present, event Y will occur. In fact, at this point event Y cannot fail to occur. The presence of all necessary conditions is the sufficient cause for the occurrence of event Y.

- - - - - - - - - - - - - - - - - - - - - - - - - - - - - - - - - - - - - - - - - - -

**THINK about It**

(?)

**2.1**   For each of the following events, describe two *necessary* causes:

1. Getting an A on a class exam.

    a . _____

    b . _____

2. Being at work on time.

    a . _____

    b . _____

Possible necessary causes are discussed at the end of the chapter.

- - - - - - - - - - - - - - - - - - - - - - - - - - - - - - - - - - - - - - - - - - -

If you are following us so far, you may see a problem when you look for the cause of an event. (We did warn you that our everyday language of causation leaves a lot to be explained.) Consider the causal analysis of our baseball team's wins. We agreed that a number of conditions are necessarily present if a team is going to win, such as good pitching, hitting, and fielding. And we just said that *all* these conditions together make up the sufficient cause of a win. But wait a minute. Are there not literally hundreds of necessary conditions? We were talking about survival, too. Doesn't a baseball team need air to breathe? For that matter, doesn't a ball need air to slow it down? Consider how many home runs Babe Ruth would have been able to hit if he hit every ball in a vacuum. (Of course, in a vacuum he wouldn't have been able to breathe, and even if he held his breath he would soon realize that the ball was going to be coming across the plate a lot faster without air to slow it.) Has identifying the cause of an event become an impossible task? We hope not; but we must proceed carefully.

## Selecting a Cause

As the philosopher J. L. Mackie (1974) noted, when we talk about causes "we tend to be selective, to be more ready to call some kinds of factors causes than others" (p. 34). And while Mackie suggested that there are "no firm rules" governing our choices of events as causes, he did identify some systematic tendencies in the way we make decisions about causal factors. We are, for example, more likely to attribute a cause to the occurrence of some event than to something that is merely present. A spark, for example, is more likely to be considered the cause of an explosion than the presence of flammable materials. Actively studying for an exam is likely to be considered a cause of an A rather than a book to study from (or, for that matter, air to breathe!). Also, we are more apt to consider causal something that is intrusive than something that typically occurs or is ongoing. We are more likely, for instance, to say that a severed artery caused the blood to flow than to say that the pumping of the heart produced the loss of blood. Finally, often what we consider to be causally related is something that is abnormal, novel, or unusual (Taylor, 1967). While we may not pay much attention to an average pitching staff, we may single out the pitching staff as a cause of a team's winning if the pitchers are having an unusually good season. We don't, in other words, talk about a team's winning because it needs air to breathe or gravity to bring a ball back to earth. These are necessary conditions that simply aren't worth mentioning. They can be taken for granted. When people look for the cause of an event, they generally seek something that stands out from the background of all those conditions that must be present if the event is to occur.

To aid your thinking about causes, we might emphasize the distinction between conditions and causes (Einhorn & Hogarth, 1986; Mill, 1843/1950). As we pointed out, the totality of conditions that are necessary for an event to occur can be considered the cause of the event. However, many of these conditions are not typically seen as causally relevant (for example, air to breathe for our ball players). When people talk about what caused an event, they tend to choose some of these conditions as causes. Their choice, as we saw, is often based on what makes an event stand out from the background of conditions that are present, what the philosopher John Stuart Mill (1843/1950) referred to as the event that is "superficially the most conspicuous" (p. 197).

You may see that an analysis of this topic of causality has revealed something about why it is that disagreements about causal factors sometimes arise. If we consider an event as nothing special or not particularly different from what we might usually expect in a situation, then we are not likely to suggest that this factor is causally relevant. However, if we judge a condition to be intrusive or unusual, to stand out from its context, then we are apt to say that it is causal. For instance, although both losing and winning baseball teams need air to breathe and pitchers to pitch, if the pitchers are doing unusually well, they are likely to be seen as causal. Thus we find that our decision regarding causal factors will be affected by the way we view the situation or context in which the event occurs. We are not all likely to define a situation or context in the same way, and consequently our causal reasoning may not be the same as someone else's.

To see how different definitions of a context can influence our thinking about causes, imagine that a watch face is hit with a hammer and the glass breaks. Would you consider the cause of the breakage to be the force of the hammer hitting the glass? Most people probably would. Without any additional information it makes sense, given what we understand about everyday physics, to say that the hammer hitting the glass caused it to break. Now assume that the incident occurred in a watch factory when the glass was being tested for its ability to stand up to the kind of rough treatment that a watch might receive when it was worn on someone's wrist. Given this context, many people would now suggest that the cause of the glass breakage was a defect in the glass (based on Einhorn & Hogarth, 1986, p. 4).

**THINK about It**

**2.2**   A person is driving down a city street when a ball rolls in front of the car. Running after the ball is a small girl. The driver swerves to avoid the girl and smashes the car into a fire hydrant.

Without any additional information, what would most people say caused the accident?

We believe most people would say that the sight of the girl running into the street caused the driver to try to miss her, and so to hit the water hydrant.

Can you suggest some additional information that might lead people to consider a different cause of the accident?

_____

_____

_____

At the end of the chapter we provide a brief analysis of how additional information might change the causal attribution process.

# • • • • • • • • • •
# Criteria for Determining a Causal Relationship

We are not without help in determining the cause of something. For one event to be considered the cause of another, three major criteria generally have to be met (Hume, 1739/1969): (1) covariation of events; (2) time-order relationship; and (3) elimination of plausible alternative causes. As you will see, the problem is to make sure that all three criteria have been met. Too often, people are willing to make causal inferences without sufficient consideration of all three criteria.

## Covariation of Events

The *covariation* principle states that for event $X$ to be a cause of event $Y$, event $X$ and event $Y$ must vary together. As one changes, the other must change. They must "go together," be co-related, or, in the terminology of the scientist, be correlated. The nature of this relationship need not be in any particular direction, nor does it always have to be in the same direction. That is, as one event changes, the change in another event can be in the same direction or in a different direction. More time spent studying is likely to "go with" more answers correct on a test; more time spent studying also may "go with" less time spent on the test. What is important to assess is whether one thing changes as the other changes.

Covariation is something with which you are very familiar. Everyday experiences teach us about events that are correlated. Consider the covariation between dark clouds in the sky and the appearance of rain, or between failure to do chores and parents' nagging, or between high school grade point average and success in enrolling in college. Have you not noticed that as the amount of daylight decreases, the number of people turning on lights increases? Or what about the covariation that typically exists between people's height and their weight? We learn about covariation by observing the relationship between two events on many different occasions.

The degree of correlation between two events can be measured by means of statistical procedures. For example, one statistical measure is based on the degree to which a relationship is linear; that is, the degree to which the relationship can be summarized by a straight line. For our purpose, however, it is important only that you understand that the relationship between two events can vary in strength as well as in direction. The *strength* of correlation can be thought of in terms of how well we can predict a change in $Y$ when we know about changes in $X$ (Shaughnessy & Zechmeister, 1990). The stronger the relationship, the better our ability to predict. Consider the relationship between students' performance on the first test ($X$) in a large lecture course and their performance on the second test ($Y$). It is a fact that these two events (test 1 scores and test 2 scores) are often rather strongly correlated. This means that if we know how students did on test 1, we can predict with a significant degree of accuracy how well they will do on test 2. Of course, students who do well on the first test do not *always* do well on the second test, and scoring low on the first test does not lead inevitably to a low score on the second test. We usually cannot say *exactly* how well students will do on test 2 on the basis of their scores on test 1. This is what makes this relationship less than perfect. The correlation between students' grades on the first test in a course and their scores on the second test, although rather strongly related, is not perfect. On the other hand, we would be in a better position to predict students' scores on the second test after we found out how well they did on the first test than we would be after we found out how many hours they spent exercising before the exam. There might be some relationship between time spent exercising and scores on a classroom test (healthy bodies make healthy minds?), but we believe you will agree that the *strength* of the relationship would not be as good as that between two test scores in the class. Therefore, our ability to predict exam performance on the basis of the number of hours the students spent exercising will not be as good as it will be if we know their scores on the first exam.

The *direction* of the relationship between number of answers correct on the first exam in a course and number of answers correct on the second exam would be described as positive. In a positive relationship, the measures follow each other up the scale: low scores on test 1 tend to go with low scores on test 2, whereas high scores on test 1 tend to go with high scores on test 2. In a negative relationship, the measures vary in opposite directions. Consider the relationship between outside temperatures and the size of our heating bills. High temperatures are associated with low heating bills; low outside temperatures tend to be associated with high heating bills. The direction of a relationship has nothing to do with the strength of the relationship. A positive relationship, for instance, is not necessarily stronger than a negative one. That is, the terms "positive" and "negative" should be thought of not as "good" (or "strong") and "bad" (or "weak"), respectively, but simply as indicating the direction of the relationship. Test 1 scores will be negatively correlated with test 2 scores if we measure test 1 performance in terms of number of answers correct and measure test 2 performance in terms of number of errors. However, the strength of the relationship will not change when we make this change in the way we measure performance.

Knowledge of covariation is important not only when we are seeking to establish evidence for causation but also, as we have suggested, when we wish to establish a basis for predicting when an event will occur. As we saw, when two events are known to be strongly related, information about the state or condition of the first event can be used to predict the occurrence of the second event. These predictions often guide our behavior. Most of us, for example, reach for an umbrella or consider wearing a raincoat when we predict that dark clouds will bring rain. It is even possible that as children we did household chores to avoid the parental nagging that we predicted would follow if we didn't do our chores. We must keep in mind, however, that covariation is only one condition for establishing causality; covariation alone is not sufficient evidence to demonstrate causation. Covariation does not necessarily mean (imply) causation. Simply put, the fact that two events are correlated does not mean that one event causes the other; yet many people frequently make the mistake of arguing for causation on the basis of correlational evidence alone.

• • • • • • • • • • • • • • • • • • • • • • • • • • • • • • • • • • • • • • • • • • • • • • •

**THINK about It**

**?**

**2.3**   The following pairs of events are correlated. Odd as it may seem, there is evidence that these factors do covary to some degree.

1. The frequency of ice cream sales and the crime rate in a large city.
2. The amount of time students study and their grade point averages.
3. The number of mules in states of the U.S. and the number of Ph.D.'s in these states.

   a. Describe in your own words the nature of this covariation. As one factor increases, for example, do you think the other factor increases or decreases?

      1. _____
         _____

      2. _____
         _____

      3. _____
         _____

   b. Which of the pairs of events best illustrates the principle that correlation does not imply causation?   1   2   3

   Answers to this exercise are discussed at the end of the chapter.

• • • • • • • • • • • • • • • • • • • • • • • • • • • • • • • • • • • • • • • • • • • • • • •

## Time-Order Relationship

The *time-order* principle of causation states simply that if $X$ is to be the cause of $Y$, then $X$ must come before $Y$. Thus we typically define $X$ as a cause of $Y$ only if it can be shown that $X$ precedes $Y$. Such a demonstration is easier in some situations than in others.

First, consider some easy situations. Few people would have difficulty identifying which event came first if, as they watch Sally and Mary argue, they see Mary strike Sally, and then see Sally run crying to her mother. Clearly Sally got hit first and then she ran. Most people are likely to say that by hitting Sally, Mary caused her to cry and run to her mother. Anyone who has observed children at "play" has seen this causal relationship many times. A heavy rain that fills the streets and washes cars away is likely to be seen as a cause of a disaster. First it rained and then the streets flooded. You no doubt can think of many other situations in which event $X$ clearly comes before event $Y$. Now let's look at some other situations.

Assume you learn that parents who are stern disciplinarians and who use physical punishment are more likely to have aggressive children than parents who are less strict and use other forms of punishment. You might reasonably argue that the time-order relationship is: physical punishment is used and then children become aggressive. In fact, you might want to argue that because stern discipline and aggressiveness in children covary, and because discipline "obviously" came before aggressiveness, two criteria for causation have been met: covariation and a time-order relationship. Although the evidence in this case may indicate that covariation is present, we might suggest a different temporal order. Is it possible that children differ naturally in their aggressiveness, and that aggressive children are more likely to require their parents to resort to stern discipline? In other words, the discipline possibly came after the aggressiveness. In order to handle an unruly and aggressive child, the parents became stern disciplinarians. Time-order relationships aren't always what they seem to be. Of course, you knew this already. It's the old chicken-and-egg problem. Before deciding that event $X$ must precede event $Y$, we must ask whether event $Y$ might logically come before event $X$.

**THINK about It**

**2.4**   Research confirms that there is a relationship between time spent watching televised violence and aggressive behavior (Friedrich-Cofer & Huston, 1986). One way of looking at this relationship suggests that children first watch violent TV shows and then become aggressive. Can you think of a way in which the temporal order of events (and the causal implication) might be different?

_____

_____

_____

We analyze this situation at the end of the chapter.

## Elimination of Plausible Alternative Causes

The third major criterion for establishing a cause-and-effect relationship, the elimination of plausible alternative causes, is no doubt the most difficult to meet. Basically, this criterion states that you have made such a case for event $X$ as a cause of event $Y$ that there exists no *reasonable* explanation for the cause of $Y$ other than $X$. The problems associated with meeting this criterion are numerous. One way to approach this aspect of causal reasoning is by describing it in terms of the "third variable" problem.

When we discuss causation in terms of two events, say $X$ and $Y$, we must be alert to the possibility that another variable, say $Z$, is the cause of $X$ or $Y$ or both. That is, the problem for causal analysis is that we sometimes examine a situation and judge that $X$ causes $Y$ (or $Y$ causes $X$) when in fact there is a third variable that is actually causally related to $X$ and $Y$. You may well have thought about a third variable when in TAI 2.3 we asked you to decide the

**Covariation is not the same as causation.**

nature of the correlation between the sales of ice cream and the crime rate. You probably decided that there had to be something else, such as temperature, causally related to these two events. Warm temperatures bring out crooks as well as people looking for ice cream. The number of mules in any U.S. state is likely to be negatively correlated with the number of Ph.D.'s in the state because of factors associated with population density. The more rural the state, the fewer the employment opportunities for people holding advanced degrees (see Kimble, 1978).

To see how the identification of a third variable can complicate what appears to be an otherwise straightforward case for causality, consider the situation that once existed with regard to smoking and lung disease. For years many people argued that cigarette smoking was causally linked to respiratory illness and other diseases. The fact is that people who smoke cigarettes are more likely to develop respiratory problems than are those who do not smoke. Thus the covariation between these factors was known to exist for some time. And, as far as we know, no one has argued that illness comes before smoking, so it looks as though two criteria for establishing a causal relationship are present: time order and covariation. Is the third criterion also satisfied? Is there any other factor that might produce both smoking and illness? For some time people associated with the tobacco industry argued that the fact that the first two criteria are satisfied does not mean that smoking causes health problems because there are other factors that can plausibly be said to cause *both* smoking and illness. One factor sometimes mentioned is stress. Could it be that stress causes people both to become ill and to smoke cigarettes? If it does, then what appears to be a causal relationship between smoking and disease is really a causal relationship involving this third variable, stress, and the other two variables.

For a long time the argument over the dangers of smoking was based primarily on evidence that did not rule out possible third variables. Even though covariation was established, this was not enough to make an airtight case for a causal relationship. (Remember: covariation does not necessarily mean causation.) At stake in this controversy were not only lives but jobs and millions of dollars in taxes and income. Later in this chapter, when we discuss strategies for establishing causation, we will examine evidence that tends to rule out possible third variables in this smoking–disease relationship.

We can diagram the third-variable problem as:

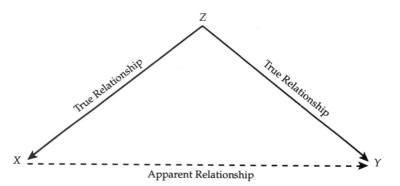

THINK about It

**2.5**   The following statements about the relationship between two events are generally true. That is, the two factors that are mentioned actually do covary (we're not just making this up!). Given that X and Y covary, do you think that X causes Y (or that Y causes X), or can you identify a possible third variable that might cause X and Y, and so prohibits us from stating that X and Y are causally related? Before thinking about possible third variables, be sure that you understand the relationship that is presented. It might be good to describe in your own words the nature of the relationship before you proceed to identify possible third variables.

1. Among people in general there is a correlation between their weight and the size of their vocabulary.

   Answer: _____

   _____

2. The grade point averages of high school drivers and the number of accidents they have are related.

   Answer: _____

   _____

3. Beginning in about the seventh grade, there is a reliable relationship between mathematical achievement scores and the gender (male or female) of the test taker.

Answer: _____

_____

Possible answers to this exercise are discussed at the end of the chapter.

● ● ● ● ● ● ● ● ● ● ● ● ● ● ● ● ● ● ● ● ● ● ● ● ● ● ● ● ● ● ● ● ● ● ● ● ● ● ● ● ● ● ● ● ● ● ● ● ●

● ● ● ● ● ● ● ● ●
# Pitfalls in Drawing Conclusions about Cause and Effect

Coming to the appropriate conclusion about a cause-and-effect relationship is not without its problems. Although you want to be able to make an appropriate decision about the true cause of an event, as we have seen, it is sometimes difficult to decide whether the criteria for establishing a causal inference have been met. You saw, for example, that time-order relationships are not always what they appear to be. There are other problems associated with the task of drawing appropriate causal inferences. We shall discuss four major pitfalls found on the road to thinking about causation. The first is a problem with assessing degree of covariation between events, which can lead us to see covariation that is not really there. The other three pitfalls are associated with a familiar every-day form of causal reasoning, which we can call the before–after argument. You will undoubtedly recognize this kind of argument, and we discuss some important principles to keep in mind when you evaluate a causal inference stemming from this type of argument.

## Illusory Correlation

Sometimes our thinking about the relationship between events leads us to the conclusion that two events covary when in fact they do not, or we judge that a relationship is stronger than it actually is. This error in thinking has been called *illusory correlation* (Chapman, 1967). It presents a problem for causal analysis because we think that one of the criteria for defining causation has been met when in fact it has not.

Often one's expectation about the degree of relationship between events is based on prior knowledge of the situation. This knowledge may be based on actual experience with the events in question or may have been learned in-directly. For example, someone may have told us about the degree of relation-ship to expect. Thus people may come to a situation with an informal theory or "intuition" about the degree of relationship that exists between two variables. The consequence of this expectation can be a tendency to see covariation that is not actually present, and to overestimate significantly any small degree of co-variation that may be present. Consider the results of an experiment that reveals this human tendency.

The experimenters presented people with data from a hypothetical cloud-seeding experiment (Ward & Jenkins, 1965). For each of 50 days, people were told whether the clouds had been seeded and whether or not it had rained. They were then asked to judge the degree of relationship between cloud seeding and rainfall. The data were purposely constructed so that there really was no relationship between cloud seeding and the likelihood of rain. Nevertheless, people judged that they were correlated. This illusory correlation appears to be the result of people thinking that cloud seeding and rain should covary. Armed with this expectation, people were more likely to notice and remember days when rain followed cloud seeding than days when rain did not follow cloud seeding.

As L. J. Chapman (1967) has emphasized, illusory correlations are likely to be the basis of "the observational errors necessary to sustain most superstitions and folklore (e.g., the report that one's luck is better when carrying a rabbit's foot), as well as beliefs in magic (e.g., the report that it is more likely to rain after a rain dance)" (p. 151). We will examine this aspect of illusory correlation in more depth in the following chapters, when we deal specifically with attitudes and beliefs. For now it's enough that you become aware of the limitations we all have when we attempt to estimate covariation; when you assess evidence for causation, be sure that the covariation criterion has been met. As when you seek evidence for other criteria of causation (such as time order), it is important to gather as much information as possible before making a judgment and to be aware of the powerful tendency to "see" what we expect to see.

**THINK about It**

**2.6**   A friend refuses to go on a trip with you until he locates his "lucky bracelet." You become impatient waiting for him while he searches, and you suggest that the idea of a lucky bracelet is ridiculous. He can't believe you would say such a thing and he tells you of many occasions when he was wearing the bracelet and something good happened.

Might an illusory correlation be present? How might it have come about?

_____

_____

_____

_____

We analyze this situation at the end of the chapter.

## The Before–After Argument

On a recent television news show, an interviewer was talking with a judge about the way cases were handled by the courts. The judge was proud of the fact that more cases had gotten to trial since his appointment to the bench than had gotten to trial under previous judges. In other words, he suggested that his presence on the bench was responsible for a speeding up of the judicial process. As far as the judge was concerned, his actions since he assumed his office were the cause of an important judicial reform. The evidence offered was that the rate at which cases were tried was slower *before* his appointment than it was *after* his appointment.

For all we know, the judge may have been right. His actions may have caused the judicial reform. Evidence based on a before–after argument, however, is generally so weak that we should be extremely cautious about accepting such reasoning (Campbell & Stanley, 1963). We are willing to accept the judge's statement that a change occurred (he supported it with figures); our problem is to eliminate other plausible explanations for the change that did occur. When the only evidence offered is that a particular situation existed before event $X$ was introduced and a different situation existed after event $X$, often many factors *in addition* to event $X$ entered into the situation. You will remember that a major criterion for establishing causality is the elimination of alternative explanations. A before–after argument often fails to meet this criterion.

### Coincidental and Natural Causes

Consider the claim made by the judge. He attributed the change in the court system to his actions, but can we think of other plausible reasons for the change? To aid our thinking, let us suggest that we first organize our discussion around two categories of alternative reasons. We will call these categories coincidence and natural causes.

Coincidence is just that; our judge's appointment was coincidental (occurring at the same time) with other events that were taking place—other events that might have caused a change. What things might have occurred about the same time a new judge was appointed? Was there also an increase in the number of prosecutors? Was a new law passed about this time which influenced the decision as to who is brought to trial? Clearly, without knowing more about what is going on about the time the judge was appointed, we should treat the judge's claim that he played a causal role as only a possibility.

Consider another category of problems. You no doubt have heard reports of people dying of "natural causes." But what does that mean? How does one die naturally (or, for that matter, unnaturally)? Generally, it is assumed such reports mean that the cause of death was a normal part of growing old. We expect some things to happen simply as part of the normal course of events. For instance, suppose you heard a report that a person was measured at age 5 years and found to be 36 inches tall, and that this same person at age 10 was

When thinking about the causes of things, remember that some events occur naturally.

found to be 50 inches tall. Without other information you probably would not think much of this fact. Children do grow, and growth of 14 inches in the five years between these ages is an expected result of natural causes—specifically, maturation.

Lots of things change naturally, and if we happen along during the time of this natural change, we may mistakenly believe that our actions are the cause of the change. To help you remember this point, you might think of the apocryphal story of the confused nature lover who, finding a young bird fallen from a nest, begins to teach the bird to fly. Through films, slides, and other visual aids, the earnest but not-too-wise bird fancier shows the young bird the art of flying. Lo and behold, after several days of concentrated instruction the bird takes off. It apparently had taken its instruction to heart and had learned the art of flying!

When we make a claim for a causal relationship, we must be careful not to put ourselves in the position of the unwitting bird lover and claim to have made a difference when the difference was brought about by "natural causes." Birds don't need to be taught how to fly, just as fish don't need to be taught how to swim or children taught how to walk. These things occur naturally.

Consider how this reasoning might be applied to the judge. Is it possible that the rate at which the courts handled cases had been gradually increasing, perhaps because of natural changes in the population of potential offenders— for example, increasing numbers of 16–24-year-olds, who are often involved in crime? An increase in the number of offenders may have necessitated an administrative change in the way cases are brought before the court. Did our judge just happen to get appointed when this change was being noticed? Would the change have occurred with or without the judge for reasons that might be considered natural in this situation? Whenever we are presented with a before-after argument for causation, we must look to see whether plausible alternative explanations exist, especially those based on coincidental events or natural causes.

**THINK
about It**

**2.7**   A school district implements a program to help children develop study skills. The year-long program includes a review of study goals and the teaching of various study strategies. A standardized test designed to measure study skills is administered before and after the program and the scores are compared. Because scores on the average are higher after the program is completed, administrators conclude that the money and time that went into this program have been well spent. Clearly the program has caused children to improve their study skills! The administrators ask the school district to seek higher taxes in order to continue this new program. Are you ready to pay higher taxes for this purpose?

   Can you identify possible alternative explanations (causes) that the administrators should consider before they raise your taxes? Try to think of both coincidental and natural causes. We suggest some alternative explanations at the end of the chapter.

_____

_____

_____

_____

_____

## Regression toward the Mean

A special problem for causal analysis appears when individuals have been singled out because of their extreme performance and are then treated in some fashion with the goal of changing their performance. Performance in this situation is likely to change even when no treatment is introduced. As in situations in which natural causes can be assumed to be operating, we may mistakenly think that a change was caused by a particular event when in fact the change was inevitable. In this case it is due to the way individuals were selected and the way their performance was measured. The phenomenon is called *regression toward the mean,* and it has complicated many causal analyses of a before-after sort. To help you to understand this concept, we begin by asking you to think about some of your own experiences involving extreme or exceptional performances.

Think for a minute about the scores you have received on school tests in a particular subject. Although some were undoubtedly high, others were probably lower than you liked. There was, in other words, some variability in your performance. Now consider the highest score you ever achieved in that subject. Can you identify some of the reasons behind your extremely good performance? (You may want to write down a few of these reasons before proceeding.) What about experiences you might have had when you were playing sports or taking part in some other highly competitive activity—a dance contest, a math competition, whatever? Was your performance on some occasions close to the best you ever did, but at other times (if you are like most of us) was your performance less than stellar? In other words, again we expect to see some variation in our ability to perform. Why? What accounts for an extremely good performance or, for that matter, an extremely poor performance?

You no doubt have observed that it is very difficult to repeat an extremely good performance. Consider what makes a championship team in a highly competitive sport, and think about why it is difficult to win the championship again the following year. A championship team will usually have many good players, discipline, teamwork, excellent coaching, and all those things that make for a superior team. If the team is to be the champions, however, everything has to click. Things have to happen just right; they have to be going your way. There can't be too many injuries to key players. More often than not the ball has to bounce in the right direction. There are, in other words, many basic factors that we would consider causal (good players and all the rest), but some chance factors are operating as well. When chance is favoring you (and you have the necessary skills and resources as well), you are likely to emerge as champion.

In a recent basketball tournament two teams were playing for a place in the title game. One team was losing by four points and there were only seconds left when a player on the losing team made a two-point shot and was fouled while he was making it. The rules say that he gets one free throw. But, of course, one point would not win the game or even tie it. The player went to the free-throw line with the intention of purposely missing the shot so that his team could get the rebound and shoot to tie the game. He did and they did. The game went into overtime and his team won. In a manner of speaking, the game was decided by the bounce of the ball off the hoop. Should the ball have careened off at a slightly different angle and gone to an opposing player, the other team would have won. (It would be an interesting exercise to see how many times, say out of ten attempts, a player can get a ball to careen exactly as he wants it to.)

If you examine the games played by any championship team, you will probably see the ball bounce to its players in difficult situations enough times to make a difference. That is one reason why it is often so hard to be a repeat winner in a highly competitive sport. Next time the ball may take a slighty different hop. Next season not all of your players may be healthy.

Similarly, when you scored near the top of the class on a difficult test, although you obviously knew what you were doing, some chance factors were operating as well. You must have studied exactly the right material, hitting especially those points that were emphasized on the test. Did the material happen to be something you especially liked or something that you had studied before? Did the instructor happen to include on the test only material presented on all the days you were present? Many factors and a lot of hard work had to come together in order for you to get such a high score. But how likely is it that everything will click so well again? The hard work may be there, but will those chance factors be present in the same combination? After an exceptional performance it is likely that you will fall toward your average on the next test. Note that we are not saying that you will never score that high again; rather, when you achieve an extreme score, some chance factors are likely to be operating, which do not necessarily always work the same way. Regression (moving back) toward the mean (your "typical" performance) can be expected after an extreme performance.

We do not mean to imply that you are more likely to regress after an extremely good performance than after an extremely poor one. Regression is just as likely when scores are selected because they are particularly poor. That is, after an extremely poor performance we might expect to see a better performance the next time simply because of the way chance factors operate. The same analysis that we applied to good performance applies here as well. Someone who does OK in a class most of the time may occasionally look extremely bad because of some chance factors. Did the test emphasize points that were presented the day a student was absent? Did a student happen not to be feeling well on the day of a test or perhaps not sleep well the night before? If so, we can expect that student's score on the next test to be somewhat higher.

How does regression toward the mean figure into a causal analysis? Whenever a group of people are identified on the basis of their extreme performance, we can generally expect the performance of the group to move toward their mean when a second measurement is made. If a group was selected because it performed very well, we expect the group to do somewhat more poorly the next time. And if a group scored very low, we expect the group to perform somewhat better the next time. We must be careful when we select people because of their extreme performances, and then introduce one or more factors with the intention of effecting a change in the group's performance. We may mistakenly believe that a difference in performance observed before and after our treatment is due solely to the treatment when actually it was the result of regression toward the mean. Of course, it is possible that our treatment did make a difference in addition to any regression effects, but if our causal analysis is to be convincing, we must be able to rule out regression toward the mean as the only factor.

---

**THINK about It**

**?**

**2.8**  People have suggested that appearing on the cover of *Sports Illustrated* magazine is a jinx on a person or a team because they never seem to do so well again. In other words, after exceptional performances that earn a cover story, people often seem to be unable to reach those heights again.

What, in the light of what you know about regression, do you think about this jinx?

_____

_____

_____

_____

_____

_____

_____

_____

We answer this question at the end of the chapter.

• • • • • • • • • • • • • • • • • • • • • • • • • • • • • • • • • • • • • • • • • • • • • •

### The Case of Missing Cases

Another problem that often goes undetected when the effect of a treatment is assessed on the basis of a difference in performances before and after the treatment is the case of missing cases. The problem is that not everyone who begins something finishes it. (Of course, we always finish what we start!) How many times have you observed someone start to diet and then stop, or try to exercise more and eventually stop trying? Changing our behavior, acquiring new knowledge, learning a skill (such as thinking critically!) are often difficult tasks. Although our intentions often are good, we sometimes fail to follow through. There are many reasons why we might not complete a task that we started, besides finding it "too hard." The important point here is that dropouts introduce a serious problem for causal analysis in a before–after situation.

Consider the evaluation of a parent-training group:

Since we have young children who are occasionally less than perfect in their behavior, we are naturally attracted to studies that deal with behavior problems in children. Groups for Parents is a packaged method that offers parents both a support group of other parents and didactic information on an integrated humanistic behavior modification approach. The authors of "Groups for Parents" (along with a few others) published a study evaluating the effectiveness of their approach in "improving both general child behaviors [and] individually targeted ones." They also reported success in increasing the parents' rates of positive reinforcement along with the rates of compliance in their children.

The method of evaluation was quite simple. Thirteen groups of parents (a total of 277) met once a week for two and one-half hours over an eight week period. About one-half of the parents had been referred by various community agencies; the rest had heard about the program from friends or other informed sources. The pre- and post-test measures used included a problem behavior checklist, positive reinforcement rates (measured by the parents), compliance rates (also measured by the parents), and client satisfaction (self-report). Approximately two-thirds (180) of those enrolled completed the entire eight-week course.

The data analyses were equally straightforward, consisting of analyses of the differences between pre- and post-test means. Significant results that concern us were reported on the problem behavior checklist, reinforcement rates, and compliance rates. In addition, a very high rate of client satisfaction at the end of the study was reported. On the basis of these results, should we enroll in these courses the next time they are available?[1]

On the basis of these results, would you recommend that parents in need of help enroll in these courses the next time they are available?

There is a serious problem of missing cases in this evaluation and it suggests that we treat cautiously the before-and-after differences. It is not the number of cases that are missing that raises the problem; it is the *kind* of cases that are missing. As only two-thirds of the parents completed the course, we want to know the likely differences between those who finished and those who did not finish. Were those parents most dissatisfied with the program the ones who quit? Was the program working more effectively for those who remained than for those who quit? Both of these questions are likely to be answered affirmatively. Therefore, when the posttraining evaluations are made, we find that those who might have been less satisfied with the program are not asked their opinion (because they aren't around anymore). Were we able to obtain pre- and posttest measures from all the participants who started the program, we might find that these before-and-after measures did not differ significantly.

It is only when we suspect that cases are missing because of some systematic bias in the procedure that we need to be concerned. Should we find, for example, that some parents were not able to continue in the program because they were forced to move from the area when the company a spouse worked for asked them to relocate, we would not be so concerned about a bias caused by missing cases. The fact that these parents were not included in the posttraining evaluation can be chalked up to reasons unrelated to the program, and without further information, we might safely assume that these missing cases were just as likely to include satisfied as dissatisfied clients.

The missing cases are not necessarily the only problem with the evaluation of this parenting group. You probably saw that other explanations—for example, those based on coincidental events or natural causes—also would need to be ruled out before we accepted the idea that participation in the parenting program caused the changes in the children and in the parents' attitudes. Was there some other event that might have occurred about this time to help parents modify the behavior of their children? Did many of the children simply improve their behavior as a consequence of normal maturation during the time of this program? And let us not forget regression toward the mean as an alternative explanation for these changes. When do you suppose parents are most likely to reach out for help? When children are behaving at their worst, perhaps? If this is the case, might we not expect, in light of what we know about regression effects, to see improvement when these children are observed at a later time?

[1]From *Rival Hypotheses: Alternative Interpretations of Data Based Conclusions,* by S. W. Huck and H. M. Sandler. New York: Harper & Row. Copyright 1979 by Schuyler W. Huck and Howard M. Sandler. Reprinted by permission.

● ● ● ● ● ● ● ● ● ● ● ● ● ● ● ● ● ● ● ● ● ● ● ● ● ● ● ● ● ● ● ● ● ● ● ● ● ● ● ● ● ● ● ● ● ● ● ● ● ● ● ● ●

**THINK about It**

?

**2.9**   A community newspaper reported that a new fitness program offered by the local community center was highly successful. Participants were asked to take several fitness tests before and after the six-week program. Of course, not everyone was able to complete the program. A thorough follow-up revealed that a few people moved out of the area, others simply got busy with other activities and stopped coming, some reported that the time of the program was "inconvenient," and several said they didn't like this particular approach to fitness. About two-thirds of the people who began the program actually finished it, and results showed that the finishing group was more healthy than the beginning group.

What do you think about these results and the claim of success? What reasons offered for failure to finish the program bother you most when you are asked to believe that the program made a difference? Why? What other problems do you see with this conclusion?

_____

_____

_____

_____

_____

This situation is discussed at the end of the chapter.

● ● ● ● ● ● ● ● ● ● ● ● ● ● ● ● ● ● ● ● ● ● ● ● ● ● ● ● ● ● ● ● ● ● ● ● ● ● ● ● ● ● ● ● ● ● ● ● ● ● ● ● ●

## Strategies for Determining True Cause-and-Effect Relationships

The methods used to discover a causal relationship vary with the situation and the available resources. Some strategies are better than others, but they may not be able to be carried out in the given circumstances. Of course, understanding some causal relationships is more important than understanding others, so that the time and effort spent on investigating a causal relationship are related to the urgency of finding a cause. Soon after the killer disease AIDS was first observed, it became apparent that society would be threatened as long as the cause of this terrible disease was unknown. Money and resources were put forward in an urgent search for the cause. Not to search for the cause of this disease when people were being afflicted without hope of a cure would have been unethical and immoral.

The opportunity to prove that a causal relationship exists beyond a shadow of a doubt does not come along very frequently. Information about causal relationships often is gathered in much the same way that a detective accumulates evidence about the perpetrator of a crime in the absence of credible eyewitness testimony or of a voluntary confession. The detective must put many pieces of a puzzle together until the picture of the crime emerges. Then the case is handed over to the prosecutor and presented to a jury with the hope that the pieces have indeed been put together correctly and that the picture is clear enough to gain a conviction. Similarly, in order to identify a causal relationship we often must rely on a variety of admittedly fallible lines of evidence in order to make a case that the event in question was truly causal. And despite the accumulation of evidence, we must live with the fact that we could be wrong, wrong in that we may have overlooked something that is revealed when evidence of a different causal link emerges.

A general strategy for determining whether a causal relationship is present is to vary the circumstances surrounding a given effect or outcome to see if the effect still occurs (Mill, 1843/1950). We will consider two specific ways in which this strategy is carried out: the method of agreement and the joint method of agreement and difference.

## Method of Agreement

The *method of agreement* asks us to identify many different situations in which the phenomenon occurs and the presumed causal event is present. If the effect occurs in all of the situations in which the presumed causal event is present, then we can argue that the event caused the effect. If the suspected cause is the only event that is common to all of the situations, then we have a strong argument for the causal nature of the event.

The logic of this argument goes like this. Consider two situations in which several possible causes are present. If the first situation in which the phenomenon occurs contains $A$, $B$, and $C$ as possible causes, and the second situation in which the effect occurs contains $A$, $D$, and $E$ as possible causes, then the only factor that is in agreement with the occurrence of the effect is $A$, and therefore $A$ may be considered the cause.

We can relate a story that illustrates the application of the method of agreement to causal analysis and also reveals a major shortcoming of this method (Wilson, 1952, p. 32). The story is about a scientist (definitely not a Nobel Prize winner!) who seeks to learn what gives him a hangover. The first night he drinks a great deal of Scotch and soda and finds that he feels rotten the next morning. The next night he drinks rye and soda and the consequences the next day are the same. On the third night he drinks bourbon and soda and the next morning once again he has a hangover. At this point he concludes that the soda, which was common to all three situations, caused his hangover.

This story alerts us to a serious limitation of the method of agreement: it is often difficult to determine whether the factor in question is the *only* factor that is present in every situation. Most situations are complex; many factors or conditions are present simultaneously. We may fail to recognize the presence of another factor that, like the factor that we are concentrating on, is also present in every situation in which the effect occurs. This other factor, like the alcohol in the scientist's drinks, could be the true causal agent.

We can use the method of agreement to help us gather evidence about potential causal factors. That is, we can try to find the one factor that remains in all the situations in which we observe the effect in question. As we noted, however, we must look carefully for any other factor that also is common to the situations, for it could be the actual cause. As you may already have realized, the method of agreement is basically correlational in nature. We have seen the problems with drawing conclusions about cause and effect solely on the basis of correlational evidence.

**THINK about It**

**2.10** Consider the problem of the young man who apparently developed an allergy to a woman he was dating. He liked the woman very much and made many dates with her. To his consternation, however, he found that he sneezed whenever he went out with her (and didn't sneeze when he was not with her). Initially, he resisted the idea that he was allergic to the object of his dreams and he decided that it must be the places where they went that brought on the sneezing. But as he had more dates with her and went to a great variety of places, he felt that the only conclusion possible was that she caused his sneezing. What do you think?

_____

_____

_____

_____

We explain what we think at the end of the chapter.

## Joint Method of Agreement and Difference

Causal inference is improved significantly when we add to the method of agreement the *method of difference.* In the method of difference we establish that when X (the assumed cause) is not present, Y (the observed effect) is also not present. By demonstrating both that when X is present Y occurs (agreement) and that when X is not present Y does not occur (difference), we provide evidence for X as a sufficient and necessary cause of Y (Boring, 1969). The joint method of agreement and difference is the basis of many scientific experiments. If two situations differ only with respect to the proposed cause, and the phenomenon is produced when the cause is present and not when it is absent, then we are led to conclude that the event in question caused the phenomenon. By way

The method of agreement has its limitations.

of illustration, consider a problem we referred to earlier, that of providing evidence for a causal link between smoking and lung disease.

Earlier we made the point that simply because two events covary—are correlated—we should not assume that there is a causal link between them. We went out of our way to provide many examples of correlated but noncausal relationships to emphasize the principle that correlation does not necessarily mean causation. Thus, when the major piece of evidence for causation is correlational only, we must acknowledge that our case is relatively weak, as we just saw in connection with the method of agreement. And should our argument for causation be related to a national controversy with millions of dollars at stake, not to mention hundreds of thousands of lives, there is obviously a need for more convincing evidence for causation than mere correlation. Such, of course, was the nature of the controversy and the stakes in the argument over the causal relation between cigarette smoking and lung disease (as well as other illnesses). As you saw, merely observing that people who smoke have a greater chance of becoming ill than those who do not smoke is correlational evidence only. Something about smokers other than the fact that they smoke may be causing poor health (for example, the food they eat or the stress they are under).

A way out of this difficulty might be to arrange to examine a group of people who smoke cigarettes and another group that has the same characteristics except that these people do not smoke. We could compare the degrees of lung damage, cancerous growths, and other health factors found in the two groups. If we could be sure that the only difference between these two groups was cigarette smoking, and the smoking group ended up decidedly more unhealthy than the nonsmoking group, then we would have a very convincing argument for a causal relationship between smoking and illness. And while this situation illustrates the application and logic of the joint method of agreement and difference in determining causal relationships, you undoubtedly realize some of the problems with this approach, at least as it is applied to this situation.

First, how do we get people to cooperate? Should we pay people to raise their children as smokers or nonsmokers? Or, once people are 21 years old and legally adults, should we simply offer money to some of them to take up smoking and reward others for not smoking? Clearly, such procedures are impractical and unethical. If we even suspected that cigarette smoking was dangerous to one's health could we in good conscience pay anyone to take that risk? But let's put this issue aside for a while and consider another problem: How do we make sure that the smoking and nonsmoking groups are really the same except for that one factor of smoking?

There are two major problems in applying this method of causal determination. The first is to establish that groups are basically the same except for the factor in question, and the second is to make sure that this group equivalence is maintained after it is established. Assuming we got people to cooperate, how would we set up two equivalent groups? The preferred procedure in many scientific studies is random assignment. Random assignment is a way to group people so that no particular characteristic (such as weight, previous condition of health, or diet) distinguishes people in one group from those in the other. One way to assign people randomly to two groups would be to flip an unbiased coin to decide in what group a person belongs; that is, heads is group *A* and tails is group *B*. Next, it would be important to hold factors constant between the two groups so that smoking remained the only difference. For example, we would not want to expose one group to the pollutants in the air of a large city while we let the other group live in the fresher air of the countryside. If group equivalance was both established and maintained throughout our period of observation and we found a difference in the health problems of the two groups, we could reasonably argue that the cause of this difference was smoking.

Although causal inference has not been (and should not be) approached in this way with human subjects, it has been used in a study of smoking with dogs as subjects (Hammond & Auerbach, 1971). Dogs can be taught to smoke cigarettes (via an opening in their air passage) and they even learn to smoke cigarettes voluntarily, approaching the smoking machine without coercion in order to take their puffs. The investigators randomly assigned male beagles to three groups: one that did not smoke, one that smoked filtered cigarettes, and one that smoked nonfiltered cigarettes. The cigarettes smoked were the same brand. How much of the cigarette each dog smoked was also held constant (at 49 mm). The dogs were fed the same diet and housed in similar cages. The experimental procedure was kept up for more than two years. While many measures were taken as indicators of the dogs' health, one result stands out from the rest. Of the dogs that smoked cigarettes, 28 died (as many as 50 percent in one group; fewer in the filtered group). None of the nonsmoking dogs died during the experiment. Dogs are not people, of course, and it may not be safe to generalize these results to human smokers. Nevertheless, the causal inference in this case is based on solid evidence and logic, and thus has serious implications for human smokers. The conclusion should be obvious.

**THINK about It**

**2.11**  A teacher wants to show that a particular method of building students' vocabulary is superior to the method currently in place at a school where she teaches. How might the joint method of agreement and difference be used to demonstrate that the new method is better than the old?

_____

_____

_____

_____

_____

A demonstration relying on the joint method of agreement and difference is suggested at the end of the chapter.

## Critical Principles of Causal Analysis: A Summary

1. People tend to see causes among events that are conspicuous, events that stand out among all the other events that are present.
2. The criteria that we use to establish a causal relationship include (*a*) covariation, (*b*) time-order relationship, and (*c*) elimination of alternative factors.
3. Covariation does not necessarily mean (imply) causation.
4. Before deciding that event *X must* precede event *Y,* ask whether event *Y* logically could come before event *X.*
5. When you seek evidence of a causal relationship, watch out for that third variable!
6. When you estimate the degree of covariation, be careful not to be influenced by expectations or beliefs about the degree of association between variables.
7. When you are presented with a before–after argument for causation, look to see whether plausible alternative explanations exist, especially those based on coincidental events and/or natural causes.
8. Performances that follow an extremely good or extremely bad performance are likely to move closer to the average.
9. When the results of a treatment are assessed on the basis of group measures taken before and after the treatment, bias is apt to be present when the same individuals are not included in the before-and-after measures.

10. The basic strategy for determining a causal relationship is to vary the circumstances surrounding a phenomenon, and to seek evidence demonstrating that only the proposed causal factor is present when the phenomenon occurs (method of agreement) and that the only difference when the phenomenon does not occur is the absence of the proposed causal factor (method of difference).

## • • • • • • • • • •
## Think about It: Discussion of Answers

**2.1**    One purpose of this exercise is to alert you to the many possible necessary causes that surround an event. Among the *necessary* causes associated with these events we suggest the following for consideration:

1. Taking the test (you *must* take the test if you are to get an A) and being enrolled in the course (that is, the instructor has to examine it and assign a grade).

2. It is necessary for you to have a job in order to get to it on time, and it may be necessary for you to be physically present to be considered on time (for example, by getting out of bed and showing up).

It may be helpful at this point to consider why other events may be merely sufficient causes. For example, studying for the test may appear necessary, but whereas one student might get an A after studying very hard, another student might not study at all and still get an A (perhaps by chance or by knowing the material before he took the course). A person might be able to get to work on time by taking the bus, by driving a car, or by some other means; under the right circumstances, each could be sufficient to produce the effect.

**2.2**    Some additional information about this situation that might change people's choice of a causal agent might be: the girl lived on a farm and was visiting the city for the first time; the girl was a block away from the car; the driver had been drinking alcohol; a sign indicating that the street was closed to traffic had fallen over so that it was no longer visible; the brakes on the car were not in working condition.

**2.3**    a. The correlations can be described as follows:

1. We have been told that the crime rate (that is, the number of crimes in proportion to the population) and the amount of ice cream sold are positively correlated. That is, as the crime rate goes up, so do ice cream sales! (See Kasarda, 1976, as cited in Kidder and Judd, 1986.)

2. When other factors (such as the difficulty of the course of studies) are held constant, we are confident that the more time one spends studying for a class, the higher the grades one gets.

3. When all 50 states are considered, there is probably a small negative correlation between the number of mules and the number of people who hold

advanced degrees (see Kimble, 1978). (Thank goodness it isn't a positive correlation! People might get confused.)

b. We suggest that the best examples of the principle that correlation does not mean causation are 1 and 3.

**2.4**   The possibility must be considered that some children naturally seek out aggressive, even violent activities, including the vicarious violence of television shows. Thus it is possible that the time-order relationship is that the tendency to engage in violent acts comes before watching violent television episodes. (This complex situation is discussed in Friedrich-Cofer & Huston, 1986.)

**2.5**   These correlations emphasize the need to watch out for that third variable.

1. Among people of all ages, young children (who naturally weigh less than adults) will know fewer words than will adults (who naturally weigh more than children).

2. We might consider intelligence and conscientiousness as possible third variables. However, we must also consider the possibility that studying takes time. The more time one spends studying, the less time one has for driving (and getting into accidents).

3. The correlation is real, and biological factors have been suggested to explain why males outperform females in math. However, the exact causal relationship is highly controversial. Before biological differences can be accepted as an explanation for the causal relationship between gender and math achievement, such third variables as variations between boys and girls in societal expectations, role models, and experiences with math-related activities (such as building model airplanes) must be ruled out. (Benbow, 1988, has an interesting discussion of these issues.)

**2.6**   An illusory correlation may arise because our friend with the lucky bracelet expects it to bring him good luck. Because of this expectation, he is likely to notice and remember the good things that happen when he wears his bracelet, and is perhaps less likely to notice and remember the bad events that happen to him. He also may selectively remember bad things that occurred when he did not wear the bracelet. (We will discuss this kind of thinking in more detail in Chapter 5.)

**2.7**   Possible coincidental events accounting for the children's change in performance might be a change in the number or quality of teachers; learning brought about through the normal routine of study and test taking over this period of time; additional money that may have become available for teachers' helpers, resulting in more one-on-one instruction; parental intervention in this area, perhaps especially likely if parents are informed about low test performance. Some possible natural causes to consider are normal maturational changes in the children over this lengthy period of time, causing children to approach their work more efficiently and seriously as they grow older; natural improvement in teachers' proficiency, especially if teachers were relatively inexperienced at the beginning of the measurement period.

**2.8**    The *Sports Illustrated* jinx may simply be the result of regression toward the mean. Athletes frequently appear on the covers of sports magazines after an outstanding (extreme) performance. Their performances after that are likely to be less spectacular. (Assume someone took your picture for the cover of *Time* magazine after your best-ever academic test performance. How likely would it be for you to appear on *Time's* cover again? Remember, we are assuming your picture was after your best-ever performance.)

**2.9**    We are concerned that the results will be biased in this before–after scenario if the people who drop out because the time is inconvenient or because they don't like this particular approach to physical fitness are the ones for whom the program is having the least effect. If the reasons for dropping out are systematically related to lack of improvement in physical fitness, then any causal inference involving the program is seriously threatened. You may also recognize that coincidental and natural causes as plausible alternative explanations for changes in physical fitness would also have to be ruled out. Are other things going on in the lives of these people that might bring about an increase in physical fitness? Is there any reason to believe that these changes might occur naturally in these people? A case might also be made for possible regression effects if, as we might reasonably assume, people seek to improve their physical fitness when they are in their worst-ever shape!

**2.10**    We suggest that before this young man breaks off the romance, he think about other factors that are present. For example, he might ask his girlfriend to change perfume, hair spray, brands of laundry detergent, material in frequently worn clothes (such as wool vs. cotton), and so on. When we apply the method of agreement it is not always easy to identify all of the factors that could be causally related to the phenomenon in question.

**2.11**    Applying the joint method of agreement and difference would involve (1) random assigment of children to the two different vocabulary methods (old and new), and (2) making sure that the method of teaching vocabulary was the *only* difference between the two groups. Random assignment should ensure that the two groups of children are essentially equal in size of vocabulary, motivation to learn, and other relevant characteristics before the training methods are introduced. If we use the same vocabulary words, and the same testing procedure and hold other important factors constant, we can be sure that the only difference between the two groups of children when a vocabulary test is given is the difference between the two vocabulary training methods. If a difference in test performance is found, then we can assume that the method of vocabulary training caused the difference.

# • • • • • • • • • •
# Recommended Readings

Many of the topics in Chapter 2 are discussed in textbooks on the philosophy of science and in books that provide an introduction to the scientific method. We're somewhat biased, but we believe an especially good example of the latter type of book is John Shaughnessy and Eugene Zechmeister's (1990) *Research Methods in Psychology,* which takes a problem-solving approach to the development of scientific thinking. You will find an excellent set of exercises to test your thinking about causal inferences in Schuyler Huck and Howard Sandler's (1979) *Rival Hypotheses: Alternative Interpretations of Data-Based Conclusions.* At a more advanced level, a classic text in this area is Richard Nisbett and Lee Ross's (1980) *Human Inference: Strategies and Shortcomings of Social Judgment.* Also at an advanced level is a book by Deanna Kuhn and her colleagues (1988), which examines the development of scientific thinking skills, especially from middle childhood to adulthood: *The Development of Scientific Thinking Skills.*

# Explaining the Behavior of Others

**Some people will never learn anything, for this reason, because they understand everything too soon.**

Alexander Pope
(18th-century English poet and satirist)

• • • • • • • • • • • • • • • • • • • • • • • • • • • • • • • • • • • • • • • • • • • • • • • • • • • • • •

In Chapter 2 you learned some basic principles to apply when you try to understand causation. We will now look more specifically at how people try to understand the causes of other people's behavior. Many of life's important problems occur within a social context, and to reach good solutions to these problems, we must attempt to understand the behavior of those who share that social context with us. This is not always a simple process, however. In this chapter we will show you many of the pitfalls that await you as you try to explain why a person acts the way he or she does. We will also show you ways in which you can improve your chances of being right when you attempt to understand the causes of other people's behavior.

• • • • • • • • •
# Introduction

There are few days when we are not called upon to think about why someone behaved in one way or another. We may be forced to think about the reasons for people's behavior when we read newspaper headlines ("Disturbed Youth Tries to Shoot President"), or when we find ourselves in an everyday predicament (Why did that driver run into my car?), or when we simply observe the people around us (Why didn't Mary come to the party?). Making causal attributions in regard to others' behavior is natural and often necessary, as when we must fix blame for a particular action. Did the youth mean to kill the president? Did that driver fail to see the stop sign? Is Mary angry with me? In Chapter 2 we discussed strategies to help us identify the causes of events; in this chapter we continue our discussion of the causal attribution process, but now our focus is on explaining behavior. As you will see, there is much more to think about than we have yet considered.

When people infer the causes of other people's behavior, they typically make a judgment as to the locus of causation of such behavior. That is, they judge that a behavior is internally caused, externally caused, or caused by some combination of internal and external factors. Internal causes are such things as an individual's personal characteristics or dispositions, emotional states, wishes and desires, and abilities. External causes include environmental or situational conditions that may elicit certain behaviors. For example, a man's extreme suspiciousness may be an internal cause of his discomfort in interpersonal relationships, but it may also be an external source of discomfort for his wife.

In general, we tend to assume that internal factors are under our control, whereas external events that influence our behavior are beyond our control or permit only very limited control (Rotter, 1966). There are many exceptions to this assumption, however. The suspicious man may recognize that there is no good reason to be so suspicious, and that his suspiciousness offends other people and causes him a great deal of personal discomfort. Despite all of the arguments he may be able to muster, however, he may not be able to change his suspiciousness one bit. His wife, however, may exert control over the external conditions that are causing her pain by choosing to divorce her suspicious husband.

• • • • • • • • •
# Determining Internal and External Causation: A Rational Model

It may come as no surprise that one of the principles for determining why people behave as they do is based on the method of agreement, which we discussed in Chapter 2. It turns out that the method of agreement is something we all tend to use naturally. In describing our search for causal conditions, for example, Harold Kelley (1973, p.108) suggests that "an effect is attributed to one of its possible causes with which, over time, it covaries." We look, in other words, for conditions that are present when the effect is present and absent when the effect is absent. (You may remember the scientist who sought the cause of his hangover.) If your cousin breaks out in a distinctive rash whenever she has to do homework, but never shows this rash when she has no homework, we are likely to conclude that the rash is caused by (an allergy to) homework.

Kelley further suggests that our attributional analyses of behavior commonly are focused on three possible kinds of causes: people, targets, and situations. In other words, is there something specific to or inherent in the *person* whose behavior we are trying to understand, is there some characteristic of the object or *target* of the individual's behavior, is there something about the particular circumstances of the *situation* in which the behavior occurs? Or does some combination of person, target, and situation determine our understanding of the causes of one's behavior?

To get a grasp on Kelley's model, let's apply it to a hypothetical scenario.

• • • • • • • • •

## The Volleyball Game

The volleyball team at Joe's college is playing for the league championship, and, knowing several players on the team, Joe decides to attend. As it's a home game, the crowd is large and supportive, and Joe sticks out like a sore thumb when he shouts derogatory and insulting comments at his team. More accurately, Joe is directing his attack at one player, a tall redhead named Vicky; he is very encouraging to the other players. It is interesting to note that Joe also makes derogatory comments to Vicky when he sees her in the dorm, at the student union, and elsewhere on campus, and has angrily refused to be paired with her to work on a chemistry project.

What are some possible reasons for Joe's behavior toward Vicky?

If you conclude that Joe behaves insultingly to Vicky because he is a jerk, hates Vicky, or has latent hostility to tall redheads because of conflicts with his tall, redheaded mother, you are basing your attributions on judgments about the *person*. You may, however, decide that Vicky is playing a terrible game, that Vicky frequently insults Joe, or that Vicky owes Joe money and won't pay him back. If so, then you have based your attribution on characteristics of the *target* of the behavior. To explain the *situation* dimension, let's assume that Gary, who knows neither Joe nor Vicky but who is sitting near Joe, starts to yell at Vicky as the home team drops further and further behind in the score. Gary has never yelled at or insulted Vicky in the past, and it is unlikely that he ever will again. Knowing this, you are apt to infer that the particular circumstances (situation) of Joe's yelling and the home team's losing have caused Gary's behavior. Or you might conclude that Gary is a fool to be yelling, but probably wouldn't be so ill mannered if Joe weren't providing an example for him. This explanation represents a combination of person and situation causes.

To understand how one's examination of person, target, and situation dimensions leads one to make either internal or external causal attributions, let's explore the model further. Kelley's model is sometimes referred to as "Kelley's

It is not always easy to determine accurately the causes of another person's behavior.

cube" because he has graphically presented the model as a three-dimensional cube, the dimensions being persons, (potential) targets, and situations. The volleyball game scenario can be represented on this cube as in Figure 3.1.

To use Kelley's cube, you might take a pencil and put Xs through all of the smaller cubes in Figure 3.1 that constitute reported instances of hostile behavior. Once you have done this, it should be evident that Joe is the only one showing hostile behavior. Thus there is low consensus as to his behavior in that other people do not share in his way of acting toward Vicky. Were Ellen, Tom, and Sue also to yell derogatory comments at Vicky during the course of the game, there would be high consensus as to Joe's behavior. That is, other people would be responding to the same target, Vicky, in the same way as Joe.

Another thing that you may notice is that Joe's hostility is directed only at Vicky; that is, it is distinctive. He doesn't show hostile behavior to any of the other volleyball players. Were he to yell insults at all of the players, his behavior would be low in distinctiveness. Finally, Joe's behavior is highly consistent. He not only yells at Vicky during the volleyball game but is also hostile to her in other situations (the dorm, the student union, chemistry class). Gary's behavior, in contrast, is low in consistency. That is, though Gary does yell at Vicky during the volleyball game, he doesn't show any hostility toward her in other situations.

Thus Kelley's analysis points to three important factors that control our attribution of the causes of behavior: people, targets, and situations. If many

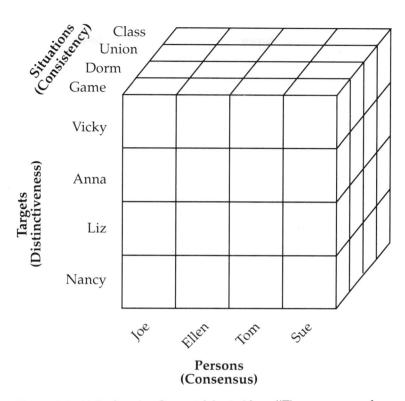

**Figure 3.1**   Kelley's cube. *Source:* Adapted from "The processes of causal attribution,"
by H. H. Kelley. In *American Psychologist*, 1974, *28*, 107–128. Reprinted by permission
of the author.

people show the same behavior, this behavior is high in *consensus*. If the behavior
is shown toward only one of several possible targets, the behavior is *distinctive*.
If the behavior is shown across a variety of situations, the behavior is *consistent*. It is the factors of consensus, distinctiveness, and consistency, according
to Kelley, that lead us to decide whether we will attribute causality to internal
or external sources (or some combination of such sources).

The manner in which we are influenced by these factors appears to be quite
predictable also. To verify this analysis, think about some of the things that you
believe may be causing Joe's behavior. Now estimate how internally or externally caused you think Joe's behavior is in terms of the following scale:

Completely internal   1   2   3   4   5   6   7   Completely external

We've already identified Joe's behavior as highly distinctive, highly consistent, but low in consensus. Kelley predicts that when we are confronted by this
pattern of high consistency, high distinctiveness, and low consensus, we are
most likely to be accurate if we make a mixed attribution; that is, see both internal and external factors to be causative (a score of 3, 4, or 5 on the scale).

Thus, you may have been thinking that Joe is a jerk (internal causation) to be making such a scene, but you may also be wondering what Vicky has done (external causation) to incur his wrath. Is she rude to him? Does she owe him money? Did she dump him?

In general, we tend to make internal attributions when behavior is low in distinctiveness and consensus but high in consistency. We probably would consider Joe as the cause of this problem if he yelled at everyone, if he were the only person doing the yelling, and if he did it in one situation after another. However, when behavior is high on all three dimensions, Kelley indicates, we are likely to make external attributions. Thus if Joe yelled derogatory remarks only at Vicky (distinctiveness), but so did everyone else (consensus), and people behaved toward Vicky in that way all the time (consistency), then we would probably say that the causes of Joe's behavior are external; that is, something other than a personal problem on his part. We would need to look to the environment or situation. Perhaps Vicky recently made money by selling a scandalous and embarrassing news item involving her classmates to the local newspaper!

• • • • • • • • • • • • • • • • • • • • • • • • • • • • • • • • • • • • • • • • • • • • • • • • • • •

**THINK about It**

**3.1**    Consider the following scenario:

• • • • • • • • •

### The Art Museum

Beth has never been particularly interested in art, so she is ho-humming her way through a tour of an art museum. Her attention is drawn, however, to a towering statue of a heroic figure that she sees at the end of a long corridor. As she approaches the statue, she finds it even more compelling, and stops to study it more closely. When she glances at her watch, she finds that she has been staring at the statue, transfixed, for over 20 minutes. Her immediate fear is that she has gotten separated from her tour group, but as she looks around her, she sees that the group is intact, most of them responding as Beth does to the statue. From then on, Beth returns to the museum frequently, primarily to see the statue.

Rate Beth's behavior on the following dimensions:

Distinctiveness:    low  1  2  3  4  5  6  7  high
Consistency:    low  1  2  3  4  5  6  7  high
Consensus:    low  1  2  3  4  5  6  7  high

Also rate Beth's behavior in terms of the locus of causality:

Internal  1  2  3  4  5  6  7  External

• • • • • • • • •

It's very likely that you rated Beth's behavior as externally caused. Now comes the real challenge. As a test of your understanding of this model, write your own scenario describing a situation in which the locus of causality is clearly something *internal* to the actor. Then turn to our discussion at the end of the chapter to see if your scenario conforms to the requirements of consistency, consensus, and distinctiveness expected with internal causality. If it doesn't, try rewriting it to conform to these criteria.

## Discounting and Augmentation Principles

Kelley acknowledges that his model is not always applied in day-to-day situations. That is, it assumes that an individual makes a large number of observations of several people in several situations over several time periods before he or she infers that a given behavior is either internally or externally caused. Kelley goes on to suggest that, for whatever reason (time constraints, lack of motivation to scrutinize a behavior, limited opportunities to observe), people often infer whether an effect is internally or externally caused on the basis of a single observation of that effect. In such a case, however, a person is rarely operating in a knowledge vacuum. "Ordinarily he (she) has observed similar effects before and has some notions about possibly relevant causes and how they relate to this type of effect. And, of course, his (her) information about the present instance is likely to indicate the presence of certain plausible causes" (Kelley, 1973, p. 113).

What typically occurs, then, is that we draw upon knowledge of similar situations, extract whatever relevant information we can from the present situation, generate a number of possible causes, and then weigh those possible causes to arrive at the most likely cause or causes. Kelley suggests that two principles are operative in this rough weighing process: the discounting principle and the augmentation principle.

Kelley explains the *discounting principle* this way: "The role of a given cause in producing a given effect is discounted if other plausible causes are also present" (Kelley, 1973, p. 113). Another way of saying this is that the more causes that seem reasonable there are in a situation, the less important we see any one cause to be. Let's take an example. Assume that you're walking across campus on a fine Saturday morning and you see your friend Keith hurrying from the gym to the cafeteria. You know that Keith is coming from an intramural basketball game, so you ask him how it went. He gives you a rushed reply: "We lost to the Killer Bees. I only got ten points. Gotta hustle if I'm still gonna make breakfast." As he passes you notice that he is carrying an ice bag and limping slightly. As we've said before, you're not operating in a knowledge vacuum; suppose you know that Keith is one of the top intramural basketball players on campus, usually scoring in the 20-point range.

**THINK about It**

**3.2**    Write down a reason or reasons that may explain why Keith scored below his average. How likely do you think your reason(s) is/are the most important one(s)?

_____

_____

_____

_____

_____

Now let's add some further information to the problem. Suppose you know that Keith doesn't exactly spend his Friday nights counting the flowers on his wallpaper, and this Friday night was no exception. Keith partied until 4 A.M. Further assume that you know his 20-point average was earned primarily in weeknight games. Finally, you recall that the Killer Bees are one of the top intramural teams at the college, and they specialize in playing tough defense. Now write down what you see to be the cause or causes of Keith's subpar performance. How certain are you that any one cause is the most important one?

_____

_____

_____

_____

_____

Some possible causes are discussed at the end of the chapter.

Let's now turn to the augmentation principle. But before we discuss this principle, please write down an answer to the following question: Which gift is most appreciated, one given by a close friend at Christmas or that same gift if it is given by your friend on the spur of the moment? Also jot down a brief explanation for your answer.

_____

_____

_____

_____

Kelley (1973, p. 114) states that the *augmentation principle* "refers to the familiar idea that when there are known to be constraints, costs, sacrifices, or risks involved in taking an action, the action once taken is attributed more to the actor than it would be otherwise." To elaborate, external causes can be seen as either facilitating or inhibiting an action. If an external cause is inhibitory, it makes an action more difficult to be carried out. Consequently, we do a little mental algebra and conclude that if there are environmental barriers to performing an act and if that act is still carried out, an exceptional internal drive must be pushing that act through the external barriers to completion. Therefore, when we see inhibiting external forces among our array of possible external causes, then we are likely to weight more heavily (augment) the importance of internal causes. Let's return to our basketball example to illustrate.

Assume that Keith's comments to you were "We beat the Killer Bees 52 to 51 and I got 32 points." Now, a possible inference comes to mind: Maybe the Killer Bees played a bad game. Probably not; they never do. So you are likely to conclude that the Killer Bees played their usual tough defensive game. Thus they are identified as a strong external inhibiting cause. How, then, are you likely to explain Keith's performance? It is possible that you say something like "I knew Keith was good, but he must really be great." That is, his good level of ability (an internal cause) is augmented until it is viewed as a great level of ability.

What happens if an external cause is facilitative? One day, in a fit of whimsy, one of your authors assigned his class a project for which they could earn a very small amount of extra credit. Students were given the option of doing something nice but unexpected for someone, and then reporting, in writing, about this experience. Their report was to tell why they decided on a particular act of kindness (washing a car, giving flowers, paying a visit, whatever), how they chose the recipient of the act (parent, sweetheart, long-lost friend), and a description of the recipient's response as well as their own response to the act.

Many students put much more effort into this project than the small amount of extra credit seemed to warrant. One student spent all weekend cleaning his grandmother's home, and another student offered apologies, complete with flowers, to a friend with whom she had had a bitter argument and had not spoken for three months. Moreover, most sudents described internal causes, such as love or affection, for selecting the particular recipient of the good deed. Nevertheless, the recipients almost invariably expressed disappointment if they found out that one of the motives for this behavior was the wish to earn extra credit. Many students echoed this disappointment, indicating that they probably would have gotten more pleasure out of their good deeds if they were not getting extra credit. The consequence of introducing a facilitating external cause, then, was that any internal causes were discounted by both the giver and the recipient. Such discounting of internal causes is exactly the effect that Kelley predicts of a facilitating external cause.

Now, reflect on your answer to our question about gift giving. Did you discount the Christmas gift in relation to the spontaneous gift? If so, how so?

# • • • • • • • • •
# "Nonrational" Influences in Determining Causation

Thus far, the attributional models that we have considered convey the impression that we thoughtfully examine a person's behavior and the environment in which that behavior occurs, and that we even carefully search our memory for related incidents of behavior, before we attribute the cause of that behavior to internal or external sources. This impression is rather deceiving. As we have said, models such as Kelley's cube represent what people *should* do rather than what they commonly do in using information to form causal attributions. Social-psychological research has clearly demonstrated that our attributions are frequently determined or influenced by much less rational and methodical means than Kelley's model suggests.

## The Fundamental Attribution Error

One nonrational influence on the attributional process is what is known as the *fundamental attribution error* (Ross, 1977), which we mentioned briefly in Chapter 1. This error in thinking has been described as the tendency of an observer to overemphasize the importance of personality or intellectual influences and to underemphasize the importance of environmental or situational influences in determining an actor's behavior (Myers, 1987). In other words, we tend to favor internal over external attributions when we explain another person's behavior. If we hear that our friend has suffered two work-related injuries in the past six months (a broken finger and a sprained ankle), we are likely to consider him accident-prone. An alternative explanation is that he works in an occupation that puts him at high risk for injury. The fundamental attribution error, however, generally prevents us from giving this alternative much weight unless it is so obvious that we can't possibly ignore it (our friend is a professional football player, say).

Even when external influences are rather obvious, the fundamental attribution error persists. Two similar studies in which students defended controversial positions succinctly illustrate this persistence. In one study, carried out in the mid-1960s (Jones & Harris, 1967), college students read transcripts of a debate in which the participants either attacked or supported Fidel Castro. Under one condition of the experiment, the students were told that each debater's position had been arbitrarily determined and assigned by the debate coach. Surprisingly, despite this information, the students concluded that the debaters who spoke in support of Castro were sympathetic to him. Thus a position that was forced on the debaters by the dictates of the situation was still (erroneously) seen as reflecting a personal disposition.

In a more recent study (Reeder, 1985), students were assigned the task of reading a prepared statement to other students in which they argued against a drinking age of 18. The student audience knew that the student speakers had been specifically instructed to prepare a statement in opposition to a law allowing 18-year-olds to drink. Nevertheless (you guessed it), the student audience concluded that the speakers were in fact opposed to the law. This conclusion, by the way, was not supported when the speakers were asked their real opinion of the law.

One factor that contributes to the fundamental attribution error is what is known as the *actor-observer effect* (Jones & Nisbett, 1971). Let's say you walk into

Beware of the actor–observer effect.

a friend's room and find her standing on tiptoe on a short ladder, painting her ceiling. Just as you enter the room, she reaches into the bucket to wet her brush, knocks the bucket of paint to the floor, and splatters everything, including you. Once you calm down, how are you likely to explain your friend's behavior? Probably by concluding that she is clumsy or careless or generally inept. But what if it were you on the ladder? My, how the tune changes: "This ladder is too short. It's too rickety. This paintbrush is too big for the bucket. You startled me." The list goes on. In other words, if you observe another person, you are likely to attribute his or her behavior to internal causes, whereas if you are the originator of that behavior (that is, the actor), you are likely to give increased emphasis to external causes in explaining that behavior.

· · · · · · · · · · · · · · · · · · · · · · · · · · · · · · · · · · · · · · · · · · · · · · · · · · ·

**THINK about It**

**3.3**   Analyze how excuses in general are illustrative of the actor-observer effect. Consider excuses you have heard people use when they were late for work, handed in an overdue assignment, missed a birthday or anniversary of a close friend, or simply didn't get the job done right. Write down your analysis in the following space:

_____

_____

_____

_____

_____

_____

_____

_____

Compare your analysis with ours at the end of the chapter.

· · · · · · · · · · · · · · · · · · · · · · · · · · · · · · · · · · · · · · · · · · · · · · · · · · ·

There is evidence that the actor-observer effect may be explained by the difference in information available to the actor and to the observer as well as differences in their focus of attention (Gergen & Gergen, 1981). Specifically, actors generally have more information about situational factors that might influence the action than observers do. In the case of your paint-spattering friend, you are unlikely to realize that she was startled. Second, research has demonstrated that "actors primarily focus their attention outward, toward the environment's obstacles, potentials, and so forth. Observers mainly focus on the actor. Other aspects of the situation—those which constrain the actor's choices—may go unnoticed by the observer" (Gergen & Gergen, 1981, p. 68). Thus, as you (the observer) focus on the actor, you fail to take into account that the ladder is short and rickety and the paintbrush too big.

Let us warn you that the actor-observer effect is not carved in stone. People in general are expected to show this bias, but many individuals stand out as exceptions to this general rule. That is, some people feel that they exert a great deal of internal control over their lives, while others see themselves as pawns of fate (and a whole bunch of us fall somewhere in between). Moreover, as you will see when we discuss self-serving biases in Chapter 4, many people are likely to see their behaviors as internally caused when it's self-enhancing to do so and as externally caused when such an attribution is self-protective. Consequently, while the fundamental attribution error is an important principle in understanding how people form causal attributions, you will see that this principle needs to be modified when you seek to explain how people determine the causes of their own behavior.

A few exceptions to the fundamental attribution error have to be acknowledged even when we are explaining another person's behavior. On occasion, we form attributions that give people the benefit of the doubt (Baum, Fisher, & Singer, 1985). If the person's behavior leads to a good outcome, we tend to attribute it to internal factors, whereas behaviors that produce negative or unpleasant outcomes are more likely to be explained by external factors. This exception to the fundamental attribution error is not universal, however. We are most likely to show such generosity when we infer causality from the behavior of people we like. With our enemies, it's a different story. The bad guys in our lives get blamed for bad outcomes but are not credited for the positive results of their efforts. We also sometimes show this attributional generosity when we explain the behavior of people who have power over us. That is, we may not like our boss, but we may still attribute his or her success to personal characteristics and abilities. Researchers (Baum et al., 1985) suggest that people do this because the alternative has unpleasant consequences for them: "Attributions that the boss is inherently incompetent makes his or her superiority seem unjust, resulting in discomfort on our part" (p. 151).

• • • • • • • • • • • • • • • • • • • • • • • • • • • • • • • • • • • • • • • • • • • • • • • • • •

**THINK
about It**

**3.4**   Bring to mind a really fanatical sports fan that you know. Describe how this person typically explains the outcome of a game in which his or her favorite team gets beaten by a rival. Does the explanation vary with the intensity of the rivalry? In what ways do this fan's explanations illustrate either the fundamental attribution error or the exceptions to the error that we have just described? Write your answers to these questions in the space provided below.

_____

_____

_____

_____

_____

_____

_____

_____

We analyze this situation at the end of the chapter.

• • • • • • • • • • • • • • • • • • • • • • • • • • • • • • • • • • • • • • • • • • • • • • • •

## Stereotypical Thinking

A particular mental set or cognitive predisposition to interpret another person's behavior in either an enhancing or a discrediting manner is clearly seen in our use of stereotypes. A stereotype is a schema that we use to categorize people. Such categorization emphasizes the similarities of all members of the category, and also emphasizes the differences between these members and those people who do not belong to the category. When we categorize people as either athletes or intellectuals, for example, we may see all the athletes as being muscular, brash, aggressive, and given to drinking vast quantities of domestic beer, while we see the intellectuals as being slim and well mannered (if a bit aloof) with distinct preferences for imported white wine and strong-smelling cheese. These categories are obvious oversimplifications. You probably know an intellectual or two who thrives on Budweiser as well as a few polite athletes.

One of the defining characteristics of a stereotype is that it is an oversimplification, and therein lies its value as well as its hazard. Stereotypes have been described as "cognitively economical" (Mischel, 1986, p. 245) in that they help us to manage large amounts of information about people and to predict the behavior of others when information is limited. In other words, after we place an individual in a category, we don't remember every bit of information we have about him or her. Rather, we focus on the characteristics of the individual that are relevant to the category. In addition, when we have very limited information about a person but we do know that he or she is a member of a given category, we are likely to assume that the individual possesses characteristics common to the category. Thus, if you are told that a man you are about to interview is a political conservative, you may conclude things not only about his politics but about his age, affluence, and taste in clothes and automobiles as well.

To pursue the adaptive value of stereotypes, let's say that you're selecting classes for the coming semester, and you choose one professor whom other students have categorized as a tough grader and another professor who is categorized as "an easy A." On the basis of these categories, you are likely to plan your study time and effort so as to maximize the possibility of getting good grades from both professors.

One of the hazards of stereotypes, even when they convey valid and useful information, is that they may also convey additional information that is of questionable utility or validity. People have consistently demonstrated the tendency to generate implicit personality theories from very limited information (Schneider, 1973). That is, given only minimal information about an individual, people readily imagine a whole network of traits that they believe to be associated with the trait identified by or inferred from the original information. This network of associations may be so complete as to give us a tentative sense of the individual's total personality structure. Unfortunately, the implicit personality theory that we create is based on very limited information, and as such probably contains many inaccuracies.

**THINK about It**

**3.5** Write down five of the most important descriptive characteristics that you commonly associate with:

physicians _____

artists _____

vegetarians _____

college students _____

lawyers _____

athletes _____

We have given this task to a group of 50 students. You can turn to the back of this chapter to see how your characterizations compare with the most common characterizations given by this group.

## The Hazards of Stereotyping

We've suggested that a stereotype can contain valid information as well as misinformation. The potential for misinformation in stereotypes is high for a number of reasons. First of all, not all information is given equal weight in the formation of stereotypes. Rather, stereotypes are particularly influenced by the *primacy effect* (Asch, 1952). You can see this effect when initial information carries greater weight in the forming of impressions than later information does. Remember the dictum "first impressions are lasting impressions"? This dictum appears to hold true even when later information contradicts the initial impression (Anderson, 1974). That is not to say that initial impressions cannot be reversed; once they are formed, however, it may take a large amount of contradictory evidence to reverse them. We will consider why this is the case when we discuss the nature of a schema in more detail.

The most obvious or *salient* cues or characteristics about a person are also likely to be given greater weight in impression formation than are less obvious (but possibly more important) cues (Freedman, Sears, & Carlsmith, 1981). These salient cues on which we base our categorizations are those things that are most easily observable about a person. These things commonly are physical characteristics such as race, gender, physique, and age. Thus, if we are white, we may base a judgment about a middle-aged black woman's intellectual potential on her skin color because it is the first (primary) and most obvious (salient) thing that we notice about her. The impact of a salient characteristic is accentuated if that characteristic is highly uncommon in the context in which the judgment is made. For example, if we find our middle-aged black woman attending classes on a predominantly black campus, her skin color decreases in salience because it is not uncommon on this campus. Her age, however, may become particularly salient because she is surrounded by young adults. Consequently, people who respond to her in terms of a stereotype may suggest that she is too old to do well in school or that she should do well because she is a mature student. Note, too, that these suggestions may be offered with no real knowledge of the woman's intellectual ability. Thus you see that our impressions are strongly influenced by what is most distinctive about this woman at first glance.

Salient characteristics of individuals may be linked to salient characteristics of situations and result in illusory correlations of the kind we discussed in Chapter 2. Remember that an illusory correlation is an inference that certain relationships exist when in fact they do not. For example, people tend to associate violent crimes with minority-group membership, and so overestimate the frequency with which minority-group members commit crimes. One explanation of such overestimation suggests that illusory correlations are particularly likely to occur when two distinctive stimuli or events occur simultaneously (Hamilton, Dugan, & Trolier, 1985).

A few years ago, a seaman was convicted of shooting and killing his electronics instructor at a naval base near Chicago. The seaman had a Middle Eastern –sounding name. An acquaintance of one of your authors, in discussing this crime, suggested that "they shouldn't let Arabs have guns; they're too violent." This stereotypic conclusion could be explained by the fact that Middle Easterners are an uncommon minority in much of this country, and that murders are uncommon occurrences. People tend to link these two uncommon events in a causal relationship, suggesting that this person's minority status is what caused him to commit murder. It's informative to note that our friend didn't focus on less salient features of the seaman and suggest that sailors or married men or residents of Illinois shouldn't have guns.

It is an unfortunate tendency not only of individuals but also of the news media to focus on salient features of individuals in reporting crimes committed by them. For instance, if a former mental patient, who is also an electrician, a model railroader, and a father of three throws a rotten egg at the governor, you know very well that the headlines won't read "Train Buff Eggs Guv." The tragedy of such reporting is that it causes us to overestimate the potential for violence in the identified population (in this case, former mental patients).

The perspective from which you view another's behavior may also contribute to the misinformation carried in a stereotype. That is, if you share membership in the same stereotypic category as the person you are judging (that is, both you and the other person are members of the same in-group), you are likely to judge that person's behavior differently than you would if he or she were not a member of your category (that is, from your perspective, he or she is a member of an out-group). One way this difference is manifested is in the tendency for members of an in-group to see this group composition as quite heterogeneous, while they see the out-group membership as quite homogeneous. In other words, as the social psychologist David Myers (1987, p. 515), has expressed it, "they are alike, we are diverse." Visitors to a foreign country commonly categorize the natives of that country as friendly or unfriendly. The natives or long-term residents of any country are unlikely to see such a categorization as very accurate. Rather, they may suggest that they have friendly neighbors, unfriendly neighbors, and even neighbors whose friendliness seems to be affected by the phase of the moon.

This tendency to perceive differences in the in-group while perceiving similarities in the out-group has been demonstrated consistently and in a large variety of groups studied in social-psychological research. For example, groups categorized by age (Linville, 1982), gender (Park & Rothbart, 1982), and sorority membership (Park & Rothbart, 1982) have all demonstrated this in-group/out-group bias. Another way in which this bias has been manifested is in the tendency to make more polarized or extreme judgments of the behavior of out-group members than of in-group members. The bad news, if you're an out-group member, is that if an in-group member judges that you've done something bad, his or her judgment is likely to be very harsh. The good news is that if the in-group member evaluates your efforts favorably, this evaluation is likely to be quite favorable.

This evaluative bias was illustrated very effectively in a study in which white subjects examined and evaluated law school applications of two candidates, one white (in-group) and one African-American (out-group) (Linville & Jones, 1980). These applications were actually rigged by the experimenters so that one application portrayed an outstanding record of achievement while the other application summarized a rather mediocre record. Beyond the academic records, only minimal information was provided about the two candidates, but included in this information was their race. Thus racial identities and academic records were presented in the four possible combinations to the raters: (1) African-American candidate, outstanding record; (2) African-American candidate, mediocre record; (3) white candidate, outstanding record; (4) white candidate, mediocre record. The white raters' evaluations of these records indicated that when they judged the two candidates with the outstanding records, they were more positive in their judgments of the African-American candidate (out-group member) than of the white candidate (in-group member). This polarity (but not favorability) of judgments was also maintained with the mediocre records. In this case, the African-American candidate was judged more harshly than the white candidate. The researchers also demonstrated that this bias was not limited only to in-group/out-group differences based on race. They replicated the study by having white male subjects judge either a white male candidate or a white female candidate, and the male judges showed the same pattern of bias, giving more extreme evaluations to the female candidate than to the male candidate.

As should be clearly established by now, we readily form attributions and pass judgments on the basis of minimal information. You will recall the fundamental attribution error as an example of such behavior. Again, the significant factor is whether we're talking about our own behavior or the behavior of someone else. When we talk about our own behavior, we are prone to be particularly sensitive to situational causes of behavior; when we talk about the behavior of someone else, we emphasize dispositional characteristics in explaining the person's behavior.

Thomas Pettigrew, a psychologist who has spent most of his career studying racial prejudice, takes the fundamental attribution error one step further in describing the *ultimate attribution error* (Pettigrew, 1979). In-group members commit this error consistently by attributing the negative or undesirable behaviors of out-group members to dispositional characteristics and discounting positive behaviors of out-group members by explaining them in terms of external causation. If the sexist male sees a woman outscore him on a physics exam, for example, he may suggest that she stole the exam, got lucky, or is having an affair with the teacher. But if the woman does poorly, our sexist student may see her performance as evidence of her inherent lack of intelligence. The ultimate attribution error is also demonstrated by our propensity to attribute desirable outcomes of in-group members' behaviors to their dispositional characteristics while attributing undesirable or negative outcomes to external forces. Thus our sexist student sees his male friend's good grades as evidence of the natural superiority of men, and his bad grades as due to bad luck, poorly prepared tests, the discriminatory grading of female teachers, and so on.

**THINK about It**

**3.6**   From the list of categories in TAI 3.5, choose those categories with which you feel most closely identified and those categories from which you feel most distanced (for example, if you are a prelaw student, you may be closely identified with the category of lawyers). The categories with which you are closely identified are your in-groups and those from which you feel distanced are your out-groups. Describe any ways in which your characterizations of your in-group categories differ from your out-group characterizations. Specifically consider the following questions.

1. Was it easier or harder to come up with five characteristics for in-groups or for out-groups?

2. What made it easier or harder?

_____

_____

3. Was either your in-group or your out-group described more favorably than the other?

_____

4. Did your in-group descriptions or your out-group descriptions match up better with the characteristics listed in the discussion of TAI 3.5 at the end of the chapter?

_____

These questions are also discussed at the end of the chapter.

## Our Personal Schema of Things

We mentioned earlier that a stereotype is a schema. A *schema* is often important in our thinking about things. It has been defined as a "knowledge structure for a fairly complex and general concept" (Zechmeister & Nyberg, 1982, p. 302). People have schemas for such concepts as "house," "person," "animal," "toy," and many other things that we think about. A schema permits efficient storage of information, as we saw in the case of stereotypes; our personal schemas also reveal our biases.

The environment usually provides us with more information than we can possibly attend to or remember later. Therefore, we look to simplify and to organize information so as to comprehend it and so that we will be able to recall it later. Suppose that you see a tall, gray-haired man dressed in jeans, a flannel shirt, and running shoes. He is wearing steel-rimmed bifocals, has a small mole above his right eye, a wedding band on his left hand, an iron-on patch on the right knee of his jeans, and the tip of a brown plaid handkerchief sticking out of his left back pocket. He attracts your attention because both you and he are having lunch at the same fast-food restaurant, across the street from the college campus, and he gets into an argument with the counterman. He speaks in an angry but articulate manner with a slight New England accent. He is carrying a red book, a sheaf of computer printouts, a stack of examination blue books, and a small but sophisticated-looking calculator. You could potentially also notice literally thousands of other things about him, but you focus or selectively attend to a few features as you try to guess who he may be. The blue books immediately make you think "professor." By his dress you guess that he's probably not from the Business School, and the printouts and calculator

Our schemas often lead us to attend to schema-consistent information, while we ignore information that is inconsistent with the schema.

lead you to conclude that he's in the Math Department. After lunch, you tell a friend about this "math prof" who made such a scene at the restaurant.

In trying to figure out who this person is, you imposed a schema on the vast array of information available to you. You focused your attention on certain characteristics (blue books, printouts, calculator) while ignoring other characteristics (such as the mole and the handkerchief) as irrelevant. This focus led to an organization that produced an articulate, older person with blue books and computing paraphenalia, who fit your stereotype of a math professor. The focus of attention and the organization of information constituted a simplification. In other words, you didn't classsify this person as a married math professor who is also a jogger, probably farsighted, and from New England; your curiosity was satisfied once you had fit this man into your simple schema "math professor." Finally, your schema is likely to reflect your own biases. Being a liberal arts major, you don't even consider that this person could be from the School of Engineering; and as you are young, it doesn't occur to you that this gray-haired man may be a graduate student.

Once a schema is established, it has some important effects on one's subsequent information processing (Baron & Byrne, 1987). First of all, you are likely to pay closer attention to information that is consistent with your schema than to information that is inconsistent with it. If you see your math professor enter the computer center, you are more likely to attend to this information as relevant than you would if you saw him enter the English Department. Second, once a schema is established, you are likely to resist any evidence that would contradict your schema, and may even try to refute such evidence. Assume that your schedule is such that you now regularly cross paths with the "math professor," and you generally do see him in the vicinity of the English Department. Rather than conclude that he may be an English professor, you may conclude that he has a close friend in the department whom he frequently visits.

It is usually easier to remember information that is consistent with one's schema than inconsistent information (Howard & Rothbart, 1980; Johnson, Petzel, & Mascari, 1987; Rothbart, Evans, & Fulero, 1979). You are more likely to remember that the professor was carrying a calculator and computer printouts than that he wore a wedding band. You might even show distortions in your memory reports that are supportive of your schema (Johnson, Petzel, Hartney, & Morgan, 1983; Johnson et al. 1987). Though you never did see the title of the book the "math professor" was carrying, you may remember it as a red math text.

Once a schema is established, it sometimes seems to have a life of its own with a very strong survival instinct. Schemas can become quite permanent and inflexible organizational structures that we impose on our world of experience. Their permanence and inflexibility reflect the fact that they lead us to focus on and interpret our experiences in ways that support and strengthen them. Once a schema is formed, it is not very likely that additional information will change it or have a corrective influence on it; it becomes self-perpetuating.

If we again consider a stereotype as one kind of schema, we can see how such self-perpetuation takes place. A person who is bigoted against African-Americans, for example, may tend to focus on the race of a criminal if that criminal is African-American, but to ignore race if the criminal is white. Consequently, the bigot is especially sensitive to and aware of crimes committed by African-Americans, and so finds it easy to think of African-Americans as criminally inclined. Such a thought is, of course, consistent with and supportive of our bigot's schematic representation of African-Americans. Should this schema be contradicted by statistical evidence in a newspaper article, the bigot may choose not to read the article, thereby ignoring the evidence, or may read the article and conclude that it simply represents the lies and fabrications of some "bleeding-heart liberal." We will meet this type of thinking again in Chapter 5, when we examine subjective validation for beliefs that we hold.

**THINK about It**

**3.7**    We have all been victims of some form of discrimination, and at the heart of this discrimination is the fact that an individual or group has assigned us to a stereotypic category (foreigner, woman, intellectual, country bumpkin, rich kid, college punk, whatever) and then responded to us as a schematic simplification rather than as a living, breathing human being. In the space provided, describe one instance in which you were stereotyped. What characteristic(s) about you was the stereotyping person or group focusing on in stereotyping you? How was their stereotype a simplification (that is, what information were they ignoring or distorting in maintaining their stereotype)? What was your emotional response to being stereotyped? Why is it important to be aware of our own emotional response to this situation if we are to guard against stereotyping others?

_____

_____

_____

_____

_____

_____

_____

_____

_____

_____

_____

Our views on this question are discussed at the end of the chapter. Do you share our views?

## Improving Causal Attributions

Frequently it makes little or no difference whether your causal attributions concerning other people's behavior are accurate. You may note a particular behavior, perhaps because it is unusual or unexpected, draw a causal inference regarding that behavior, and then go on your merry way, neither communicating your inference to the other person nor allowing your inference to influence the way you interact with the other person. In such a case, it would really be a waste of time to analyze your inferences to determine their validity. Occasionally, however, causal inferences prompt and influence very important decisions in our lives. For example, the inferences we make about why the boss passed us over for promotion, why our sweetheart has lost interest in us, or why our speech professor hasn't thus far responded favorably to our class presentations may have important implications for our subsequent behaviors in our work, our romance, or our speech class.

When we communicate our causal attributions to the target of the attribution, they may also have serious implications for the target. Consider the implications if your boss tells you you weren't promoted because your loyalty to the company is in question after your failure to attend the company picnic, if your former sweetheart tells you the relationship broke down because you are totally and irrevocably unlovable, or if your speech teacher tells you that your talks demonstrate a lack of preparation, both in content and in delivery. Each person's interpretation of your behavior offers a different potential for remediation, but if you were to attempt to remedy the situation, you would hope that the direction provided by the attribution was accurate. In short, in many situations it is clearly critical to your and/or other people's happiness and well-being for you to try to be as accurate as possible in your attributions. Let's look at some ways we can enhance the accuracy of our causal attributions concerning other people's behaviors.

First of all, causal attributions, by definition, indicate a cause-and-effect relationship. So a good way to start is to examine your attributions to see if the relationship you are proposing stands up to the criteria of causation proposed in Chapter 2. Is there covariation between events? Is the temporal order of events what it should be if the effect is to be attributed to the factor you have selected as the cause? Are there other, plausible explanations that you failed to take into consideration?

Second, you are likely to reduce attributional errors if you simply recognize that you are making an attribution, and therefore you could be right, but *you could be wrong* (Nisbett & Ross, 1980). People rarely err in the direction of having too little confidence in their causal inferences; rather, they are generally overconfident (Brigham, 1986). Such overconfidence is so prevalant and so troublesome in our efforts to arrive at accurate causal attributions that we recommend that the first premise you start with when you examine your causal attribution is *"I could be wrong."*

Overconfidence can be tempered in several additional ways. You may list reasons as to why your preferred judgment could be wrong (Koriat, Lichenstein, & Fischhoff, 1980). You may also want to generate a list of alternative causal explanations and then think of all the reasons that your favorite attribution and the just-generated additional attributions could be right or wrong. As you will see in Chapter 6, when we consider what we know and don't know, it is particularly important to emphasize why you may be wrong, as opposed to why you may be right, when you analyze your attribution.

You should also be sensitive to other people's reactions to your causal attributions. It has been suggested that "we are often given clues, frequently in the form of questions asked by other people, to the fact that we hold some opinion, or have chosen some course of action, that does not seem reasonable in light of the evidence and arguments that we currently can muster" (Nisbett & Ross, 1980, p. 288). Rather than simply being attuned to people's reactions to your particular causal explanation, you may enhance your attributional accuracy if you actively seek out causal explanations of the behavior under question from other people (Nisbett & Ross, 1980). In doing so, you may find alternative explanations that you overlooked but that are even more reasonable and better supported than yours. Now, obviously, not all critical decisions can be delayed until you've consulted with other people. For example, you wouldn't want the direction of your love life to be determined by committee decision. Nevertheless, when we seek other people's points of view, we commonly become aware of the particular set of blinders we put on when we arrive at our own point of view.

Just as we may draw on the opinions of friends, classmates, co-workers, and other people, in checking out our causal inferences, so we may draw on the resources of experts (Nisbett & Ross, 1980). For instance, if you scan the financial pages of the newspaper for stock market analyses and predictions, you are using information provided by experts to infer the outcomes of future events. If your physician tells you that if you don't lose weight, get more exercise, and cut back on the cholesterol in your diet, you will greatly increase the likelihood of a heart attack in later life, you are getting an expert opinion on a potentially important cause-and-effect relationship in your life. So one way to examine the probable accuracy of your causal inferences is to examine them against the opinions of experts. Please remember, by the way, that many experts are waiting to advise you, free of charge, on the shelves of your local library.

As you may have noticed, experts often speak in terms of statistical probabilities. Some statements are quite precise: "Brushing your teeth with Glunk reduces cavities by 45 percent over no brushing at all"; "Bag-O-Bones is an 8-to-5 favorite to win the prestigious Mudwater Derby." Others are less precise: "You are more likely to have a heart attack"; "These symptoms are associated with schizophrenia." Thinking in terms of statistical probabilities is second nature to many experts. Scientists who study human inference (such as Arkes, 1981; Nisbett & Ross, 1980) suggest that nonexperts (that's us, folks!) would do well to examine their important causal attributions in terms of probabilities also. You may, if you have the time and inclination, seek an expert opinion as to the probability that a proposed cause will lead to an observed effect. Your other option is to guess at the probabilities yourself. In such a case, your probabilities may be general categories, such as "pretty unlikely" or "kind of likely," rather than precise numerical values ("75 percent probability," "5-to-1 odds"). Even in the face of such imprecision, research has indicated that guessing at the probabilities of alternative causal explanations can increase our chances of choosing a correct alternative and rejecting incorrect ones (Arkes, 1981). Sometimes possible but unlikely causes do turn out to be the correct ones, but before you assume that they are correct, the fact that they are unlikely should cue you to examine them very carefully.

Your personal biases (that set of blinders we referred to earlier) are likely to be particularly constraining to the extent that the information you are basing your inference on has an emotional impact on you. Your inferences may be particularly prone to error if they are made in an emotionally charged situation (Nisbett & Ross, 1980). Think of those occasions in which you have gotten very angry with someone, thought all kinds of terrible thoughts about his or her motives, basic character, and ancestry, and then, with the passage of time, revised your appraisal and possibly concluded that his or her actions were somewhat justified. The lesson to be learned here is that attributions made in the heat of anger, passion, or any other intense emotion are quite prone to distortion, and that they should be carefully evaluated after you have cooled off.

One final helpful hint for enchancing the accuracy of your attributions takes us back to the start of this chapter. Kelley's cube is called a rational model because it helps us increase the probability that we will be accurate in determining the locus of causality of behavior. Though this model is not foolproof, referring to Kelley's cube will help us hedge our bets.

A causal attribution, because of its inferential basis, is not a statement of fact; it is a guess at the likelihood that an identified possible cause has in fact produced the effect in question. Those situations in which we can be certain that we completely and clearly understand the causes of someone's behavior are rare indeed. Even the simplest of situations is often difficult to analyze. One of your authors saw a friend hit himself in the shin with a sledgehammer while driving a stake into the ground. He kept right on hammering for about a minute, then stood up straight and screamed, threw the hammer in one direction, and galloped off into the woods in the other. How would you explain his one-minute latency of response? How certain are you of your explanation?

As you can see, even seemingly simple causal relationships can very easily become quite complex and difficult to explain. But there are times in your life when it is important to be accurate when you make a causal attribution, particularly when a corrective response depends on the accuracy of that causal attribution. For example, the teacher who blames a student's poor classroom performance on a bad attitude when in fact that student has a reading disability is not doing much to help the student improve. At those times when your causal attributions do have an impact, we urge you to dig in and think critically, with the goal of improving the chances that your causal attributions will be right.

**THINK about It**

**3.8**   Describe a situation in which a person (such as a teacher, a friend, or a parent) tried to explain your behavior but was in error in identifying the cause of the behavior. Explain that person's error in terms of a principle or principles discussed in this chapter. How did you feel in this situation? Did the erroneous explanation have any serious consequences for you?

_____

_____

_____

_____

_____

_____

At the end of the chapter we consider the importance of such self-reflection for your own behavior. (As a bonus, we will explain the sledgehammer incident!)

• • • • • • • • • • • • • • • • • • • • • • • • • • • • • • • • • • • • • • • • • • • • • • •

## Principles of Effective Thinking about Others: A Summary

1. Acknowledge that your preferred causal attribution in a given situation could be wrong. Further, move beyond this simple acknowledgment to an examination (listing?) of the pros and cons of your chosen attribution as well as the pros and cons of alternative attributions.

2. Examine your attribution to see if it stands up to the criteria of causality discussed earlier (covariation, temporal ordering, and absence of alternative explanations).

3. Be sensitive to others' responses to your attribution as possible indicators that your attribution is not a readily embraced one. Lack of agreement does not necessarily mean that your attribution is wrong, only that it requires careful scrutiny.

4. Determine whether your attribution is consistent with expert opinion.

5. Try to estimate how probable it is that the cause you have identified would have actually occurred and led to the behavior in question. Causal attributions of low probability are more likely to be wrong than attributions of high probability.

6. Reevaluate attributions made in the heat of emotion after you have calmed down and achieved some distance from the emotion-laden situation.

7. Evaluate the behavior under question in terms of its consensus, distinctiveness, and consistency. Remember that behaviors of high consensus, high distinctiveness, and high consistency are likely to be externally caused; behaviors of low consensus, low distinctiveness, and high consistency are likely to be internally caused; and behaviors of low consensus, high distinctiveness, and high consistency are likely to be the products of an interaction between internal and external causes.

8. Keep in mind that the methods suggested above can only increase the probability that your causal attributions will be accurate; they cannot guarantee accuracy.

## Think about It: Discussion of Answers

**3.1**    Beth's behavior is high in distinctiveness in that she is generally bored by art museums; this time, however, she is fascinated by a particular work of art. Her behavior is also high in consistency in that she returns to the art museum repeatedly to view the statue. Finally, her behavior is high in consensus in that other members of the tour react to the statue as Beth does. This pattern of high distinctiveness, high consistency, and high consensus is usually seen in behaviors that are externally caused. In this case, the statue is of such exceptional beauty that it has a strong impact on almost everyone who sees it.

In your scenario, the actor's behavior should be low in consensus, low in distinctiveness, and high in consistency to conform to a pattern of internal causation.

**3.2**    First, you were to suggest reasons for Keith's subpar performance on the basis of only one obvious cause, his injury. When additional possible causes were introduced, however—too much partying and tough opponents—the singular importance of Keith's injury is minimized by the potential contribution of these other causes. This exercise, then, should give you an example of the discounting principle at work.

**3.3**    When a person presents an excuse, that person is, in effect, proposing that his or her behavior is pardonable or justifiable because its cause was beyond his or her control. External causes are much more likely to be beyond our control than are internal causes. Consequently, most excuses explain or justify behavior in terms of external causes.

**3.4**    Sports fans are by definition very closely identified with their favorite team, so closely that they see the team as an extension of themselves. For example, sports fanatics don't say, "My favorite team won"; rather, they say, "We won." Because of this identification, sports fanatics tend consistently to explain their team's losses in terms of external causes—bad breaks, biased referees, dirty play by the opponents, and so on. If another team continually dominates the sports fanatic's favorite team, then the sports fanatic may emphasize that this team is truly outstanding ("the team of the decade," "the team of the century"). In this way, sports fanatics can still believe that their team is very good despite its losses to its uniquely talented opponent.

**3.5**    In tabulating the descriptive characterisics supplied by the 50 students, we grouped descriptions that were synonymous or very similar in meaning. Here are the top five descriptions associated with each concept:

*Physicians:* (1) intelligent, smart; (2) caring, understanding, compassionate; (3) wealthy, rich; (4) busy, hardworking; (5) well educated.

*Artists:* (1) creative; (2) bizarre, strange; (3) free-spirited, nonconformist, individualistic; (4) liberal, tolerant, open-minded; (5) talented, gifted.

*Vegetarians:* (1) healthy, health-conscious; (2) environmentally or ecologically conscious; (3) limited in diet, picky about food; (4) caring, sensitive; (5) liberal.

*College students:* (1) fun, wild, exciting; (2) stressed, pressured, fatigued; (3) intelligent, bright; (4) diligent, dedicated, studious; (5) poor, broke and open-minded, tolerant, liberal (tie).

*Lawyers:* (1) articulate, convincing, persuasive; (2) deceptive, dishonest; (3) wealthy, rich; (4) intelligent, smart; (5) strong-willed, powerful and ambitious, success-oriented (tie).

*Athletes:* (1) athletic, fit, strong; (2) driven, highly motivated, dedicated; (3) competitive; (4) agile, quick; (5) glorified, famous, popular and egotistical, proud, high self-esteem (tie).

**3.6**    People sometimes find it difficult to generate as many as five important characteristics of out-groups because their knowledge of out-groups is limited. On the other hand, they may have such a rich knowledge of in-group characteristics that they might find it difficult to decide just which five characteristics are the most important. In addition, in responding to this task, people generally come up with more positive or favorable characteristics for the in-groups than they do for the out-groups. Finally, when the generated characteristics are compared with a norm, as in TAI 3.5, in-group descriptions commonly are more discrepant from the norm than are out-group descriptions. The reason is that out-group descriptions are more likely to be based on the most obvious characteristics of any given category. In-group descriptions reflect more intimate knowledge of the category under consideration and are therefore likely to include characteristics that are not obvious to the casual observer.

**3.7**    In this exercise we continue to explore the hazards of stereotyping by asking you to draw on your own personal experiences. People resent being stereotyped because it robs them of their individuality. This resentment is commonly accompanied by such negative feelings as frustration, anger, and perhaps even helplessness. If you treat people as stereotypes rather than as individuals, you should fully expect that they will show these feelings in response to you. It is important to reflect upon your own emotional response to being stereotyped because doing so helps you reach an empathic understanding of what others are feeling. That is, if you can remember how you felt in such a situation, you can more easily reach not only an intellectual but also an emotional understanding of what the victim of stereotyping may be experiencing.

**3.8**    Again, we are asking you to draw on your own world of experience to apply a principle presented in this chapter. It can be very frustrating when another person tries to explain your behavior with causes that just don't fit. Perhaps, if you can recall your own frustration in such a situation, it will help you exercise caution when you seek to explain the behavior of others. Our causal explanations can have serious consequences for those over whom we have influence or control. This fact should further reinforce our awareness of the need to think carefully and critically when we attempt to understand and explain these people's behavior.

And now, on to the explanation of the sledgehammer incident. Your author and a few of his friends were building a cabin. The unfortunate sledgehammer victim had been convincingly demonstrating his lack of aptitude for carpentry for the better part of the day. His carpentry was so bad, in fact, that he had been assigned the menial task of measuring the rough dimensions of the (soon to be) cabin porch and marking these dimensions with stakes. After the incident, he explained that he was feeling so shamed and frustrated by his inept performance that he had vowed to himself not to do another thing to embarrass himself for the rest of the day. Almost immediately after making this vow he hit himself in the shin with the hammer. He contained his pain for as long as he could, hoping that no one had noticed. Finally the pain got the better of him, and off he went, howling into the woods. We noticed!

## •••••••••
## Recommended Readings

Many of the concepts discussed in Chapters 3 and 4 are central to the discipline of social psychology. David Myers' (1987) book, *Social Psychology,* provides a thorough and highly readable overview of the field. Within the discipline of social psychology, social cognition deals specifically with the topic of understanding and explaining other people's behavior. Susan Fiske and Shelley Taylor have done an outstanding job of summarizing basic theory and research in this area. Their 1984 book is titled, appropriately enough, *Social Cognition.* Nisbett and Ross's (1980) book, *Human Inference: Strategies and Shortcomings of Social Judgment,* was already recommended in Chapter 2. Their chapters on the identification and remediation of inferential errors (Chapters 9, 10, 11, and 12) are particularly relevant to the topics discussed in Chapters 3 and 4 of this book. Finally, two classic articles, though written at a fairly high level, are worthy of consideration: David Schneider's 1973 article, "Implicit Personality Theory: A Review" (*Psychological Bulletin,* vol. 79, pp. 294–309) documents our tendency to draw sweeping conclusions about an individual's personality from only limited observations of the person's behavior; Walter Mischel's 1973 *Psychological Review* article, "Toward a Cognitive Social Learning Reconceptualization of Personality" (vol. 80, pp. 252–283), convincingly argues for the importance of situational factors in addition to dispositional factors in determining an individual's behavior.

# Reflecting on Self

**There are two sides to every question: my side and the wrong side.**

Oscar Levant
(20th-century American humorist)

**Oh wad some power the giftie gie us
To see oursels as ithers see us!**

Robert Burns
(18th-century Scottish poet)

• • • • • • • • • • • • • • • • • • • • • • • • • • • • • • • • • • • • • • • • • • • • • • • • • • • • • • • • •

**Just as we must seek to understand the behavior of other people in order to solve many of the critical problems that face us, so we must struggle to understand the causes and motivations of our own behavior. This is indeed a struggle, as we often engage in deceptions that are self-protective or self-enhancing. That is, though we don't intentionally seek to deceive ourselves, we may be less than honest with ourselves when we take more credit than we are due or shift the blame when we should in fact accept it. Sometimes, as you will see, these self-deceptions are harmless and perhaps even adaptive. At other times, however, they seriously interfere with our attempts to make effective adaptations to the demands placed upon us. In this chapter we will examine some common forms of self-deception people engage in and see how these self-deceptions can be self-defeating as well. We will also explore ways in which you can combat such self-deceptions.**

• • • • • • • • • •
# Introduction

As you saw in Chapter 3, our attempts to explain and understand other people's behavior may be hampered by demonstrable errors and distortions in our thinking. Of course, one could argue that it's always going to be difficult to explain another person's behavior, because as an observer you do not have access to the same fund of information as does the person whose behavior you seek to explain (the actor). But what if the actor and observer are one and the same person? In other words, what if you are trying to determine, understand, and explain the causes of your own behavior? The task should be greatly simplified and your accuracy should be greatly increased because now you have access to a whole fund of information ranging from personal traits and motivations to environmental influences and your individualized reactions to those influences. So, maybe you are smarter when you set out to explain your own behavior. Or are you?

• • • • • • • • • •
# Self-Serving Biases

Just as we are prone to distortions and errors when we explain other people's actions, so we are prone to distortions when we explain our own behaviors or estimate our own abilities. As you might expect, these distortions often enable us to think of ourselves in a very favorable light. These kinds of favorable distortions are referred to as self-serving biases. In fact, people rarely see themselves as average or below average on anything. Thus these self-serving biases frequently result in statistical absurdities. For example, an analysis of the questionnaires that students fill out when they apply to take the Scholastic Aptitude Test revealed that 70 percent rated themselves above average in leadership ability while only 2 percent rated themselves as below average; in respect to ability to get along with others, none of the approximately 1 million students sampled saw themselves as below average, while 25 percent saw themselves as being in the top 1 percent (Myers, 1987)!

We often take undue credit for success in our lives, but readily shift the blame to someone or something other than ourselves when things turn out poorly for us. Consider these blame-shifting gems obtained from drivers' descriptions of accidents on insurance forms: "An invisible car came out of nowhere, struck my car and vanished"; "As I reached an intersection, a hedge sprang up, obscuring my vision, and I did not see the other car"; "A pedestrian hit me and went under my car" (Myers, 1987, p. 87). We will discuss in more detail this particular selective attribution of causation later in this chapter.

A list of relatively common ways in which people kid themselves would include the following (Myers, 1987):

1. They overestimate how likely it is that other people agree with their opinions.

People have a tendency to evaluate themselves favorably, which sometimes produces statistical absurdities.

2. They overestimate how likely another person would be to commit the same unethical act they just committed.
3. They underestimate how vulnerable to harm or misfortune they might be.
4. They underestimate how common their virtuous behaviors actually are.
5. They overestimate the accuracy of their judgments and beliefs.

If this list has you questioning your own motives and explanations of your behaviors, it may be deflating, but it may also have a very beneficial effect. It has been proposed that

> self-directed attention is necessary in goal-directed behavior. Only when people are self-aware . . . are they consciously oriented toward the accomplishment of goals and guided by personal standards regarding acceptable behavior. Thus, competent, moral, and efficient behavior generally requires some degree of self-reflection. (Leary Miller, 1986, p. 60)

Most psychologists would agree that a foundation stone of effective behavior is to be found in the ancient Greek dictum "Know thyself." They also would agree, however, that people show an amazing capacity to deceive themselves concerning the causes of their behavior.

· · · · · · · · · · · · · · · · · · · · · · · · · · · · · · · · · · · · · · · · · · · · · · ·

**THINK
about It**

**4.1**   Self-deceptions frequently involve convincing ourselves that there are good reasons that we can't do something we are in fact capable of doing but just don't want to do. The student who is faced with a long and tedious night of study, for example, might reason that it's not worth studying because he won't be able to understand the material. Describe a situation in which you or someone you know well converted a "don't want to do" into a "can't do" formulation. Also describe the consequences of this conversion on subsequent attempts at this behavior.

_____

_____

_____

_____

_____

_____

_____

Compare your description with ours at the end of this chapter.

· · · · · · · · · · · · · · · · · · · · · · · · · · · · · · · · · · · · · · · · · · · · · · ·

## The Utility of Self-Deception

You have been introduced to the concept of schema as a means of organizing and simplifying the large amount of information present in any given situation so as to make the information manageable and coherent. And just as we form schemas about other people (remember our math-professor schema), we form schemas about ourselves. These self-schemas are frequently identified as one's basic personality traits—honesty, intelligence, enthusiasm, and the like. Further, these self-schemas have been described as serving six basic functions, some of which should be familiar to you from the discussion in Chapter 3. Any given self-schema, according to this description (Tedeschi et al., 1985, p. 3):

1. Directs selection from available information: accepts congruent information (i.e., information that supports the schema) and screens out incongruent information (i.e., information that contradicts the schema).
2. Organizes incoming information to be consistent with self-schema.
3. Revises incoming information to fit the schema by adding information relevant to it and altering inconsistent information.
4. Speeds the processing of relevant information.

5. Facilitates the memory of schema-relevant information.
6. Reconstructs memory so events fit self-schemas.

Consider Craig, a young man who thinks of himself as an honest person, but who, like most people, is not honest at all times and in all situations. Craig may screen out information by forgetting that he has taken notebook paper from his roommate's desk without permission, organize some of his acts of dishonesty into that supposedly harmless and acceptable category of "little white lies," and revise the incoming information that he has just cheated on an out-of-bounds call in a tennis match by adding the (perhaps incorrect) information that his tennis opponent is cheating on most of the line calls, so the normal rules of the game no longer apply.

The various self-schemas that we have do not exist in isolation from one another. Rather, they may be linked with each other and organized under more comprehensive schemas. For example, the schematic traits of honesty, kindness, generosity, and intelligence may be organized under the more general schema of "good person." Further, the schemas of coordination, persistence, competitiveness, and, again, intelligence may be organized under "good athlete." Thus the schemas, particularly the superordinate or more comprehensive ones, help to define the core elements of one's self-concept. The basic self-concept held by a person who fits the organization we just described would probably be "morally good and athletically skilled."

Our self-concept gives us a sense of consistency, a basic sense of who we are. Challenges to one's self-concept are likely to be particularly threatening because they challenge this basic sense of identity. Consequently, in the face of such a challenge, we may distort incoming information so as to make it consistent with our self-concept. Researchers have identified a number of conditions under which people are likely to resort to self-defensive, but not necessarily accurate, modes of processing information. Let's examine some of the more common ones.

One common way of protecting and maintaining a positive self-concept is by explaining the causes of the negative events in our lives in self-defensive ways while attributing the occurrence of positive events to self-enhancing causes. For example, we may attribute the rather dismal outcome of our last romantic relationship to interfering parents, our former sweetheart's immaturities, or just plain bad luck. On the other hand, we may feel sure that our present romance is doing well because of our charm, wit, intelligence, and breathtaking good looks.

Although we can offer an almost infinite number of causes for our behavior, most of the important causes can be reduced to a few simple dimensions (Weiner, Frieze, Kukla, Reed, Rest, & Rosenbaum, 1971). The first dimension is *internality versus externality*. That is, does one attribute causation to something that is inherent in oneself or to external forces? If you attribute your A on a psychology quiz to your basic intelligence, for example, you are making an internal attribution, whereas suggesting that you got a good grade because the quiz was ridiculously easy constitutes an external attribution.

The second dimension (in no particular order of importance) is *stability versus instability*. This dimension identifies how likely you think the identified cause or causes are to occur again in similar situations. Referring back to the quiz-grade example, you would expect intelligence to be stable over time, whereas if your psychology professor has a reputation for giving difficult quizzes, you may see this easy quiz as being out of character for her. Consequently, you wouldn't expect to see another easy quiz in her class. Thus the easy-quiz explanation, under these conditions, attributes your grade to an unstable cause.

The third dimension is *globality versus situation-specificity*. This dimension examines how likely you think the identified cause of the present outcome is to have pervasive effects in many areas of your life as opposed to having effects that are specific only to this situation and perhaps very similar situations. Let's say that you've explained your A on the psychology quiz as being due to your basic genius. As this is a global attribution, you expect to get a lot of mileage out of this particular cause. That is, intelligence is likely to enable you to get good grades in other courses, solve problems effectively on the job, say interesting and witty things at parties, and on and on. However, if you suggest that your good grade is due to a particular aptitude for psychology, you might expect to continue to get good grades in psychology, but such an attribution doesn't also suggest promising results in English, fine arts, or physics classes, nor does your psychology aptitude suggest that you will be good at financial matters or fascinating at parties.

The fourth dimension, *controllability versus uncontrollability*, obviously involves attributing causes to factors that are under one's control versus factors beyond one's control. If you attribute your quiz grade to the kinds of questions the professor chose for the quiz, you are making an attribution that suggests that you have no control over the situation. If, on the other hand, you explain your A by saying that you studied long and hard for the quiz, this attribution suggests that you have a great deal of control over the situation.

**THINK about It**

**4.2**  Which of the four dimensions of attribution do you think has the greatest influence on the way we behave? In other words, if you make an attribution today, which of the four dimensions of attribution do you feel will have the greatest effect on the way you behave tomorrow? Explain your choice.

_____

_____

_____

_____

You can compare your response to this question with that of two experts in the field by turning to the discussion at the end of the chapter.

• • • • • • • • • •
# Depressed Thinking

Lyn Abramson, Martin Seligman, and John Teasdale (1978), in their classic article on the relationship between causal attributions and depression, propose that the internality, stability, and globality dimensions have specific effects on a person's mood and behavior. They suggest that depression is fostered when a person habitually makes internal, stable, and global attributions for negative outcomes in his or her life (that is, events that have turned out badly because the person has been helpless to control the direction of the outcome). Let's consider the relative contributions of each of these dimensions to depressive symptoms.

The internality dimension is believed to account for the loss of self-esteem seen in depresssion. That is, if one assumes that a negative outcome is the result of an internal cause (such as one's own stupidity), then one is assuming a personal helplessness (I am helpless, but other people aren't). On the other hand, if one attributes a negative outcome to an external cause (such as an incredibly difficult test), such an attribution is likely to imply a universal helplessness (I am helpless, but so is everybody else). Obviously, judging oneself as unique in one's inferiority is much more deflating to one's self-esteem than is assuming that we are all in the same boat in our inability to cope.

The stability dimension is seen to account for the chronicity of depression. In other words, some people get over depressing experiences rather quickly, whereas in other people the depression hangs on or becomes chronic. If you attribute the depressing event to an unstable cause, the future may still look bright, because this cause is likely to disappear or at least be changed. If, on the other hand, the depressing event is attributed to a stable cause, that cause is still going to be out there, just waiting to happen again. Consequently, the future, like the present, looks gloomy.

The globality dimension is believed to account for the pervasiveness of depression. In other words, a person may get depressed about problems she is having at work, but she isn't depressed only from nine to five. That is, she may see her ineffectiveness on the job as being due to global factors that are likely to have significant impact on many areas of functioning. Thus her inability to balance the books at her office may be interpreted not as indicative of poor accounting skills but as evidence of basic stupidity, which is going to make her ineffectual also as a wife, mother, real estate agent, bridge player, and so on.

There is ample support for the existence of a depressive attributional style (Peterson & Seligman, 1984; Sweeney, Anderson, & Bailey, 1986, among others). However, while we all experience a depressed mood from time to time (we get the blues or get up on the wrong side of the bed), we don't all get clinically depressed. Does this mean that only those people who get seriously and chronically depressed show self-defeating distortions in their attributions while nondepressed people are more accurate in their attributions? Not really. In fact, there is some evidence that depressed people may be less biased in some of their perceptions than nondepressed people.

Depressed people are sometimes more accurate than nondepressed people in estimating the amount of control they have over various tasks (Alloy & Abramson, 1979; Golin, Terrell, Weitz, & Drost, 1979). Nondepressed subjects also have been shown to overestimate the importance of their successes while underestimating the importance of their failures (Johnson, et al., 1983). Finally, with specific reference to attributional style, depressives have been shown to be more evenhanded than nondepressed people in their attributional patterns (Johnson, Petzel, & Munic, 1986; Raps, Peterson, Reinhard, Abramson, & Seligman, 1982). That is, depressed people are likely to use the same or quite similar attributional patterns to explain both positive and negative events in their lives, thereby taking relatively equal credit for their successes and blame for their failures. Nondepressed people tend to attribute their successes to internal, global, and stable causes, while attributing their failures to external, unstable, and situation-specific causes. Nondepressed people, in other words, are likely to show a self-enhancing bias in magnifying their responsibility for their successes and a self-defensive bias in minimizing blame for their failures.

**THINK about It**

**4.3**   In Chapter 3 we examined excuses in connection with the fundamental attribution error. Let's now take a closer look at excuses. Think of the last time you made up an excuse for an undesirable behavior on your part. Briefly describe the excuse:

_____

_____

_____

_____

_____

_____

_____

Now rate the excuse on the following dimensions:

Likelihood that I or something about me (internal) versus someone or something in my environment (external) was the cause:

Internal   1   2   3   4   5   6   7   External

Likelihood that the cause has widespread effects on many of my behaviors (global) versus is a highly focused cause that influences only the behavior being explained (specific):

Global   1   2   3   4   5   6   7   Specific

Likelihood that the cause will occur consistently in future stiuations (stable) versus infrequently and unpredictably (unstable):

Stable   1   2   3   4   5   6   7   Unstable

The discussion at the end of the chapter shows how the "ideal" excuse is rated on these dimensions.

• • • • • • • • • • • • • • • • • • • • • • • • • • • • • • • • • • • • • • • • • • • • • • • • • • • • • • •

## • • • • • • • •
## Enhancing Our Attributional Accuracy

You should not conclude that you are doomed forever to give biased and inaccurate causal attributions for the positive and negative events in your lives. Not all of our attributions are biased and inaccurate, nor do we even bother to give causal attributions for many of the events in our lives; "when the causes of behavior are conspicuous and the correct explanation fits our intuition, our self-perceptions can be accurate. . . . It is when the causes of behavior are not obvious even to an observer that our self-explanations become more erroneous" (Myers, 1987, p. 116). Thus, if you drop a brick on your foot and find yourself hopping around, you don't have to go digging for obscure reasons for your behavior. Moreover, when the outcome of a behavior fits commonly held expectations, people are likely to be accurate in their causal attributions. For example, when an intelligent woman studies hard and does well on that psychology quiz we keep talking about, she is most likely accurate if she attributes her good grade to ability and effort rather than to luck, divine inspiration, or ESP.

Conformity to commonly held expectations is not a foolproof way of assuring attributional accuracy, however, because it's hard to know just what is meant by "commonly held." Let's say that a bigoted white man, upon learning that a Vietnamese man has been charged with murder, attributes the murder to the "inborn nefariousness (evilness) of Orientals." While his family members and perhaps his circle of friends may accept such an attribution (birds of a feather . . .), once he moves out of this circle, he is very likely to find that this attribution is rejected by people who don't share his bigoted beliefs. On the other hand, it's hard to imagine any sizable constituency arguing against the expectation that smart people who study hard will probably get good grades. Generally, expectations can be commonly held for one of two reasons. On the one hand, they may be well supported by available evidence. On the other hand, they may be held because, even though there is no strong evidence to support them, neither is there any strong evidence to refute them. Consequently, when we judge the adequacy of our commonly held expectations, we should ask two questions:

1. Is this expectation held by most people or just by members of my in-group?
2. What is the adequacy of the evidence supporting this expectation?

- - - - - - - - - - - - - - - - - - - - - - - - - - - - - - - - - - - - - - - - - - - - - -

**THINK about It**

**4.4**    Later we will examine in greater detail the criteria for good evidence. At this point, however, let's say you are charged with the task of evaluating the evidence or lack of evidence regarding "the inborn nefariousness of Orientals." List several questions that you would want to answer before you would determine whether or not you have good evidential support for such a statement.

_____

_____

_____

_____

_____

_____

_____

_____

_____

_____

_____

Compare your questions with those in the discussion at the end of the chapter.

- - - - - - - - - - - - - - - - - - - - - - - - - - - - - - - - - - - - - - - - - - - - - -

## Cognitive Dissonance

As we have suggested, we don't make causal attributions for all of the events in our lives. In fact, we make causal attributions for only a few of the effects that we cause to occur. A number of factors influence whether or not we will bother to make causal attributions. First of all, we are much more likely to attempt causal explanations of effects that are of personal relevance than of effects that are trivial (Nisbett & Ross, 1980). Every time we move a muscle, we cause an effect, but these effects generally go unnoticed or at least unexplained. If, however, an effect is ego-involving—that is, somehow affects our self-esteem—we are much more likely to seek a causal explanation.

Second, unexpected effects prompt causal explanations (Hastie, 1984). Consider this situation. You're walking to class one morning, and as you pass friends, you get the usual stream of "Hi," "Howyadoin," "Whaddayasay," and "Have a good one." You don't stop to analyze why each person has chosen his or her particular greeting, but should one of the greetings be "Good evening," you're likely to start a causal analysis: "Is he crazy? A smart guy? Trying to be funny? Disoriented? What's the story?"

A third factor that apparently prompts causal explanations is a negative outcome of our behavior (Diener & Dweck, 1978; Peterson & Seligman, 1984; Wong & Weiner, 1981). A negative outcome may be simply a special instance of an unexpected outcome. As we saw at the start of this chapter, we tend to think quite highly of our talents and abilities. Consequently, we may expect our efforts to lead to positive outcomes even when such expectations are unrealistic. As long as things are running smoothly, we let them keep right on running. It is when things suddenly grind to a halt (that is, in an unexpected negative outcome) that we are likely to say to ourselves, "Whoa! What's going on here?" (Well, maybe not exactly "Whoa . . .")

Elliot Aronson (1984) has devoted much of his career as a social psychologist to studying two conditions in which our actions have ego-involving, unexpected negative consequences: (1) we consciously and knowingly do something stupid, and (2) we do something to harm another person. Aronson proposes that either of these conditions creates *cognitive dissonance* in the actor. When things are dissonant, they are disharmonious or out of tune with each other. Just as the strings on a guitar can be out of tune, so can the ideas one holds. Cognitive dissonance, then, is defined by Aronson (p. 116) as "a state of tension that occurs whenever an individual simultaneously holds two cognitions (ideas, attitudes, beliefs, opinions) that are psychologically inconsistent."

As we have emphasized, we like to see ourselves in a favorable light. Contributing to this high opinion is likely to be the belief that we are intelligent or at least have good judgment, and also that we are humane. Doing something stupid or harming another person flies in the face of these beliefs, and so creates cognitive dissonance. This dissonance creates an uncomfortable tension, and our discomfort motivates us to do what we can to reduce the tension. We do not reduce the tension simply by arriving at a causal explanation of the behavior. If an explanation is to reduce cognitive dissonance, it also has to be a justification (an excuse, if you will). For example, you may explain your cruelty to another person by saying, "I'm in a bad mood," but such an explanation does not effectively justify the cruelty. However, saying that the other person "came looking for trouble and found it" justifies (to yourself) your cruelty and reduces the tension caused by the dissonance.

## Sour Grapes and Sweet Lemons

If you consider Aronson's first condition for cognitive dissonance, you may be prompted to wonder why anyone would consciously and knowingly do something stupid. What Aronson means is that cognitive dissonance is very likely to occur when a person puts a lot of thought into an action, carries out the action, and still ends up looking like a fool. Such a sequence is common when we make an important decision or choice that turns out to be poor in comparison with other choices we might have made. In this same situation we may attempt to reduce postdecisional dissonance in one or both of two ways: the sweet-lemon rationalization and the sour-grapes rationalization.

In the *sweet-lemon rationalization*, people emphasize the positive qualities of their choice while ignoring the negative characteristics. When we engage in the *sour-grapes rationalization*, we emphasize negative characteristics of the unchosen alternative while ignoring positive aspects. Let's say you're confronted with the decision whether to buy one of two used cars, the Rag Top 409 or the Creampuff Gran DeLuxe. You carefully weigh all of the pros and cons that you can think of and finally decide on the 409. You happily drive home, singing the old Beach Boys song "She's real fine, my Four-o-nine, my Four-oooohh-nine," pull into your driveway, brake to a stop, and *clunk*, your transmission drops out, right there on the blacktop. You run into the house and phone the dealer, and he says, "Sorry, friend, no warranty on that beater. It's your baby now." So you're stuck. After all your careful deliberation, there go your 800 bucks, right down the tubes. Despite the fact that you like to think of yourself as having good judgment, right now it looks like you're a certifiable bonehead. But are you really?

It is likely that at this point the cognitive dissonance wheels start to spin (unlike the wheels on your 409). You remember a friend who bought a Creampuff Gran DeLuxe, had it in for repairs every other week, and got only eight miles to a gallon (sour grapes). Later you notice how many Creampuffs are involved in the accident reports in the local newspaper (sour grapes). In addition, you start thinking that since the car is undrivable, you'll sure save a lot of money on automobile insurance and gas (sweet lemon). Then you have the brainstorm that if you put the top down and fill the 409 with dirt, your mom will have the most unusual planter for her peonies in the history of ornamental horticulture (sweet lemon to the extreme).

The sweet lemon technique is a way of resolving cognitive dissonance.

**THINK
about It**

**4.5**    In general, fraternities and sororities played a more dominant role in the campus life of the 1950s and early 1960s than they do now. In fact, many students seemed to embrace their Greek society with the fervor of a religious zealot rather than the interest of a member of a social organization. It is interesting to note that hazing of pledges (that is, exposing prospective members to prolonged physical and psychological abuse) was more common 30 years ago than it is now. Explain how the principle of cognitive dissonance might be applied to link hazing with zealous commitment to one's fraternity or sorority.

_____

_____

_____

_____

_____

_____

_____

Our analysis is at the end of the chapter.

## The Just-World Hypothesis

The justification that one gives for doing harm to another person is commonly guided by the just-world hypothesis (Lerner, 1970; Lerner & Miller, 1978). Simply put, the *just-world hypothesis* is the belief that victims get what they deserve. This idea may have its roots in the Puritan ethic, the belief that virtuous behavior will have its rewards in both this life and the next, and, by implication, that sinful behavior will be punished both here on earth and in the hereafter. Researchers have convincingly demonstrated that when a person suffers a misfortune, other people are likely to attribute at least part of the responsibility for the misfortune to the victim's poor judgment, stupidity, or basic immorality even when there is no evidence to support the assumption. This tendency is vividly seen when people are asked to judge the complicity of a victim in her own rape (Burt, 1980; Lerner & Miller, 1978). They judge the victim as somehow sharing responsibility with the rapist for the commission of the crime. We like to believe that we live in a just world (and hold the comforting belief that we are good people, deserving of our rewards), and the fact that a terrible crime was committed against a good woman challenges this belief. Thus we experience cognitive dissonance. We can reduce our dissonance by either rejecting our belief in a just world or increasing our belief in the culpability of the victim. Research demonstrated that, in general, people are much more likely to do the latter than the former. We are living examples of the just-world hypothesis when we say that the person deserved it, provoked it, was asking for it, and so on.

In summary, then, Aronson (1984, p. 119) argues that

> we humans are motivated not so much to *be* right; rather we are motivated to *believe* we are right (and wise, and decent, and good). Sometimes, our motivation to be right and believe we are right are working in the same direction. . . . Occasionally, however, the need to reduce dissonance (the need to convince oneself that one is right) leads to behavior that is maladaptive and therefore irrational.

## Impressing Others

In Chapter 3 we examined how we explain the behavior of other people. So far in this chapter, we've directed our attention primarily to the way we explain our behavior to ourselves. Let's turn now to what happens when we explain our own behavior to other people.

When we explain our behavior to other people, our explanation often takes the form of *impression management* (Goffman, 1959). That is, our explanations may deviate from the truth insofar as we feel a need to convey or maintain a certain image to our audience. For example, the professor who chews out a student because he is in a bad mood may tell a shocked colleague who observed the tirade, "It's very painful for me to be harsh with students; I love them so. I just have to build a fire under this particular student so she will realize her as yet untapped potential." In the blink of an eye, the moody professor becomes a self-sacrificing saint of courage and imagination.

Not everything we do has impression management as its goal, but many of the things we do are done for an audience. Why do you buy and wear the clothes that you do, wear your hair in a particular style (or even bother to comb it), use deodorant, decorate your room, and so on? You may do so to please yourself, but you also are likely to do so to convey a certain impression to other people. In fact, you perhaps feel pleased with yourself when you are successful in conveying the desired impression.

A factor governing our tendency to engage in impression management is self-monitoring. *Self-monitoring* is the observation and modification of one's own behavior in response to situational cues. Research suggests that there are wide individual differences in self-monitoring (Snyder, 1974, 1979, 1987). We can easily imagine that the explanation given by our grumpy professor was generated by a frown or a look of dismay from the professor's colleague. If the colleague's reaction to the scene had been "Way to go, Tiger," we might have gotten a different explanation from Professor Grouch. As you might expect, the more strongly an individual tends to self-monitor, the more likely the person is to engage in impression management.

**THINK about It**

**4.6** Mark Snyder and his colleague Steve Gangestad (1986) have developed a scale to measure the tendency of people to self-monitor. Here are some questions from their scale.[1] Answer them true or false:

T F 1. I guess I put on a show to impress or entertain people.

T F 2. I find it hard to imitate the behavior of other people.

T F 3. I would probably make a good actor.

T F 4. In a group of people I am rarely the center of attention.

T F 5. I can look anyone in the eye and tell a lie with a straight face (if for a right end).

T F 6. I have trouble changing my behavior to suit different people and different situations.

T F 7. I can make impromptu speeches even on topics about which I have almost no information.

T F 8. I have never been good at games like charades or improvisational acting.

T F 9. I'm not always the person I appear to be.

T F 10. At a party I let others keep the jokes and stories going.

The discussion at the end of the chapter explains how to score your responses.

## Self-Handicapping

When we face a task that is important to us and in which there is a distinct possibility of failure or poor performance, we may engage in a form of impression management known as *self-handicapping* (Berglas & Jones, 1978; Jones & Berglas, 1978). That is, one develops possible excuses for failure before the fact (before taking part in the challenging task) rather than after the fact. Before an exam any classroom has its share of students who complain about the excessive demands made by their boss in their part-time job, lack of sleep, or everything coming due in one week. Now, students could keep this information to themselves, but it often seems particularly important that this information be shared with others. The concept of self-handicapping indicates that such sharing helps these students protect their self-esteem in the face of potential failure.

Self-handicapping is especially likely to occur when our behavior is readily observable by others, and can be negatively evaluated by others. In fact, some

[1]From "On the nature of self-monitoring: Matters of assessment, matters of validity," by M. Snyder and S. Gangestad. In *Journal of Personality and Social Psychology*, 1986, *51*, 125–139. Reprinted by permission of the author.

research indicates that, in general, when one's behavior is not public, one engages in very little self-handicapping (Kolditz & Arkin, 1982). Another factor that influences the likelihood of self-handicapping is the impact success or failure in the given activity has on one's self-esteem. That is,

> we would expect people to self-handicap chiefly in situations in which the self-relevant implications of failure are more threatening to the individual than is failure itself. People should be willing to risk self-handicapping only when the possible threats to self-esteem outweigh the potential consequences of failure. (Leary & Miller, 1986, p. 54)

Thus, for some students, what others think of them may be more important than their actual performance on an exam.

What's so bad about self-handicapping? After all, it's very common, and it helps to protect our self-esteem in the face of potentially negative evaluations by others. One problem is that we may start to believe our own excuses. Researchers have distinguished between self-handicaps and reported self-handicaps (Leary & Miller, 1986; Leary & Shepperd, 1986). Self-handicaps actually interfere with performance, whereas reported self-handicaps do not; they just provide excuses in case the performance should be poor. For example, the student who seeks out distractions the night before his biology final is self-handicapping; the student who studies hard for the exam but tells classmates she had numerous distractions while she was studying is engaging in self-reported handicapping.

A major problem with reported self-handicapping is that we run the risk that it may become real self-handicapping. A student who reports being distracted many times before an exam for which she actually studied hard and about which she feels fairly confident (reported self-handicap) may look for distractions when she is studying for a particularly difficult test (that she "knows" she will flunk). This impact of self-handicapping on performance was demonstrated in an interesting study of members of the Princeton swim team (Rhodewalt, Saltzman, & Wittmer, 1984). The researchers measured self-handicapping tendencies of the swimmers at the start of the season. Then they monitored the swimmers' practices over the course of the season. They found that the swimmers who were high in the tendency to self-handicap did not practice as hard before important meets as did the swimmers low in the self-handicapping tendency. The two groups did not differ in effort put forth in practice before unimportant meets. Common sense tells us that we should try hardest at those things that are most important to us. Unfortunately, self-handicapping produces just the opposite effect.

Another problem with self-handicapping is that it can become habitual, even a way of life. As you are aware, we often learn through reinforcement. When we are rewarded for behaving in a certain way in a given situation, we become more likely to show that same behavior in the same or similar situations. Consider what may occur when a student goes out and gets drunk the night before a final exam (setting up, of course, a good excuse for failing the exam). What, you may ask, could possibly be a reinforcement for such behavior?

The reward may be the relief the student feels in acknowledging, "Now, whatever happens, I have an excuse. I don't have to put my self-esteem on the line."

Self-handicapping can be a very consistent form of reinforcement because it is under the learner's control. A person can always get drunk, find distractions, or employ a favorite way of creating excuses, but one can't always be sure of a successful performance. One explanation of alcohol abuse is that it may be a chronic form of self-handicapping in which the person doesn't accept the normal risks of failure that most of us cope with, but may be able to maintain the belief that he or she is a person of great potential and ability whose magnificence is obscured by a drinking problem (Berglas, 1985).

**THINK about It**

**4.7**   We will provide you with examples of behavior, and we want you to indicate whether the behavior is likely to be a self-handicap (SH), a reported self-handicap (RSH), or neither a self-handicap nor a reported self-handicap (NSH).

Stef could not adequately prepare for her history exam because her notes were stolen from the rack of the lunchroom.

Circle one:   SH   RSH   NSH

Art practices hard and long for a piano competition, but then complains about a lack of practice time.

Circle one:   SH   RSH   NSH

Alicia has a large pizza one hour before she is to run in an important track meet.

Circle one:   SH   RSH   NSH

John carefully prepares his presentations for his speech class, but when he gets up in front of the class he gets so nervous that he forgets most of his talk.

Circle one:   SH   RSH   NSH

Elaine gets a good night's sleep before her Graduate Record Exam, but the morning of the exam she tells her friends that she didn't sleep a wink.

Circle one:   SH   RSH   NSH

Herb, who is not in very good physical condition, decides to lift weights and run five miles immediately before a tennis match with his girlfriend.

Circle one:   SH   RSH   NSH

See if your answers match ours in the discussion at the end of the chapter.

When we are confronting the possibility of failure, self-handicapping can protect our self-esteem; however, it can also produce failure.

# Thinking Rationally about Yourself

So far, we've presented some fairly good arguments for actually engaging in self-deception. That is, it may help you maintain a high opinion of yourself, and possibly make you resistant to depression. These arguments are only half-truths, however. Let's examine them further and try to get a more complete picture.

A very basic human motive is self-efficacy; we want to be competent and successful in those life challenges that are important to us. Obviously, our goof-ups threaten this motive. A negative outcome (goof-up), as you will recall, is a strong cue for us to launch into an attributional analysis of what went wrong. Now, you can take this analysis in one of two general directions: you can take the self-defensive direction of casting about for an excuse (any excuse) that will minimize your responsibility for the outcome, or you can take the more honest approach of attempting to understand, in an unbiased, although sometimes self-deflating, way your own responsibility for the outcome. The first direction usually enables one to come up with a quick, tension-relieving explanation, but that explanation frequently is not a completely accurate (and sometimes is a very inaccurate) determination of causality. The good news is that you have temporarily protected your self-esteem, but the bad news is that because you don't accurately identify your mistakes, it is very difficult to learn from them. Thus a self-defensive attributional analysis rarely serves the important motive of self-efficacy.

In explaining their own fallibility, people may engage in either characterological or behavioral self-blame (Leary & Miller, 1986). A person who engages in *characterological self-blame* attributes the cause of a negative outcome to some personal characteristic that is relatively resistant to change. For example, one might attribute one's poor performance on a physics exam to basic stupidity and one's romantic difficulties to an inherent nerdiness. Characterological self-blame hinders us from learning from our mistakes, because such learning usually requires us to change our behavior but characterological self-blame implies a cause that is unchangeable or highly resistant to change ("That's just the way I am.") Consequently, there is little adaptive value to characterological self-blame.

*Behavioral self-blame,* however, enhances our ability to learn from our mistakes. The reason is that behavioral self-blame leads us to identify changeable behaviors ("What am I doing wrong?" and *not* "What is wrong with me?") as the cause of the negative outcome. For example, the poor grade in physics that we initially explained as due to basic stupidity could also be behaviorally explained as due to a lack of preparation or as a failure to choose a major that best capitalizes on one's aptitudes. The direction of remediation varies in the latter two attributions, and those directions are clearly indicated: study harder in one case and find a more appropriate major in the other. Contrast the direction we get from these behavioral attributions with the lack of specific direction we get from the characterological attribution of basic stupidity. Contrast also the sense of hope we get from a behavioral attribution as opposed to a characterological attribution. It should come as no surprise that depressed people are more likely to engage in characterological self-blame than are nondepressed people (Janoff-Bulman, 1979). Thus, if you are looking for a way to keep honest in your causal attributions while remaining resistant to depression, behavioral self-blame is the way to go!

· · · · · · · · · · · · · · · · · · · · · · · · · · · · · · · · · · · · · · · · · · · · · · · · · · ·

**THINK about It**

**4.8**   Most ice skating instructors emphatically maintain that "if you can learn to walk, you can learn to skate." People seem to respond to this statement in one of two ways: either they believe it or they don't. On the basis of what you know about behavioral and characterological self-blame, describe how the believers might differ from the nonbelievers.

_____

_____

_____

_____

_____

_____

_____

_____

_____

We discuss this situation at the end of the chapter.

• • • • • • • • • • • • • • • • • • • • • • • • • • • • • • • • • • • • • • • • • • • • • • • • • • • •

## • • • • • • • •
## Rethinking Your Attributions

Psychologists have determined that people commonly overestimate the contribution of ability and underestimate the contribution of effort when they determine the nature of internal causes. A technique known as *attribution retraining* (see Forstelling, 1985) very simply involves teaching people to give greater weight to effort and less weight to ability than they typically do.

Attribution retraining makes good sense for at least three reasons. First of all, we are surrounded by people who have overcome limited ability with extra effort. Unfortunately, we can also find plenty of people who waste precious abilities through lack of effort. Second, effort can, over time, become ability. For example, a student may enter college with substandard reading skills. Now, he may give in to this limitation by reading as little as possible, or he may enroll in a reading skills development program, be sure to read all class assignments, and try to read also for enjoyment. Through effort, this student may improve his reading ability over time to the point where it is no longer a handicap; the nonreading student is just likely to fall further and further behind.

A third factor that suggests that attribution retraining is a good idea is that it works. Studies with children (Dweck, 1975), college students (Wilson & Linville, 1985), and elderly nursing home residents (Rodin & Langer, 1977) have demonstrated that focusing on effort to explain negative outcomes commonly leads to improved performance on subsequent tasks.

The message, then, is that when you are confronted with a negative outcome, take a long, hard look at the quality and quantity of your effort in pursuit of your desired goal. In such an examination, you should ask at least two questions. The first question, obviously, is "Did I try hard enough?" The second question is less obvious, but perhaps even more important: "Did I plan and apply my effort in the most efficient ways?"

**THINK about It**

?

**4.9** Take a look at the last major academic performance (test, paper, oral report, whatever) for which you received a disturbingly low grade. Analyze this performance according to the following questions:

1. Did I try hard enough? _____ Explain your answer.

_____

_____

_____

_____

2. Did I plan and apply my efforts in the most efficient and effective ways? _____ Explain your answer.

_____

_____

_____

_____

3. Do I understand what are the most efficient ways to study? _____ Explain your answer.

_____

_____

_____

_____

These questions are discussed at the end of the chapter.

## Setting Goals

People are sometimes accurate when they attribute a negative outcome to a lack of ability. This is commonly the case when they set unrealistic goals for themselves. The ultimate consequence of setting unrealistic goals, of course, is failure and all of its concomitant feelings of helplessness, ineffectiveness, and wanting to give up (Abramson et al., 1978). Goals are sometimes unrealistic not because they are ultimately unattainable but because they are beyond our present capabilities. However, subgoals on the way to these unrealistic goals may be attainable. In other words, one can improve one's chances of success by taking it one realistic step at a time.

Albert Ellis, an eminent American psychotherapist, says that two important goals many people hold dear are always to be approved of by other people and always to prove themselves thoroughly competent, adequate, and achieving (Ellis, 1962; Ellis & Harper, 1975). Although Ellis says that these are critical goals to many people, they are also irrational goals that cause those who strive for them much frustration and misery. Specifically, Ellis (1962) argues that it is not irrational to enjoy being approved of by other people; it is irrational only when we conclude that we really must be (need to be) approved of by *all* those who are important to us. Moreover, it is not irrational to want to strive for competence; it is irrational only when this striving is based on the idea that we must be *completely* competent, adequate, and so forth.

To think that you must always be approved of is unrealistic. No matter how hard you try, you simply can't ensure that everyone will approve of you. Some people may disapprove of you for their own irrational and arbitrary reasons (such as your religion, skin color, age, where you go to school). Also, constant striving for the approval of others requires a great deal of effort—so much effort that you end up with little time or energy for anything else (Ellis & Harper, 1975). "Striving ceaselessly for approval means living your life for what *others* think and want you to do rather than your *own* goals. It also usually means playing the patsy and buying others' approval at the expense of selling short your own desires and values" (p. 93).

Ellis and his colleague Robert Harper also point out that an unquestioned and constant need for approval often backfires. That is, other people may see this need and its related behaviors as signs of weakness and think less of you for it. They may also see constant approval-seeking behavior as a kind of pestiness and be annoyed by it. Finally, they may see the chronic approval-seeker as lacking substance, conviction, and vitality, and therefore as less desirable and possibly downright boring. The conclusion is that "you'd better accept yourself (try to discover your own fundamental desires and values) and remain vitally absorbed in various people, things, and ideas *outside* yourself" (Ellis & Harper, 1975, p. 93).

Ellis and Harper make a strong case for the proposition that the need to be thoroughly competent, adequate, and achieving is also irrational. First of all, they argue that this need requires one to attain the unattainable: perfection. Second, slavish adherence to this goal leads one to identify one's personal worth in terms of what one has accomplished, or, more accurately, is currently accomplishing. The consequence of this identification is that the individual has no stable sense of self. Rather, self-worth fluctuates daily, like the stock market, depending on one's most recent successes or failures. Third, people committed irrationally to achievement commonly are also committed to competing with other people in order to demonstrate their personal adequacy.

If you constantly seek to prove your self-worth by defeating or outdoing others, you run into three major problems: (1) Such egocentric competitiveness often interferes with interpersonal cooperation in the attainment of goals; (2) people may find your constantly competitive stance quite unpleasant; (3) the strategy substitutes an unrealistic goal (always be better than others) for the much more realistic and manageable goal of attaining success by trying to improve upon your own past performance.

Ellis and Harper (1975) argue that

> if you inordinately strive for success and feel anxious about failing, you will fear taking chances, making mistakes, doing the wrong thing, or doing many things you would really like to do. By insisting on outstanding achievement, you will leave yourself the pitifully narrow choices of (a) making mistakes and feeling depressed about them, or (b) refusing to try to do things for fear of making mistakes and feeling self-hating about them. (pp. 104–105)

To these two "pitiful" choices we would like to add a third: engaging in self-deceptions and self-handicapping and ultimately failing in your pursuit of self-efficacy by failing to learn from your mistakes.

**THINK about It**

**4.10** People with superiority complexes often adopt these complexes to defend against underlying feelings of inferiority. Often, however, this defense backfires and leads to even more severe feelings of inferiority. The ultimate failure of a superiority complex as a defense against feelings of inferiority can be understood in terms of the principles presented in this section on goal setting. Explain this failure according to these principles. Can you provide any real-life examples to support your analysis?

_____

_____

_____

_____

_____

_____

_____

_____

_____

_____

See how your analysis compares with ours at the end of the chapter.

# •••••••••
# Critical Thinking Principles Related to Self: A Summary

Most of the principles set forth in Chapter 3 are applicable to explanations of-fered for one's own behavior. We propose the following additional principles for your consideration:

1. Avoid self-handicapping. Most people recognize excuses for exactly what they are: signs of weakness or self-doubt. Moreover, self-handicapping in-terferes with our learning to be effective in dealing with the challenges of life.
2. When you seek to remediate internally caused negative outcomes, remember that characterological self-blame is counterproductive, whereas behavioral self-blame is productive.
3. Carefully analyze the quantity and efficiency of your effort when you seek to remediate a negative outcome.
4. Set short-term subgoals to long-term goals and focus on the attainment of these short-term goals.
5. Avoid setting irrational goals for approval and perfection. Rather, recognize that slavish pursuit of such goals is likely to lead to rejection and failure in the end.
6. Set goals that you will enjoy pursuing. You are more likely to be successful in pursuit of such goals.

# •••••••••
# Think about It: Discussion of Answers

**4.1**    The "can't do" formulation demonstrates the power of both self-talk and self-deception. When we tell ourselves (self-talk) that we can't do something, we ordinarily stop trying to do it or only go through the motions. As a result, we are in fact unsuccessful in meeting the challenge we are faced with. Our failure makes it easy for us to believe that we really can't meet this challenge. In other words, it becomes easy for us to engage in self-deception. Once we believe this self-deception, we are likely to avoid the challenge in the future or make only halfhearted attempts to meet it. Thus we create a self-fulfilling prophesy of failure, which supports our self-deception. Unfortunately, people who habitually lock themselves into this vicious cycle of self-deception impose limits on themselves that need not be imposed; commonly they fail to realize that many of the "can't do's" in life can be converted into "can do's" with effort and perseverance.

**4.2**    Leary and Miller (1986) argue that one's perception of controllability may be the most important of the four dimensions in its influence on subsequent behavior. That is, controllability may be of a higher order than internality, stabil-ity, and globality, because these other dimensions derive much of their effect on behavior from the way they combine to predict controllability. For example, if we get a poor grade and attribute it to an internal and stable factor such as lack of intelligence, we can exert little control over this cause. If we attribute our poor grade to lack of effort, however, we can change our behavior and possibly do better next time. Put simply, the controllability dimension is important because when good things happen under our control, we can take credit for them, and when bad things happen as the result of behaviors or conditions under our control, we can change such behaviors or conditions so that we won't again experience the same kind of negative outcome.

**4.3**    This exercise gives you some experience in doing an attributional analysis of your own behavior. Let's see how your analysis agrees with ours. In terms of the three attributional dimensions under consideration, the ideal excuse tends toward the external, unstable, and situation-specific dimensions. An external cause is less likely than an internal cause to be under your control; therefore, it absolves you of responsibility. An unstable cause is reassuring to the person you are presenting your excuse to, because it indicates that this event is unlikely to occur again. For example, not every weekly assignment will be handed in late, just this one. Finally, while excuses can be located anywhere on the global–situation-specific dimension, made-up excuses tend to fall at the situation-specific end of the continuum by virtue of the fact that they are made up. That is, global excuses are likely to be fairly catastrophic in that they have widespread effects (car accidents, hospitalizations, deaths in the family). Catastrophes commonly leave records such as accident reports, hospital bills, and death notices. Catastrophes also frequently have witnesses. Situation-specific excuses are less likely to leave records or have witnesses. Thus, if you tell your English professor that you didn't hand in your term paper on time because you were in a car accident and didn't make it to any classes that day, the professor could simply ask for proof in the form of an accident report. If your excuse is made up, you won't have this proof. On the other hand, if your excuse is situation-specific, such as "My dog ate my term paper," there is no tangible record of proof your professor can use to test the credibility of your excuse. Thus the professor has to choose whether or not to believe you (and any good excuse maker can differentiate the softies from the flint-hearts).

**4.4**    If you simply look at the three key words in the phrase "inborn nefariousness of Orientals," you will see that each of these words generates important questions that you have to answer when you evaluate the evidence supporting this statement. The word "nefariousness" suggests the following questions:

1. What do we mean by nefariousness? Are we talking about any kind of evil acts, or only criminal acts, or only certain criminal acts, or only murder?

2. Is there any evidence that Orientals differ from other racial groups in frequency of evil or criminal acts?

3. If such differences exist, are they always in the direction of greater wrongdoing among Orientals?

4. If Orientals are also found to perform more of certain kinds of good acts, what does this say about their overall nefariousness?

Examination of the word "Orientals" suggests several questions as well:

1. Are we talking about all Orientals or only about Vietnamese?
2. If we find that the citizens of any Asian country differ from the citizens of any country outside of Asia in frequency of evil/criminal acts, can we conclude that this finding applies to Orientals in general?
3. The Vietnamese man in this example was a recent immigrant to the United States. Can we generalize his behavior to all Orientals or even to all Vietnamese?

The word "inborn" suggests that the nefariousness is genetically determined and is relatively uninfluenced by environmental conditions. This assumption stimulates the following questions:

1. What evidence is there that evil/criminal behavior in general is genetically determined?
2. What evidence is there that any such genetic factor, if it does exist, varies from one ethnic group to another?
3. What evidence is there that such a genetic factor, if it exists, is peculiar to Orientals?
4. What environmental or cultural factors could also account for any observed differences in evil/criminal behaviors among ethnic groups?

This list of questions is by no means exhaustive. We hope that many of your questions are similar to ours. We further hope and expect that you have added some more good questions to our list.

One point should be clear by now: It would be very difficult to provide conclusive proof of the "inborn nefariousness of Orientals" because this concept is so vague. Unfortunately, concepts that are difficult to prove because of their vagueness are also difficult to disprove. Consequently, in-group members frequently find it quite easy to support each other in the maintenance of their particular prejudices, and bigots often find comfort in their sweeping but unprovable pronouncements.

**4.5**    The hazing experienced was painful, prolonged, and often dangerous. One would have to consider oneself very stupid or, at the very least, to have very poor judgment, to have gone through this ordeal to achieve a relatively minor goal (membership in a Greek society). Consequently, the importance and uniqueness of the goal had to be magnified. Otherwise new members would have been left with the cognitively dissonant awareness that despite their fond belief that they have good judgment, they had just done something really stupid. That is, they had just endured months of grief for a social payoff of friends and recognition that could have been achieved in less painful and more productive ways.

**4.6**    To score your responses to Snyder and Gangestad's self-monitoring scale, count the number of odd-numbered questions that you endorsed as true and the number of even-numbered questions that you rejected as false. The higher the score, the more inclined you are to self-monitoring. Extreme scores in either direction are not particularly desirable. That is, people who score very high in self-monitoring may ignore their own feelings and attitudes in situations so as to present a socially desirable front to other people. On the other hand, people who score very low on self-monitoring may be relatively insensitive to cues guiding socially appropriate behavior, such as tact and respect for other people's points of view, when they share their feelings and attitudes.

**4.7**   Alicia, the trackster, and Herb, the tennis player, are engaging in actual self-handicapping in that they both are likely to do poorly in their events, and they have consciously chosen to engage in activities (pizza eating and exhausting exercise) that will directly contribute to their poor performance. Both Art, the pianist, and Elaine, the GRE taker, are engaging in reported self-handicapping in that they are making up false excuses, and as these excuses are false, their behaviors are not likely to be affected. Though Stef of the stolen notes and John, the nervous speaker, are both obviously handicapped in their performance, they are not engaging in any form of *self*-handicapping. Their handicaps are not of their own choosing; they are beyond their control.

**4.8**   People who give up learning to ice skate after one or two tries almost invariably report, "I can't skate; I have weak ankles." These are the nonbelievers and they are attributing their failure to an internal and relatively unchangeable characteristic. Thus they are guilty of characterological self-blame. Their blame may not be accurate, either; skating instructors argue that most cases of "weak ankles" are really attributable to ill-fitting or poorly constructed skates. Believers, on the other hand, believe that skating is a skill that they can learn and that the only reason that they are continually sprawled on the ice is that they have not yet mastered the behaviors necessary to be skilled skaters. The believers are engaging in behavioral self-blame, and are more likely to persist and become competent skaters.

**4.9**   Again we ask you to apply a principle to your own experiences. For some of you, this application may help improve your academic performance. We discuss a model for efficient and effective study in Chapter 6. If, after studying this model, you are still having trouble answering parts 2 and 3 of this question, we recommend that you discuss these questions with a teacher or a student counselor.

**4.10**   The person with a superiority complex may be seeking to achieve both of the irrational goals discussed in the goal-setting section of this chapter. This person may want not only to be approved of but to be the most approved-of, most respected, most admired person. This particular expression of a need for approval often places one in a continuously competitive relationship with others. This ceaseless competitiveness may very well alienate people, leading to their disapproval and rejection. The person with the superiority complex may also constantly strive for perfection because perfection provides a direct contradiction to feelings of inferiority. However, if perfection is the individual's only defense against feelings of inferiority, we know that this defense is destined to fail; as the old saying goes, nobody's perfect. Thus we see that the individual's attempts to ward off feelings of inferiority fail in at least two ways: these attempts alienate other people, and they lock the person into the pursuit of unattainable goals.

## Recommended Readings

Bernard Weiner got the attribution-theory ball rolling at high speed with this now classic book, *Achievement Motivation and Attribution Theory* (1974). More recently (1988), Lyn Abramson's book *Social Cognition and Clinical Psychology: A Synthesis*, examines the role that attributional processes play in adaptive and dysfunctional behaviors. The impact of attributions on self-concept, mood, motivation, and psychological health is considered. Also of recent vintage (1988) is *Self-deception: An Adaptive Mechanism?* by Joan Lockard and Delroy Paulhus. This book reviews research and theory relevant to the issue of self-deception, but provides only a qualified "It depends" response to the question posed in the title of the book. Both Abramson's and Lockhard and Paulus's books are written primarily for professional audiences but are quite comprehensible to nonprofessionals as well. Elliot Aronson's book, *The Social Animal* (1984), was written primarily for undergraduate students. Winner of the American Psychological Association's National Media Award, this is a finely written book worthy of a cover-to-cover read. The chapter on self-justification is particulary relevant to Chapter 4 of this book, and provides excellent coverage of cognitive dissonance theory. Finally, in *A New Guide to Rational Living* (1975), Albert Ellis and Robert Harper convincingly demonstrate that unrealistic goals are the source of much human frustration and misery. Further, they offer guidelines for developing and maintaining more realistic goals.

# BELIEVING AND KNOWING

# Analyzing Beliefs

**Nothing is so firmly believed as that which we least know.**

Michel de Montaigne
(16th-century French philosopher)

Many everyday events occur naturally by chance. They are simply coincidences that frequently provide an interesting and stimulating aspect to everyday life. Nevertheless, sometimes people reject chance and natural processes as explanations for an event and choose to believe that an event is due to some unknown factor, one that cannot be explained. This factor sometimes is associated with occult forces, or is said to be the result of ESP (extrasensory perception). The cognitive biases surrounding beliefs of this sort can be shown to affect our thinking in a wide variety of ways. In this chapter we examine factors that influence people's belief in the probability of everyday occurrences. A major topic is how our thinking about events may lead us to see events in the way we expect to see them, and even to bring about a change in the way events occur.

• • • • • • • • • •
# Introduction

Headline in the *National Enquirer*, October 14, 1975: "ESP EXPERIMENT DEFIES ODDS OF 10 BILLION TO 1."

This account followed on page 4:

> In the most spectacular ESP experiment ever, famed psychic Uri Geller achieved an incredible success that defied odds of "more than 10 billion to one," say astonished experts.
>
> As Geller soared in a balloon high over Princeton, N.J., people all over America and across the Atlantic received telepathic messages he transmitted in a dramatic test sponsored by The ENQUIRER.
>
> Readers were requested to use a coupon that accompanied the article to record their results—and send them to The ENQUIRER . . .
>
> "Geller must have incredible psychic powers. There's no mathematical explanation for what happened," [said a Dr. Boyette]. (Reported by Dick Saxty)

Nature offers us a plethora of dazzling and not-quite-explainable (to the casual observer) displays. There are, for instance, geysers that spout like clockwork (Old Faithful) and "falling stars" in the night sky. We often don't give much thought to these wonders of nature, and accept them for what they are, natural wonders. Other "mysterious" phenomena, however, are sometimes given a great deal of attention, at least by some tabloids and among certain groups. Some people offer supernatural explanations that stretch the imagination: voodoo death, out-of-body experiences, channeling, spontaneous self-combustion, bigfoot. Others include the somewhat less bizarre but still mysterious phenomena of extrasensory perception (ESP). At one time or another probably most people have discussed the possibility of ESP.

ESP is traditionally considered to include the following paranormal experiences (experiences beyond the power of science to explain):

*Clairvoyance*: the ability to sense something in the absence of physical stimulation of the sense organs (such as the ability to predict the contents of a sealed envelope).

*Telepathy*: transmission of one person's thoughts to another (as the *Enquirer* claimed for Uri Geller in the "most spectacular ESP experiment ever").

*Precognition*: perception of an event in the future (such as a dream about an event that later actually happens).

*Psychokinesis*: the effect of a mental state on a physical object (such as influencing the roll of dice by thought alone).

Many people claim to have experienced ESP and many others express a belief in ESP, to the extent that estimates based on national surveys indicate that as many as 80 percent of American adults believe moderately or strongly in ESP (see Singer & Benassi, 1981). Other reports (such as Miller, 1986) reveal that almost two-thirds of American adults read astrology reports and that as many as 39 percent give some credence to them. Belief in occult phenomena is said to be on the rise (Marks & Kammann, 1980).

In this chapter we take a look at belief in paranormal phenomena. Our main concern, however, is not to convince you that such phenomena are not real. We agree with those who suggest:

> It would be foolish to deny the *possibility* of ESP, or for that matter, the fountain of youth. We must acknowledge that most wonders of modern science were once crazy conjectures: atoms, meteorites, germs, artificial fertilizers, genes, antibiotics, and all the rest. Who among us wants to be the historic fools of our era, like those who doubted the round earth of Columbus, the centrality of Copernicus' sun, Fuller's steam engine, or NASA's moon landing? (Marks & Kammann, 1980, pp. 155–156)

Not to mention black holes in space and genetic engineering!

We also are not about to investigate the nature of specific paranormal phenomena. We focus rather on the nature of the cognitive and personal biases that frequently support people's *belief* in these phenomena. As we shall see, these biases can affect our belief in other, more commonplace events as well.

Just how prevalant and potent these biases are can be seen by a look at two characteristics of people's belief in ESP-type phenomena. First, consider the fact that there exists no good scientific evidence for the existence of paranormal phenomena such as ESP. To be acceptable to the scientific community, evidence must be both *valid* and *reliable*. Evidence is valid when it can be demonstrated that an event is caused by the factor under consideration and not by something else. It is necessary, for example, to show that the results of an experiment that is supposedly providing evidence for ESP are not due to artifacts of the testing procedure or to inadequate measurement. Reliable evidence is something that can be obtained over and over again by independent observers. Scientists are careful to repeat experiments in order to rule out the possibility that the original results were simply a chance occurrence. Claims for evidence of paranormal phenomena have not proven to be both valid and reliable. Nevertheless, as we have seen, numerous surveys reveal that a majority of people maintain that such phenomena are real. Thus many people apparently believe in something that currently is supported by no valid evidence—that is, evidence that cannot be explained in some other plausible way. (Remember: We are not referring to belief in the *possibility* that something like ESP could ever exist; we are talking rather about belief that it *really* exists.) What kind of thinking is the basis for this belief?

Another aspect of belief in ESP that reveals powerful cognitive biases is the difficulty of changing people's beliefs about ESP. Even when it is obvious that paranormal processes could not be responsible for the events that were observed, many people stubbornly cling to explanations based on "psychic" powers. Why will people not give up their belief in ESP? What sustains these beliefs in the face of clear evidence to the contrary?

We hope you agree that biases as influential as these are worthy of investigation. The thinking, or rather the *mis*thinking, that is generally assumed to be the basis of belief in the paranormal illustrates important factors that no doubt serve to create and sustain our beliefs about many diverse phenomena (Marks & Kammann, 1980; Singer & Benassi, 1981). Your awareness of these factors should lead you to think more critically about what it is that you do believe and why you believe it. This information is relevant to such diverse problems as what kind of insurance policy you should buy, what neighborhood you should live in, and what sustains prejudice against certain groups of people.

· · · · · · · · · ·
## To Believe or Not to Believe: The Intransigence of Occult Beliefs

As we noted, belief in psychic phenomena and the occult is widespread. Thus it is perhaps not surprising to learn that when two social psychologists set out purposely to mislead students in several large introductory psychology classes into thinking that an amateur magician was really a psychic, and that the simple magic tricks that he performed were evidence of his psychic abilities, an overwhelming majority of the students (77 percent) believed the person was psychic and that the demonstrations of "mindreading" and other magician's tricks were really psychic phenomena (Benassi, Singer, & Reynolds, 1980).

The goal of this social psychology experiment was not to show that people, in this case college students, can be duped into believing that someone is psychic (especially when that someone comes dressed up in a purple robe, with a medallion around his neck, sandals on his feet, and long hair and beard). The psychologists had set out to show that by varying the information about the performance given to the students before they saw the magician, they would produce a change in the students' belief. The magician was introduced as a psychic in only one condition of the experiment; as we saw, the response from the students was clear: they believed. In another condition, the man was introduced as what he was, an amateur magician. In a third condition, not only was the man introduced as a magician but it was specifically mentioned that he had no psychic powers and that his tricks were just that, only tricks. The psychologists expected that the information provided the students in the latter two conditions would reduce their tendency to believe in psychic phenomena. This expectation was confirmed; fewer students believed that the man had psychic powers when they were told that he was only a magician. Yet their written responses after the performance made it clear that despite the disclaimers, many students continued to believe that the man was psychic, if not an agent of Satan! In the strongest debiasing condition, when students were explicitly told that the performer had no psychic abilities, the data indicated that more than half (58 percent) of the students still believed that the magician was psychic.

Evidently belief in the occult and in psychic phenomena is not only widespread, it is remarkably intransigent (resistant to change). What accounts for this intransigence in the face of logical alternative hypotheses? Let's consider two general hypotheses (Benassi et al., 1980). First, the students in these experiments had strong prior beliefs in psychic phenomena. These students would have reported a belief in psychic abilities without ever having seen the magician. Once a personally significant belief is established, people generally are motivated not to abandon it even when disconfirming evidence is presented

(Festinger, Riecken, & Schachter, 1956). A second hypothesis offered by the researchers for the obvious stubbornness of students' beliefs in psychic phenomena is that the students' reasoning was deficient. It is possible, the investigators suggested, that the students trusted their own intuitions and failed to analyze in critical fashion the information that was presented to them. In a moment we will look at possible bases for both of these hypotheses.

---

**THINK about It**

**5.1**   Consider people with whom you have come into contact who indicate a belief in ESP. Write down two reasons people generally give for their belief:

1. _____

2. _____

Compare your reasons with the ones we provide at the end of this chapter, which we believe are the two most commonly given for belief in ESP and similar phenomena. You will want to think critically about these reasons in light of what you learn about certain cognitive biases in thinking.

---

## Vividness of Personal Experience

When the researchers considered some of the possible deficiencies in human reasoning that might explain why subjects in their experiment failed to think critically, they mentioned the possibility that students' personal experience of the magician's performance may have had a greater impact on them than the verbal information they received (Benassi et al., 1980). The researchers' description leaves no doubt that the students were greatly impressed by this performance: they "paid rapt attention," and even "chanted loudly and in unison with him while he bent the rod." It was clear that many students were visibly moved by the experience. After the performance some sat in their chairs, "shaking their heads or staring vacantly into space." Others rushed up to the "psychic" to learn more about his powers. The researchers "had the feeling that if [he] wanted to found a cult, he could have done so on the spot" (p. 341).

This report matches the experiences of a professional magician by the name of James Randi. Perhaps you have heard of Randi. He has been on many TV talk shows, and he has widely publicized his readiness to give $10,000 to any supposed psychic who performs a feat that Randi cannot duplicate by ordinary sleight of hand. Randi is an avowed skeptic and a vocal critic of those who take advantage of a naive public by claiming to have powers greater than those represented by a magician's simple talents (see, for example, Randi, 1986). Randi reports that people often cannot accept the fact that they have been tricked:

Vivid personal experiences create believers.

> In my appearances before many hundreds of thousands of persons in the last thirty
> years, I have consistently denied any possibility that what I do is done by super-
> natural means. Yet some of my audience will argue with me at great lengths that
> some of the illusions I've presented are impossible of explanation by any other
> reasoning. Though I should certainly be the one who knows the answer to that,
> these people are unable to accept the obvious fact that they have not been able to
> solve a puzzle. (Randi, 1975, p. 17)

Vivid personal experiences make believers out of many of us. "I wouldn't
have believed it unless I'd seen it with my own eyes" is a familar statement
to all of us. Certainly some events are difficult to imagine unless we are actually present to experience them personally. Have you ever seen a holographic
image projected in front of you? Laser-produced holograms are sometimes part
of exhibits at science fairs and in some museums. They are also used in amusement parks, such as Disney World, where a three-dimensional image of a ghost
can be seen sitting next to visitors in a haunted house. It is difficult to explain
the experience of a hologram to someone. You simply have to experience a
hologram to appreciate it, and once you have experienced it, it is unforgettable.

But we don't conclude that holographic images are supernatural phenomena
(at least most people over the age of 5 don't). Why? One likely reason is the
setting. The situation in which we experience an event can influence our interpretation of that event. Museums of science and various science fairs have the
purpose of explaining nature to us. We expect to see dazzling scientific displays
in these settings. Although most of us can't explain how a hologram is made,

we accept it as part of the wonders of physical science. At an amusement park we expect to have entertaining tricks played on us. However, project a holographic image during a séance conducted by a "medium" to communicate with the dead and the event may be interpreted neither as a scientific display nor as a trick. Without a disposition to analyze events critically, we simply may interpret this vivid personal experience as the context in which it occurs suggests that we should.

But what do we think when we are confronted with a seemingly unexplainable event in a situation that offers few or no clues to the cause of the event? A good magician such as a James Randi can usually provide such a situation. The news media frequently describe "unusual" phenomena and "unexplained" (as yet) events. In such circumstances, people reasonably consider many possible explanations. An explanation based on psychic powers may be among those they entertain. Of course, even to consider an explanation based on psychic phenomena necessarily means that some credence is given to the existence of ESP (and, as we saw, most people do give some credence to it). Thus many people find themselves experiencing something that appears to provide evidence to support their belief in ESP. What happens when they are told that this demonstration that was so personally convincing was nothing more than a magician's trick? Or that the "unexplained" event reported in the newspaper has a simple scientific explanation?

You should see elements of cognitive dissonance in this situation, as well as elements of our tendency toward self-efficacy, aspects of human cognition that were discussed in Chapter 4. To acknowledge that what we believed was ESP was merely a trick, or that a simple scientific process can explain what we thought was a supernatural event, would mean that our hypothesis was wrong: it wasn't ESP. And if ESP doesn't explain what happened in this situation, then perhaps it doesn't explain phenomena in other, similar situations. Our beliefs are being called into question. Cognitive tension is present: our belief in ESP, even if only briefly entertained, is not in line with what we have been told. Either what we were told is not true or our beliefs are incorrect and we must chalk this experience up as a failure to think critically. We suggest that many people, especially those who lack important attitudinal dispositions identified with critical thinking (see again Chapter 1), are unable to admit that they were wrong and to consider in an objective way the evidence that has been presented to them. They resolve cognitive dissonance by believing that they really are right: it is ESP. Despite evidence to the contrary, such as the disclaimer of an honest magician or an explanation by a social psychologist, people continue to maintain that their beliefs in ESP are correct. An important by-product of this cognitive resolution is that people do not have to accept the fact that they are capable of being fooled. As Randi pointed out, this is something that many people simply are not willing to accept. It may be that people are seeking self-efficacy—that is, to see themselves in a good light. If they haven't been fooled, then they can continue to maintain the idea that they are perceptive, intelligent, and generally not the kind of person who is easily tricked.

**5.2**    Describe three vivid instances in your personal experience that reminded you (maybe even convinced you) of ESP-type phenomena. Search your memory for any recollections of personal experiences that could fall into the categories of clairvoyance, telepathy, precognition, or psychokinesis. We have no doubt that you can identify some.

1. _____

_____

_____

2. _____

_____

_____

3. _____

_____

_____

At the end of the chapter we report three instances from our own personal experience that reminded us of so-called ESP-type phenomena.

## Availability

Vivid and engaging personal experiences are often remembered when more abstract information is forgotten. When later you are called upon to remember instances of a category of events, it is likely that these vivid experiences will be easily recalled. Most people have little difficulty in recalling at least one personal experience that "could be" evidence of ESP. This phenomenon leads us to a judgmental heuristic (strategy) that is the basis of our thinking about many kinds of experiences. When we follow the *availability heuristic,* we use the number of instances of a phenomenon that quickly come to mind as a gauge of the frequency with which the phenomenon occurs: if we can quickly recall many instances—that is, many instances are available to us—we assume that many more instances could be recalled with some effort; if we can recall few instances, we assume that few instances exist to be recalled. The influence of this heuristic on our thinking was the subject of a series of experiments by two well-known social psychologists, Amos Tversky and Daniel Kahneman (1973). We will first review briefly the outcome of these experiments and their interpretation, and then we will look at people's thinking about ESP-type events in light of the availability heuristic.

Several of the experiments were quite simple (see Tversky & Kahneman, 1973). For example, in one experiment the psychologists simply posed to a group of subjects such questions as the following: How many Russian novelists can you name? How many flowers can you name? After the subjects had estimated the number of instances that they could recall, the researchers asked them to produce instances of these categories by writing them down. The correlation between subjects' estimates and their actual knowledge of instances of these categories was quite good when they were averaged over many categories. How might someone perform this task? Tversky and Kahneman reasoned that people quickly try to think of as many instances of a category as they can; that is, people retrieve from memory names associated with the particular category in question. If many instances are available, then we might reason that given enough time, we can recall more instances of this category, so we give a large estimate. If a quick memory search produces no or few names, then we might reason that there isn't much available that is relevant to this question—that is, even if we were given ample time we could produce few instances—so we give a small estimate. It appears that we often rely on the immediate availability of instances in memory to estimate the overall frequency of instances that we can recall.

Well, you might say, what's wrong with that? And we must admit that there isn't anything actually wrong with our use of the availability heuristic. As the results of these experiments demonstrated, people were rather accurate in their estimates of frequency when (apparently) they used the availability heuristic. The problem is that it isn't hard to demonstrate that we sometimes are led to make an incorrect inference by relying on the availability principle. Consider another question posed to subjects in these experiments. Decide whether each of the letters R, K, L, V, and N appears most frequently in the first or third position in English words (excluding words of fewer than three letters). (You might try this experiment on a friend.) Many people who were asked about these letter positions said that a majority of these letters appear more commonly in the first position than in the third. When they were further asked to estimate the ratio of first to third positions, subjects said that the letters were about twice as likely to be first as third. In fact, all of these letters occur more frequently in the *third* position than in the first when all English words are considered. It appears that subjects erred because they made use of the availability heuristic. Because it is easier to think of words beginning with a certain letter than it is to think of words with a letter in a later position, words beginning with these letters are more easily recalled than are words with letters in the third position. (Try it. How many words can you quickly think of that begin with L? that have L in the third position?) Because the first-letter words were more available, subjects incorrectly estimated that the overall frequency of this category was greater than that of the third-letter category.

• • • • • • • • • • • • • • • • • • • • • • • • • • • • • • • • • • • • • • • • • • • •

**THINK
about It**

**5.3**    Consider the following questions about the frequency of causes of death
(see Fischhoff, Slovic, & Lichtenstein, 1977). For each pair of possible causes
of death, decide which cause (A or B) you think is more frequent (circle one):

1. (A) pregnancy, abortion, and childbirth, or (B) appendicitis
2. (A) all accidents, or (B)  stroke
3. (A) homicides, or (B) suicides

We give the correct answers at the end of the chapter.

• • • • • • • • • • • • • • • • • • • • • • • • • • • • • • • • • • • • • • • • • • • •

Though the availability heuristic serves us well in many situations, it can
lead our thinking astray in others (e.g., Curt & Zechmeister, 1984). When we
try to answer such questions as "What is the most frequent cause of death,
accidents or strokes?" we begin to understand how the availability heuristic can
mislead us. We generally attempt to recall instances of each of these causes of
death that we have read about or have experienced personally. Examples of
accidental deaths are likely to be more available than those of strokes because
of the news media's differential coverage of these events. How many headlines
have you seen publicizing a death by stroke? Strokes simply aren't very sensational (unless thay happen to members of an Antarctic exploration team or a
U.S. president). Accidental deaths, however, are news. Stories in the media about
spectacular accidents are attention-getting and are likely to be remembered.
Everyday reports from friends and acquaintances also tend to be biased toward
more spectacular and sensational events. How many times has someone told
you about another person who was killed in an accident? Contrast that impression with your estimate of the number of times someone told you about a person who died of a stroke. Even if you had been told about more stroke-related
deaths (although this seems unlikely), the lurid details of a story about an accidental death are likely to be remembered better than the details of a report
about someone whose death was due to a stroke. In other words, your memory
for these two classes of events is likely to be biased toward the more vivid
category of events. Our "personal experience" with accidental deaths is likely
to suggest that accidental deaths are more frequent than deaths due to strokes,
when they are not.

It is generally acknowledged that the media also serve to increase the
availability of explanations based on psychic processes and occult phenomena
(Singer & Benassi, 1981). A UFO (whether or not it later turns out to be a weather
balloon), a deserted ship floating at sea (whether or not it later is discovered
that the crew was washed overboard), an accurate psychic prediction of an important future event (whether or not it turns out to be only one correct guess
in a thousand attempts) can be news. Newspapers frequently consider stories
of this kind to be a source of amusement for their readers (Klare, 1990). Later
retractions, corrections, and admissions of error do not always appear, and if

they do, they are rarely given as much attention as the original story. So the stories we read tend to be ones that apparently confirm the existence of psychic phenomena. As a consequence, "puzzling events for which explanations might otherwise be conceived in terms of scientific phenomena or of fraud may tend to be explained as paranormal phenomena when the media bring this category so obtrusively to our attention" (Singer & Benassi, 1981, p. 50). Indeed, the ease with which we can produce examples of psychic phenomena may give them an appearance of plausibility. And, as we have suggested, once we are led to consider psychic explanations, we may run into cognitive dissonance that we can resolve only by holding on to those beliefs.

**THINK about It**

**5.4**   Our belief about the likelihood of events plays a role in many everyday decisions. Some of these decisions are very important. For example, we may believe that earthquakes are likely in a particular part of the country. Should we decide to live there, we might think about buying earthquake insurance to protect us from loss from this type of disaster. If we believe that a particular neighborhood or town has a crime rate higher than average, we may consider not moving there even when there may be other advantages to such a move. Although earthquakes may be likely to occur in a region where we wish to reside, and there actually may be a better-than-average chance of being mugged in a particular neighborhood, we will want to be sure that an availability heuristic is not misleading us about the true likelihood of these events. (Earthquakes and crime do get a lot of media attention.) Consider the following hypothetical statement from an alderman in a large city: "The city has a serious rat problem. We must have a comprehensive plan for dealing with rats. A resident in my district told me that he was bitten by a rat. I even saw a rat in my garage." How might an availability heuristic be at work here?

_____

_____

_____

_____

Our analysis is provided at the end of the chapter.

## Representativeness

The tendency to believe that certain phenomena are psychic happenings is aided by a common judgmental process referred to as *representativeness*. A person is said to use representativeness when the likelihood of an event is estimated by the degree to which the event is judged as similar in essential characteristics to the concept or process in question (Kahneman & Tversky, 1972). In other words, we often look to see if the event in question matches (that is, represents well) our idea of something. Does the event have attributes similar to those that we believe are characteristic of a particular concept?

When we are confronted with an event that seems mysterious or puzzling, we, normally curious creatures that we are, consider possible explanations. As we have seen, explanations involving occult or psychic forces are easily brought to mind, and thus are available as explanatory causes. The representativeness process is at work when we judge that an explanation based on occult forces fits a rare or unusual event better than does a more mundane but natural cause. That is, mysterious events are sometimes judged to represent mysterious causes (Singer & Benassi, 1981).

We have already suggested that when the students in the magician-as-psychic experiment saw someone perform feats that they could not explain in ordinary terms, they quickly reached for an available explanation that fit the event. An explanation that fits, given no other information, is one based on ESP. This is not irrational or stupid thinking; rather, it is simply a failure to think critically about a conclusion suggested on the basis of the common judgmental heuristic of representativeness.

**THINK about It**

**5.5**    Consider the following information about a graduate student named Tom W.:

Tom W. is of high intelligence, although lacking in true creativity. He has a need for order and clarity, and for neat and tidy systems in which every detail finds its appropriate place. His writing is rather dull and mechanical, occasionally enlivened by somewhat corny puns and by flashes of imagination of the sci-fi type. He has a strong drive for competence. He seems to have little feel and little sympathy for other people and does not enjoy interacting with others. Self-centered, he nonetheless has a deep moral sense. (Kahneman & Tversky, 1973, p. 238)

In which of the following fields of graduate study would you judge that Tom W. is most likely to be currently enrolled? Rank-order (1 = most likely) the following:

1. Business administration. ___

2. Computer science. ___

3. Humanities and education. ___

We discuss this exercise at the end of the chapter.

Events often occur without plan or purpose: coincidences do happen.

## Chance and Coincidence

The coming together of two events at the same time or in the same space in the absence of any intention or plan for them to do so is called a coincidence. If an important meeting happens to occur at the same time as the showing of our favorite television event, we bemoan the coincidence. We also label it a coincidence when we happen to meet a close friend at the supermarket. In most cases we attribute coincidences to the operation of chance factors. ("How lucky I was to run into you!") In other words, we find coincidences part and parcel of everyday living; in fact, they add some spice to our normal routine. They also attest to our belief in chance happenings.

Why is it, then, that on occasion we want to reject a theory of chance to explain a coincidence and substitute a theory of psychic forces or supernatural causes? The precipitating experience is usually a coincidence that appears too unusual to be due to chance (Marks & Kammann, 1980). Suppose when we play a game with dice we wish very hard for a certain number to appear, and it does. We are likely to be pleased but are not apt to rush out and proclaim to the world that we have telekinetic powers. After all, it happened only once, and such an outcome might easily be explained by chance, especially if we had been wishing for all sorts of numbers before the last 20 throws and this is the first time that we got the number we wanted. But what if we were asked to predict the outcome of the throw of an unbiased die on each of eight throws, and we were correct each time? Our intuitive notion of probability will not yield the exact probability of such a feat, but most of us will realize that such a coincidence is highly unlikely to occur by chance. In fact, the probability of succeeding by chance would be about one in a million (Randi, 1975). (You might appreciate why some scientists at the Stanford Research Institute were impressed when the alleged psychic Uri Geller did exactly this when a die was shaken in a metal box and he was asked to predict the face showing when the box was opened.)

If one should correctly predict the outcome of eight throws of a die, there are only two possible explanations. Such an outcome, no matter how improbable, could be due to chance, and thus by definition still be a simple coincidence. Or it is not chance, and we must look for an explanation elsewhere. It is possible (although not necessarily probable) that someone could wish the sun not to rise tomorrow and it would not. (In that case, of course, we wouldn't be around very long to care.) Thus even very unlikely events logically must be seen as possible. Most of us, however, work under the assumption that when the probability of an event is very low by chance, then something other than chance is probably the cause.

What often is called an "unexplainable coincidence" is an event that *appears* to be accounted for neither by chance (that is, the likelihood of its occurrence by chance is deemed to be very low) nor by ordinary processes (that is, a natural process is not evident). So-called psychic phenomena often fall into the category of unexplainable coincidences. Such events as predicting the throw of a die eight times in succession seem too unlikely to have been due to chance, yet no natural explanation seems to be available. In fact, some scientist-observers suggested that Uri Geller's remarkable success at predicting the throw of a die was indeed evidence of paranormal forces (Targ & Puthoff, 1974). The magician James Randi's (1975) analysis of the situation surrounding Geller's amazing ability to predict led to a more worldly explanation: Geller cheated.

The concept of chance ("How likely is that to happen by chance?") is so much a part of everyday thinking that it will pay us to look more closely at the way we think about chance events.

## Simple Probability

Our experiences with events that seem unlikely to be the result of chance often impress us, and it is good that they do. The unusual noise we hear in our car engine when we cruise at high speed might be passed off as a chance agitation of a mechanical monster or it could be treated as a sign of impending engine failure and a signal for us to look for a service station. In our effort to make sense of the world around us we are often in the position of having to decide whether the occurrence of an event was due just to chance or to "something real." One reason we sometimes say that a particular coincidence "simply couldn't happen by chance" is our misunderstanding of probability and chance factors (Marks & Kammann, 1980). This possibility suggests that we look more closely at our understanding of the nature of chance, if for no other reason than to make sure we get to the service station in time.

Consider the following two questions about the probability of occurrence of events. Try to answer each question correctly, but don't look for pencil and paper or head for the computer. Simply do some mental calculations.

1. What is the probability of selecting an ace of spades from a regular deck of shuffled cards?
2. What is the likelihood of rolling a 7 when two dice are thrown?

Your answers to these questions are intended to demonstrate that your basic notion of probability is likely to be correct. No doubt your answer to the first question was "1 in 52." You probably reasoned that inasmuch as there are 52 cards in a normal deck and you are interested in only one of these cards, then, in an unbiased selection, you should have 1 in 52 chances of getting the ace of spades. Your thinking provides us with an elementary definition of probability. We find the probability of anything by dividing the number of events that we are interested in (the favorable outcomes) by the total number of possible outcomes (both favorable and unfavorable). To select the ace of spades, one favorable outcome, we must identify the total number of outcomes, which is 52. So far, so good, we hope.

Now consider question 2. This is really an extension of question 1. If you applied the same rule, then you first identified the number of favorable outcomes there were. A quick calculation reveals that you can roll a 7 by throwing 5 and 2, 6 and 1, and 3 and 4. Since there are two dice, these pairs can be rolled in two ways (say, 5 on the first die and 2 on the second or vice versa). Thus there are six favorable outcomes when two dice are rolled. The problem then is to decide how many total possible outcomes there are when two dice are thrown. This is a bit more difficult, but some thought should reveal that there are 36 possibilities. The correct answer is 6 in 36, or 1 in 6.

You probably had no problem with question 2 unless you miscalculated one of the elements to the problem, as the teenage son of one of the authors did when he was presented with this problem. He said there was a 1 in 12 chance of rolling a 7 because there were three ways to get a 7 and 36 possible outcomes. Perhaps you made a similar error. Clearly, our application of the basic probability formula produces an error when *either* the number of favorable outcomes *or* the total number of possible outcomes is judged incorrectly. Our teenager got 1/12 by dividing 3 by 36. As you will see, we often get in trouble by misjudging elements in the probability equation. We want to emphasize that when we err in deciding about probabilities it is often not because we do not understand the concept (that is, the definition) of simple probability, but because we do not put the right numbers into the formula. That we all tend to make errors when we calculate probabilities quickly, magicians know well, and so do others who purposely misdirect our thinking.

## • • • • • • • • • •
# Probability and Availability

Consider another question. The same rules apply: no electronic help.

A group of 100 people are asked to guess a number between 1 and 10. What is the probability (relative frequency) that the number 7 is guessed?

1. 1 out of 100.
2. 7 out of 100.
3. 10 out of 100.
4. 17 out of 100.

Before putting you on the spot, we might first phrase this question slightly differently and give you a chance to change your answer. Suppose the question read this way:

Each of 100 people is asked to pick a number between 1 and 10 from a hat containing the ten numbers on equal-sized slips of paper. (Numbers are replaced and mixed up before each selection.) What is the probability that the number 7 will be selected? That is, how many of the 100 people would you expect to pick 7?

Do you see the difference between the two questions? The second way of phrasing the question emphasizes the randomness of the event. In this case you should estimate that the probability that a 7 (one of ten possible numbers) will be selected is 1 in 10, or approximately ten 7s out of 100 random selections. If you said "10 out of 100" was the answer to the first question, you probably misjudged the number of favorable events; that is, the number of times people are likely to guess 7. When you ask 100 people to guess a number between 1 and 10, would you expect approximately ten people to give you each of the ten numbers? Probably not, because of a bias in thinking about numbers that may not have occurred to you. Let us illustrate the problem by citing the results of an experiment conducted by two New Zealand psychologists (Marks & Kammann, 1980).

They asked several instructors of large classes to give students the following problem:

"I am thinking of a number between 1 and 10, for example, a number like 3, but it's not 3. Write down the first number that comes to your mind." (The "sender," by the way, was told to concentrate on 4. Who knows, it might work!)

This problem resembles closely a mindreading demonstration used by Uri Geller as well as another popular so-called psychic, The Amazing Kreskin. The problem, as you can see, eliminates the number 3, which is done purposely by professional mindreaders to affect people's guesses.

Their results, based on the responses of 197 college students, revealed the following percentages of guesses for the increasing numbers 1 through 10 (including 3, as some people still wrote that down): 2.0, 3.0, 5.1, 3.6, 12.7, 18.8, 32.0, 11.7, 10.7, and 0.51 percent. You can see that the odds that someone will guess a 7 are 32 out of 100, or almost 1 in 3. When you attempted to answer the first question given earlier, only if you took into account the fact that people's guesses are not evenly distributed and are actually biased toward the number 7 would you estimate that the probability of guessing a 7 is closer to 17 out of 100 than it is to 10 out of 100 (and, as you saw, the odds may be twice that). It is also possible, as an astute critic mentioned to us, that the odds of guessing a number may be affected by people's interpretation of the phrase *"between* 1 and 10." If some people interpret this to mean only the numbers 2 through 9, then the possible choices are reduced even more. The very low probabilities associated with guesses of 1 and 10 seem to suggest that many people do not, in fact, consider these numbers. Don't think that it is only New Zealand subjects who think this way. A similar experiment performed in the United States by one of the authors with students in sections of an introductory psychology class obtained similar results: people's guesses reflect obvious biases toward certain numbers.

The results of these informal experiments emphasize that the concept of equality rarely applies to people's thinking about the instances of a category. In other words, whether it be a category of numbers between 1 and 10 or a category of colors or a category of cars or almost any other category, our thinking is not likely to reflect equal consideration of all the possibilities. Certain numbers, specific colors, particular makes of car are more available than others. When we are asked to name an instance of a category, we must not mistakenly assume that all instances are equally likely to be named. It is important to ask ourselves why some events might be named more often or more quickly than others.

● ● ● ● ● ● ● ● ● ● ● ● ● ● ● ● ● ● ● ● ● ● ● ● ● ● ● ● ● ● ● ● ● ● ● ● ● ● ● ● ● ● ● ● ● ● ● ●

**THINK
about It**

**5.6**   A favorite question of so-called mindreaders goes something like this: "I am thinking about two simple drawings. I will concentrate on them while you try to draw them on a sheet of paper."

Let's forget for a moment about ESP. Consider all the possible objects in the world. In the universe, even! What do you think is the probability that one of the pictures drawn by someone will be a house? One in a million? One in a billion?

The probability that someone will draw a house is approximately _____ .

Data bearing on this question are provided at the end of the chapter.

● ● ● ● ● ● ● ● ● ● ● ● ● ● ● ● ● ● ● ● ● ● ● ● ● ● ● ● ● ● ● ● ● ● ● ● ● ● ● ● ● ● ● ● ● ● ● ●

● ● ● ● ● ● ● ● ●
## Probability and Representativeness

We aren't done yet; there is more to be learned about estimating everyday probabilities. Once more, please try to answer the following two questions.

1.  When an unbiased roulette wheel is spun one time, the odds of ending up with the ball in a red pocket are slightly less than 50:50. If after ten turns

of the wheel the ball has landed on black each time, what are the odds that on the 11th spin the ball will be in the red pocket?

    a. Slightly less than 50:50.
    b. Exactly 50:50.
    c. Slightly more than 50:50.
    d. Much more than 50:50.

2. Compare the following sequences of outcomes of unbiased coin tosses (H = heads, T = tails). Would you say that by chance *a* is more likely, that *b* is more likely, or that the two are equally likely?

    a. HTHTHTHT.
    b. THHTHTTH.

Consider first your answer to question 2. This may be considered a trick question in that the correct answer is that the two outcomes are equally likely. The problem has been used to illustrate how the representativeness heuristic leads people to avoid sequences that don't look random (Kahneman & Tversky, 1972). It seems that people tend to look to see whether a particular sequence of events represents their concept of randomness. The two sequences in question 2 have an equal likelihood of appearing, but one seems more random than the other. People expect an unbiased coin to produce about an equal number of heads and tails, but their intuitive notion of randomness is that these occurrences should not be systematic. So they are likely to judge one sequence (the more random-appearing one) as being more likely. They use the representativeness heuristic when they look to see if the example that was given fits their concept of randomness.

Attempts to answer question 2 often highlight another characteristic of our thinking: a belief that what works in the long run also works in the short run. This bias in our thinking has been called a belief in the law of small numbers (Tversky & Kahneman, 1971). Consider the fact that we are better able to estimate the characteristics of a population when very large samples are drawn than when small sample sets are examined. Eating a large slice of a pie will tell us more about the pie's overall taste than will nibbling the crust. You probably know this already. The problem is that people have a tendency to use the rule of large numbers when they look at small numbers. They expect that what will happen in a large set of numbers (or over the long run) will happen in small sets (or over the short run). Thus many people who are asked question 2 will suggest that heads and tails should not alternate systematically (even though this is a short-run problem). They fail to realize that only a few sets based on small samples will exactly reflect the population characteristics; the majority of small sets will not look like the population. Imagine a sequence of 1000 outcomes of an unbiased coin toss. In the middle of this series of 1000 heads and tails, mentally insert the two sequences of eight outcomes in question 2. In this imaginary sequence of 1000 outcomes, does either *a* or *b* look less random? Probably not, because when you look at the long run you no doubt see that *a* and *b* seem to fit right in. On the other hand, if you saw 1000 outcomes alternating systematically between heads and tails, like those in *a*, you would probably think (with good reason) that chance was *not* operating.

Because of our belief in the law of small numbers we also tend to see sequences of events as self-correcting (Tversky & Kahneman, 1971). You may have recognized question 1 as the famous "gambler's fallacy." The odds that a ball will land on red (or black) in a single spin of the roulette wheel (in a fair gambling house) do not change with the number of prior red or black outcomes. In our example, the odds that the ball will land in a red pocket after ten balls have landed in a black pocket are still slightly less than 50:50. Our intuition, however, is that to be fair a process must be self-correcting, and that after a given number of outcomes in one direction it must go in the other direction; that is, that the odds of the ball's landing in a red pocket are now greater than 50:50. When we think this way, we are again applying the law of small numbers. What we know to be true in regard to large numbers (many, many spins of the wheel) we feel must work for small numbers (relatively few spins). But nature (that is, chance) doesn't necessarily work that way. Not all samples are going to be representative of a population, and representativeness as a rule is going to decrease as the size of the sample decreases.

· · · · · · · · · · · · · · · · · · · · · · · · · · · · · · · · · · · · · · · · · · · · · · · · · · · · · · · · · · · ·

**THINK
about It**

**5.7**  If there are 23 people in a room, what would you estimate is the probability that two people have the same birthday? Indicate your answer by circling one of the following:

1. 100:1 (that is, 1 in 100).
2. 10:1 (1 in 10).
3. Greater than 50:50.

The answer is provided at the end of the chapter.

· · · · · · · · · · · · · · · · · · · · · · · · · · · · · · · · · · · · · · · · · · · · · · · · · · · · · · · · · · · ·

We conclude this section with one more question. What is the probability that a watch that has simply stopped and has been put away in a drawer will start ticking again when it is picked up?

We don't really know what is the exact probability that a stopped watch will start when it is picked up, but we will wager that in most people's minds the probability is much lower than it actually is. Note that we are not talking about broken or smashed watches, which perhaps have defective or missing pieces. We are asking about a watch that one day quit ticking and was laid aside. When it is picked up later, what is the likelihood that it will start ticking?

It turns out that there are data bearing on this question. Generally speaking, we can judge that about half of such watches will start ticking, at least for a few seconds, when they are picked up and jiggled, and perhaps the oil

What works in the long run may fail in the short run.

inside is softened by the warmth of someone's hands. Several investigators (Marks & Kammann, 1980; see also Randi, 1975, pp. 199–200) asked local jewelers to try this with watches that had been brought to them for repairs. In one case they found that more than 57 percent of the watches started when they were picked up, shaken, and warmed by the jewelers' hands. When a small group of students tried this, more than 80 percent of the stopped watches started working.

Fixing "broken" watches is a favorite trick of magicians (and alleged psychics). Uri Geller, the psychic superstar of the 1970s, would announce on television and on radio shows that people should go and collect watches that had stopped. While they held them, he said, he would use his telekinetic powers to start them running again. About one-half to three-fourths of these people probably still think that Geller has psychic powers. To be impressed by this demonstration people must ignore the probability of favorable outcomes and judge that the starting of a watch is not representative of a chance event. That is, some people no doubt believe that the starting of a watch is more representative of some mysterious psychic process than it is of ordinary processes.

In the October 14, 1975, story in the *Enquirer* (the one we referred to at the beginning of the chapter), it was noted that Geller, perched high above the earth in his balloon, also concentrated "for precisely 10 minutes on repairing broken watches and appliances." It was further stated that "almost half the total who responded reported that Geller helped them repair broken watches and appliances." Well, are you surprised?

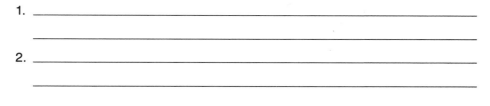

**THINK about It**

**5.8**   What do you think about the following all-too-familiar scenes?

1. A person has a lifelong fascination with astrology and suggests that you change a dinner date with her because of today's signs, which, according to her, "have been right in the past."

2. Someone you know is convinced that ESP is real because on "many occasions" he has experienced precognition. For example, he tells you that just yesterday he knew someone was about to call him just before the person did call him, and last week he dreamed about being in an accident and this week he had an accident. These coincidences, he suggests, are so striking that they can be explained only through ESP.

Can you identify one or more biases in thinking that are present in each of these scenarios?

1. _____

_____

2. _____

_____

## Subjective Validation

*Subjective validation* is the basic human tendency to misread unfavorable or neutral evidence as giving positive support for one's own beliefs (Marks & Kammann, 1980). In other words, once we have accepted a particular idea, we tend to find evidence supporting that idea, even when there is no real evidence or when the evidence actually is the opposite of what we believe.

> Our beliefs are not automatically updated by the best evidence available. They often have an active life of their own and fight tenaciously for their own survival. They tell us what to read, what to listen to, who to trust, and how to explain away contrary information. (Marks & Kammann, 1980, p. 176)

Beliefs, in this view, tend to be self-perpetuating.

Some of the more prevalent kinds of subjective validation fall under the heading of *expectancy effects*. We find what we expected to find. Consider the results of a clever study involving a somewhat unusual task (Cordaro & Ison, 1963). The researchers asked observers to record the behavior of worms. Specifically, the observers were requested to record the number of head turns and body contractions made by planaria (flatworms). The observers were told to expect a high incidence of turning and contracting among half of the worms, and to expect a low incidence of turning and contracting among the other half. Actually, the worms under observation were essentially identical. The only thing that varied was the observers' expectations. The results showed that more than twice as many head turns and body contractions were reported when the observers held high expectations of body movement as when they had low expectations.

Results such as these have been documented numerous times, in many situations and with various tasks (see Rosenthal, 1966). The findings illustrate the effect of observer expectations on what is being observed. How do we account for these expectancy effects? Did the observers fake their reports in order to meet the expectations given to them? The possibility that observers sometimes falsify data cannot be ruled out; however, typically the errors are unintentional and arise from the way our expectations influence the observation process.

Consider the case of the planaria. The head turns and body contractions of these little beasts are no doubt difficult to observe. Was that a head turn or not? When the situation requires a decision and the evidence is unclear, we are apt to be influenced by what we think we should see. If a large number of head turns is expected, then it seems likely that the slight movement we saw (or did we really see it?) was a head turn. Conversely, when we expect a low frequency of head turns, that slight movement we witnessed (or did we?) might more reasonably be classified as "not really a head turn" and not recorded.

Now consider the behavior of more complex organisms, such as students, psychics, children, mental patients, persons we don't like—in other words, people in general. As we saw in Chapter 3, we are continually making judgments about the behavior of others. Moreover, it is clear that we usually have ideas about how people *should* behave. We expect bright students to do bright things. We expect people in mental hospitals to do strange things. If we believe in ESP, we expect to see instances of ESP. The evidence for expectancy effects should alert us to the possible biases that can operate when we look at a situation through the colored glasses of a strongly held belief. (You may remember that in Chapter 2 we discussed the role of expectancy in producing illusory correlations.) The lesson should be clear: We must critically evaluate the "evidence" we have obtained in light of the expectancies with which we gathered it.

**THINK about It**

**5.9**    Assume, if you will, that someone holds the belief that people with blue eyes are more intelligent than people with green eyes. How might subjective validation operate to sustain such a belief? List three kinds of "evidence" for the superiority of blue-eyed people over green-eyed people that might be obtained by someone who is unaware of subjective validation effects.

1. _____

_____

2. _____

_____

3. _____

_____

     We also have been collecting evidence and it is summarized at the end of the chapter.

## Self-Fulfilling Prophecies

     Our beliefs influence what we do and whom we listen to, and, in the form of expectancies, affect our perceptions of a situation. Our beliefs also may have the power to affect people in a way that leads them to behave in a manner that is consistent with our predictions, making things, so to speak, come out as we expected. This process has been called a *self-fulfilling prophecy* (Darley & Fazio, 1980). Consider that when we think about a particular situation we often make predictions (prophecies) about what will happen in this situation. How many times have you heard people (perhaps yourself) say something like: "I know that no one will like me at that party." "If I go for that interview I'm sure I won't get the job." "This is going to be the best semester ever." A prophecy is self-fulfilling when our beliefs prompt ourselves or others to behave in ways that fulfill our predictions (prophecies). We should emphasize that a prophecy is self-fulfilling when what happens would not have happened in the absence of the role played by our beliefs; an expectation becomes reality because of the way that a person acts to change the situation.

     Consider the following experimental demonstration of self-fulfilling prophecies (Fazio, Effrein, & Falender, 1981). Students in an introductory psychology class were asked to participate in an experiment called "Personality Interviewing." As part of this experiment the subjects answered a series of questions that were characteristic of either introverted persons ("What things do you dislike about loud parties?") or of extroverted persons ("What would you do if you wanted to liven things up at a party?") The students were randomly assigned to these conditions so that we can assume that subjects in each of these groups were on the average neither particularly introverted nor extroverted. (In fact, a pretest affirmed that the groups were similar on the introversion–extroversion dimension.)

     The experimenters sought through their questions to influence the subjects' self-perceptions and to assess whether the subjects would then behave in a way consistent with the self-perception the experimenters had induced. After answering the experimenter's questions, the subject was asked to remain for a period in a waiting room with another person. This person, unknown to the subject, was an accomplice working with the experimenter. The conversation between the subject and the accomplice in the waiting room was recorded. Also recorded was the distance from the accomplice the subject sat. After being in the waiting room for a period of time, the subject was asked to finish the experiment by filling out a self-perception inventory that asked the subject to rate his or her characteristic behaviors (talkative–quiet, friendly–unfriendly, and the like).

The results of the experiment revealed that students who had been asked a series of questions designed to identify them as more extroverted than the other subjects were more likely to initiate a conversation with the other person in the waiting room, tended to sit closer to the person, and perceived themselves as significantly more extroverted on the self-perception scale they completed at the end of the experiment. Moreover, the waiting-room accomplice (who did not know what questions had been read to the subjects) rated these subjects as significantly more extroverted than those subjects who had been encouraged to think of themselves as introverted. In other words, subjects apparently came to perceive themselves as extroverted (or introverted) and subsequently behaved in a way that caused others to perceive them as extroverted (or introverted). A (false) belief about oneself came to be true when the subjects behaved in a way consistent with that belief.

Self-fulfilling prophecies have been seen to play a role in the classroom. In fact, in at least one case, teachers' expectancies have been said to bring about actual changes in pupils' IQ during a school year (Rosenthal, 1966; Rosenthal & Jacobson, 1968.) Children were randomly assigned to teachers who were told that the children "would show unusual academic development" during the school year, and to a control group for which no such expectation was suggested. The children whom the teachers expected to improve did in fact show significantly greater improvement than control children, although there were no differences in academic ability between the groups of children at the beginning of the year. The investigator responsible for these research findings pointed out:

> If experimenters can, and if teachers can, then probably healers, spouses, and other "ordinary" people also can affect the behavior of those with whom they interact by virtue of their expectations of what that behavior will be. (Rosenthal, 1966, p. 412; see also Darley & Fazio, 1980).

**THINK about It**

**?**

**5.10**  After reading about self-fulfilling prophecies, can you think of concrete ways in which a (false) belief can be made to come true? Assume that the following expectations have no basis in fact; there is no evidence that the outcome would occur naturally. For each, suggest how a self-fulfilling prophecy might occur, and a prophecy come true.

1. A company boss tells her (not yet very competent) employees that they are "the best."

The incompetent employees could perform exceptionally well if _____

_____

_____

_____

_____

2. A party is predicted to be a disaster.
   The prediction could come true if _____

_____

_____

_____

3. Someone seeking a romantic relationship with another person consults a palm reader and is told that "the new year will bring you together."

   The prediction could come true if _____

_____

_____

_____

The discussion at the end of the chapter provides some suggestions.

# Principles of Critical Thinking about Beliefs: A Summary

1. Be aware that we often rely on an availability heuristic to estimate the frequency of a phenomenon by noticing the ease with which we can bring to mind instances of that phenomenon.

2. We use a representativeness heuristic when the likelihood of an event is estimated by the degree to which the event is judged to be similar in essential characteristics to the concept or process in question.

3. Recognize that chance (mere coincidence) sometimes is the best explanation available.

4. We can err in estimating probability when we fail to identify correctly either the number of favorable events or the number of possible outcomes, or both.

5. We must be careful not to believe that what works in the long run (for a large sample or population) will always hold for the short run (for a small sample).

6. We have a tendency to believe (mistakenly) that nature is always self-correcting (the gambler's fallacy).

7. We humans have a tendency to see what we expect to see, so the evidence we gather to support a belief must be critically evaluated in terms of these expectations.

8. Our beliefs (even though false) can come true when they lead us or other people to behave in a way that is consistent with our expectations (self-fulfilling prophecies).

## • • • • • • • • • •
## Think about It: Discussion of Answers

**5.1**    Our experience suggests that the two reasons most frequently given for a belief in phenomena such as ESP are: (a) personal experience ("I've experienced it"), and (b) lack of knowledge or thoughtful consideration of alternative explanations ("There isn't any other way to explain some of these things"). The power of personal testimony, of course, does not go unnoticed by those who seek to influence our thinking. We recently came across an advertisement for a series of books about "mystic places." On the cover was a picture of a woman quoted as saying: "I never thought I would believe it. Until it happened to me."

**5.2**    We have had the following experiences that led us to entertain (if only briefly) the idea that ESP is real:

1. Someone we were thinking about called us on the phone at the very moment we were thinking about him (telepathy?).
2. A person we dreamed would get into trouble did get into trouble soon after our dream (precognition?).
3. A number we picked for a lottery did in fact appear (clairvoyance?).

Although the idea that ESP might be involved was briefly entertained, it was just that, a bit of entertainment.

**5.3**    In each pair, alternative *a* is the *least* frequent. Surprised? You might be interested in what happened when several social psychologists presented these questions and others like them to subjects with the request that subjects both give an answer and rate their confidence in the answer. The respondents were often wrong in their choice of answers and expressed a high degree of confidence that their (wrong) answers were correct (Fischhoff et al., 1977).

**5.4**    Although there may be a citywide problem with rats, we would want to find out whether the estimate of the frequency of rats is biased by the information that is available to the alderman. A rat-bites-man story is something we are likely to remember, and seeing a rat in our garage can be rather unsettling. When we think about a rat problem, these instances no doubt will easily come to mind. An availability heuristic may suggest to the alderman that there are lots of rats running around. But so far, we may be talking about one or at most two rats!

**5.5**    Perhaps you can feel the representativeness heuristic at work. We often hold certain stereotypes about people in various occupations. Called upon to estimate the likelihood of Tom W.'s being a graduate student in the areas named, we attempt to judge how well Tom W.'s characteristics represent the essential characteristics of the stereotype that we hold for each of these fields. Daniel Kahneman and Amos Tversky (1973) gave this description to graduate students in psychology and asked them to rank the likelihood that Tom was a graduate student in each of these above areas (as well as some other fields). The mean ranks showed clearly that Tom was considered most likely to be a computer science student. Humanities and education as a category was ranked well down the list, with business administration somewhere in between. Other data collected as part of this study revealed that the graduate students' predictions of Tom's chosen field did not take into account their knowledge about the frequency of graduate students in the United States in each of these fields. The subjects were obviously aware that there are many more graduates in the fields of humanities and education than there are in computer science; so one of those fields would be the best guess for Tom. However, people tended to rely more on the representativeness heuristic than on their knowledge of actual relative frequency. In what field did you think Tom was enrolled?

**5.6**    The New Zealand psychologists David Marks and Richard Kammann (1980) posed this question to several hundred students at two universities. A house or building accounted for 94/702 or 13 percent of the drawings. If we throw in responses depicting a square or a triangle, which easily could be part of a house, you account for 228/702 or 32 percent of the drawings. In fact, just eight drawings accounted for 69 percent of the responses. Rather interesting results when you think of the billions and billions of objects in the universe! Want to go into the mindreading business?

**5.7**    This question frequently is used to illustrate just how poor our intuitive judgments about probability can be. The answer to the birthday question is *c*, greater than 50:50. Many people are surprised by this fact because they relied on the representativeness heuristic (Kahneman & Tversky, 1972). Apparently most people briefly think about the large number of days in the year (365) and the fact that only 23 individuals are represented. To suggest that one of these many days of the year would be represented twice just doesn't seem to be very likely. That is, two people with the same birthday seems unrepresentative of our intuitive notion of chance. Interested readers can see John Allen Paulos's stimulating book, *Innumeracy: Mathematical Illiteracy and Its Consequences* (1988, p. 2), for a complete mathemathical explanation of the birthday problem. Briefly, first the number of ways that 23 dates can be chosen is determined, using a multiplication principle. Then the number of instances when no two dates are the same is calculated, and the proportion of the total number of ways is determined. This proportion is subtracted from 1.00 to yield the proportion (probability) that at least two of 23 people will have a common birthday. As noted, this proportion or probability reveals that fully half the time that 23 randomly selected people are gathered together, two or more will have a common birthday.

**5.8**    When someone's astrological sign appears to predict his or her future, or when someone experiences an event that "could be" ESP, the events may be vividly etched in that person's mind. Memories of these events are available as "evidence" to support a belief in psychic phenomena. Moreover, the ease with which these instances come to mind is likely to lead someone to think that they occur more frequently than they actually do.

1. Anyone familiar with astrological signs knows that many events might be considered to verify an astrological prediction. How many people are guilty of selecting from among the many everyday events those that "fit" their astrological prediction? We can also assume that people are not likely to remember *all* the occasions when an astrological sign did *not* predict the future.

2. When we think about why someone telephoned when we were wishing to hear from that person, we want to consider how many times we were thinking about another person and he or she did *not* call. Did someone call once when we were thinking about her, and not call 99 times when we were thinking about her? We also must remember that such coincidences *are* likely to occur, and in fact their probability may not be as low as you suspect. Is it possible, for example, that we have been thinking about that person more frequently than usual because she has not been seen or heard from for some time? That is, are we worried or at least curious about her situation? Given this state of affairs, are the odds that low that we might be thinking about that person about the time that she calls? (Or does she actually call relatively frequently, so that the "coincidence" is rather probable?) Do dreams predict future events? Keep in mind that accidents happen to everyone; minor ones occur almost every day. Is it that unusual that a dream about an accident occurs just before one happens? How many times have we dreamed about someone being in an accident and no accident happened? A person who doesn't think critically may decide that these events are more representative of something mysterious than simply chance coincidences.

**5.9**   We have been watching green-eyed people carefully the last few days with this hypothesis in mind. (This is an easy exercise because we happen to be blue-eyed.) We can report that:

1. We saw a green-eyed person drop his drink on the floor at a party we attended. No blue-eyed person (whom we saw) did anything so stupid at the party.
2. A green-eyed student in one of our classes got a D on a paper she handed in.
3. The gardener who takes care of the lawn of our neighbor is green-eyed, whereas our neighbor who is a business executive is blue-eyed.

What more evidence do we need? On the other hand, perhaps we should try the same exercise for the next few days but with the opposite expectation in mind! What do you think we will see this time?

**5.10**   1. The evidence regarding the effect of self-fulfilling prophecies suggests that there is good reason to believe in the "power of positive thinking." If the employees believe their boss, or even if they entertain the hypothesis only briefly that they are "the best," they may look around for evidence that she is right. It won't be difficult to find examples of some things that are done well (just as it isn't hard to find evidence that an astrological sign predicts something we do). Having seen evidence that the boss is right, the employees may incorporate this belief into their thinking about themselves and gain confidence in themselves to tackle more difficult tasks and assignments. An expectation about them leads them to behave in a way that fulfills that expectation.

2. It probably has happened to all of us. We just *know* that a party or other social affair is going to be a disaster. You know who will be there! It isn't the kind of party we like! Given this expectation, is it any wonder that we look for people and events at the party that support our belief, and not look for people and events that do not meet our expectation? If our seeking of evidence that we are right leads us to feel more and more unhappy or even angry, do we then begin to behave in a way that irritates our host or the person we came with? Has the party turned out to be the disaster that we predicted because our behavior helped to bring about what we predicted?

3. The belief that the new year will find us growing closer to the one we love may prompt us to behave in a way that makes it easier for the one we idolize to approach us. That is, our behavior may change in ways that make this togetherness actually occur. Does believing that we will be closer together put us in a cheerier mood? produce greater self-confidence? yield more consideration toward this other person (because he or she is "destined" to be with us)? or make us more available? Of course, critically thinking about the situation without the help of a palm reader may also suggest ways we can make this outcome happen.

## •••••••••
## Recommended Readings

We have trouble restraining ourselves when we make recommendations for additional readings on the topics discussed in this chapter. There is a multitude of good ones to choose from. Among our favorites—works from which we noticeably drew much material—are *The Psychology of the Psychic,* by David Marks and Richard Kammann (1980), and books by James (The Amazing) Randi, including *The Magic of Uri Geller* (1975) and *Flim-Flam: Psychics, ESP, Unicorns, and Other Delusions* (1986). As Isaac Asimov says in a review reprinted on the cover of John Paulos's book *Innumeracy: Mathematical Illiteracy and Its Consequences* (1988), "This pleasant book would improve the quality of thinking of virtually anyone." Paulos addressed the 1990 CSICOP conference in Washington, D.C., the themes of which were "Scientific Literacy" and "Critical Thinking in Higher Education." CSICOP is the acronym for Committee for the Scientific Investigation of Claims of the Paranormal. The 1990 conference is reviewed in the Fall 1990 issue of *Skeptical Inquirer.* This publication is must reading for anyone interested in thinking critically about everything from health fads to horoscopes to ghostbusters. It is the official journal of CSICOP (Box 229, Buffalo, N.Y. 14215-0229).

# Knowing about Knowing

**To be ignorant of one's ignorance is the malady of the ignorant.**

Amos Bronson Alcott
(19th-century American philosopher and educator)

It's a particularly disconcerting experience to think we know something only to find out that we don't. The student who exclaims, "I thought I knew it!" after an exam that clearly demonstrated that the student did *not* know it at least knows exactly what we mean. Another vexing experience of this sort is to say we are "sure" that we know the right answer to a question and find out that our answer is wrong. This chapter examines some of the reasons why we may think we know something when we do not. Also discussed are strategies to improve your comprehension and retention of information, as well as ways to increase the likelihood that what you think you know is what you do in fact know. The goal, as you will see, is to become a good "cognitive monitor" and an "active processor" of information.

• • • • • • • • • •
## Introduction

Have you ever been in the position of thinking that you knew something was true but then finding out that what you thought was true was not? If you're like the rest of us, you probably have been in this situation more than once. The realization that what we thought was true actually was not true sometimes can be a painful experience, as when we find that a grade on a class exam is lower than we anticipated because we (mistakenly) "thought we knew it." Although often we know what we know and don't know, sometimes we think we know something when we don't. Why?

The bases for why we think we know something can be rather subtle, as research by several cognitive psychologists has shown (Hasher, Goldstein, & Toppino, 1977). The psychologists asked college students to help construct "a new test of the general knowledge of college students." The task given to the students was to judge whether various plausible assertions were true or false. To make their judgments, each student used a 7-point scale, where 1 = definitely false, 4 = uncertain, and 7 = definitely true. Put yourself in the position of these helpful students and judge the truthfulness of the following statements:

1. Kentucky was the first state west of the Alleghenies to be settled by pioneers.
2. The People's Republic of China was founded in 1947.
3. French horn players get cash bonuses to stay in the U.S. Army.
4. Zachary Taylor was the first president to die in office.

As you can see, it was not an easy task. The second and fourth statements are false, and the first and third are true.

The goal of this research was not, however, to show that students are uncertain about what they know to be true, nor was it even to prepare a new general knowledge test; rather, the purpose of this psychology experiment was to investigate the effect that repetition had on judgments of a statement's truthfulness. On three occasions at two-week intervals the students listened to a list of sentences and made judgments using the 7-point scale. Some of the sentences were repeated on these occasions, although students were not told about this aspect of the procedure. The researchers found that the average rating of a repeated sentence increased across the three sessions. That is, with repetition, a statement came to be viewed as more true. This effect occurred whether or not the statement was really true or false.

Have the words of the English poet Matthew Prior been validated?

> Till their own dreams deceive 'em,
> And oft repeating, they believe 'em.

This chapter explores what we know about what we know, a subject that psychologists call *metacognition*. The prefix "meta" means about or around, and "cognition," of course, refers to knowing. Therefore, metacognition is "about cognition," or what we know about knowing. Are we better at math tasks than at verbal tasks? Do we know that a particular bit of information—for example,

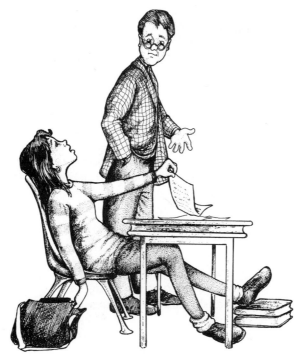

Sometimes we think we know something when we don't.

an answer to a trivia question—is stored in our memory even if we can't retrieve it? When we read a passage knowing that we will be tested on its contents, can we accurately predict how well we will do? These are all aspects of knowing about knowing—that is, of metacognition.

## Metacognition: The Case for Cognitive Monitoring ●

Metacognition can be viewed as having both a knowledge component and a regulatory component (Brown & Palincsar, 1982). The knowledge component represents what we know about cognition. It is likely to include knowledge about people, tasks, and strategies (Flavell, 1979). Consider the following questions about our metacognitive knowledge:

*People knowledge:* What do you know about yourself and other people as processors of information?
Can you remember 20 digits presented to you at a rate of one a second? Do you occasionally forget answers that you previously learned in preparation for a test?

*Task knowledge:* What do you know about the goals of a given task and the difficulty of achieving them?
Are essay tests easier than multiple-choice tests? What is required to score well on a standardized test such as the LSAT or MCAT?

*Strategy knowledge:* What do you know about the best ways to approach a task in order to achieve a specific goal?

What should you do to prepare to give a speech without looking at notes? What is the best way to learn the meanings of new words?

The second major aspect of metacognition, the regulatory component, has to do with regulating our cognitive processes. We might think, as many contemporary psychologists do, of people making use of various "executive processes." The intended analogy is with a boss or executive who is responsible for supervising a particular activity. An executive typically must plan how an activity will be carried out, monitor the effort made to carry it out, and, when the task has been accomplished, evaluate it in terms of the stated goals of the project. Of course, to regulate our cognitive activities adequately we have to use what we know about cognition, or the first category of metacognition. Thus these two aspects of metacognition, knowledge and regulation, interact in our everyday thinking.

Metacognitive processes are critical to nearly all important cognitive activities, such as those involved in communicating and comprehending information (including reading and writing), language acquisition, memory, problem solving, and social cognition (Flavell, 1979). Contemporary views of human intelligence also emphasize the role of metacognitive processes in intelligent behavior (Sternberg & Detterman, 1986), and learning of metacognitive skills is seen as important for human development and for theories of education (Brown & Palincsar, 1982; Flavell, 1979). In short, there are few human cognitive activities that do not include some form of cognitive monitoring if they are performed appropriately.

● ● ● ● ● ● ● ● ● ● ● ● ● ● ● ● ● ● ● ● ● ● ● ● ● ● ● ● ● ● ● ● ● ● ● ● ● ● ● ● ● ● ● ● ● ● ● ● ● ● ● ● ● ●

**THINK
about It**

?

**6.1**    Consider the two chief aspects of metacognition, knowledge and regulation, as well as the particular aspects of each. We have suggested that the knowledge component includes person, task, and strategy knowledge, whereas regulation involves planning, monitoring, and evaluating. Now consider the task of reading a biology chapter in preparation for a test.

1. What type of metacognitive knowledge is relevant to this task? Can you identify one example each of person, task, and strategy knowledge?

Person: _____

_____

Task: _____

_____

Strategy: _____

_____

2. What kinds of regulatory activities might you perform in planning, monitoring, or evaluating the outcome of this task? Can you suggest one example of each of these types of regulatory activities?

Planning: _____

_____

Monitoring: _____

_____

Evaluating: _____

_____

At the end of the chapter we provide some examples of the kinds of knowledge and regulatory activities that might be associated with this task.

## Thinking about What Is to Be Learned

There are two immediate benefits to thinking carefully about what we have been asked to learn before we attempt actually to learn it. By thinking about the topic under consideration we activate relevant schemas that facilitate comprehension and help us to organize new information with information that we already know. Also, thinking about what is to be learned is important so that we can plan how to study efficiently. For example, we will probably want to spend more time studying material that is unfamiliar or that is particularly difficult than material that is familiar or easy to learn.

## The Role of Schemas

As we saw in Chapter 3, *schemas* are organized knowledge structures. They "represent knowledge that we experience—interrelationships between objects, situations, events, and sequences of events that normally occur" (Glaser, 1984, p. 100). Schemas, in other words, are our organized prior knowledge, and, as such, are critical for understanding and remembering new information. Given the task of learning something new, we typically attempt to integrate new information with what we already know. Without some prior knowledge we frequently find that comprehending new material is difficult.

The following passage will help to illustrate this point. Please read the next paragraph carefully.

The procedure is actually quite simple. First arrange things into different bundles depending on make-up. Don't do too much at once. In the short run this may not seem important, however, complications easily arise. A mistake can be costly. Next, find facilities. Some people must go elsewhere for them. Manipulation of appropriate mechanisms should be self-explanatory. Remember to include all other necessary supplies. Initially the routine will overwhelm you, but soon it will become just another facet of life. Finally, rearrange everything into original groups. Return these to their usual places. Eventually they will be used again. Then the whole cycle will have to be repeated.[1]

Having read the passage, use a 7-point scale, where 1 = difficult to understand and 7 = very easy to understand, to rate your comprehension of the passage.

We can assume that your rating is not very high; why else would we give you such a passage? The words are familiar and every sentence has a subject and a verb, but something is missing. The passage just doesn't seem to make sense.

When passages like this one were presented to college students as part of a psychology experiment, they, too, rated them difficult to comprehend (Bransford & Johnson, 1972; Nyberg, 1975). Well, at least some of the students did. Some of the students were given some additional information about this passage, information that it turns out was quite important for comprehension. Before these students read the passage they were told that it was about washing clothes. You might try reading the passage again with that information in mind. The students who were given an appropriate schema did not find the passage particularly difficult to comprehend, and when their memory for the contents of the passage was tested, they remembered nearly twice as much as did the students who were not told the topic before they read it.

We are not always conscious of the schemas we possess, but everyone has many schemas available and often we share this knowledge with other members of our culture (Bower, Black, & Turner, 1979). Think of the schemas you have for visiting the dentist, attending a college lecture, and going to a restaurant. Many people possess similar knowledge about the kinds of events that typically are associated with these activities and about the relationships among those events. We know that when we eat out, for instance, someone will probably show us to a table, the table will have appropriate place settings, a menu will be provided, we will typically eat before we pay, and so forth.

Our schemas are necessary to fill in what is missing from our everyday experiences. When we see someone emerge from a store holding a package, we infer that the person purchased something in the store. When we hear that someone "flew to New York," we will probably judge that the trip involved purchasing a ticket from an airline representative or a travel agent, going to the airport, boarding a plane, and so on. When we read that "the carpenter hit his thumb," we are likely to infer that a hammer was being used to strike a nail and that the carpenter missed. We make these inferences on the basis of

---

[1]From a dissertation by S. E. Nyberg, State University of New York at Stony Brook, 1975, entitled "Comprehension and Long-Term Retention of Prose Passages." Reprinted by permission of the author.

our organized knowledge about buying things, traveling by airplane, and building something with hammer and nails.

It is important that *before* you study material to be learned you survey it to determine what kinds of organized knowledge are relevant. When you learn new information you want to make available related prior knowledge. If an assigned passage is about weather and climate, for example, you will want to ask yourself what you know already about this topic. What is the weather like where you live? What kinds of unusual weather conditions have you experienced? A good idea is to look briefly through the new material to see if familiar concepts are mentioned. One specific strategy is to examine the main headings in a text and to think about what you know about the topics that are identified by these headings. Doing this will activate relevant knowledge that should aid your comprehension and retention of the material to be learned.

## Ease of Learning Judgments

Another reason for thinking about what it is that you are to learn is to help you plan how to allocate your study time in an efficient manner. Generally, material to be learned will vary in difficulty. You will have had more experience with some kinds of material than with others, and no doubt your aptitudes and interests make some things easier to learn than others. An optimal allocation of study time is one that distributes time and effort in direct proportion to the difficulty of the material. You are not likely to be successful if you study most those things that you already know or that are easy to learn and study least those things that are difficult to learn.

Looking over material to be learned in order to determine what will be easy or hard to learn may seem like an obvious study strategy, but there is an important assumption behind it. We must assume that we are able to discriminate accurately between what is easy and hard to learn. It appears that this is a skill that we acquire gradually and may not be well developed in everyone. Research has shown that less academically successful grade school children are not as able as their more successful classmates to distinguish between material that is easy and hard to comprehend or remember (Owings, Petersen, Bransford, Morris, & Stein, 1980). Researchers presented "easy" and "hard" stories to fifth-graders for study. The easy stories contained such sentences as "The tall boy had played basketball." The hard stories used such sentences as "The hungry boy had played basketball." You can see that in the easy condition the subject and predicate of the sentence are appropriately related, whereas in the hard condition the sentence elements are inappropriately related. Results of this experiment revealed that the more successful students were more likely to identify the appropriately written stories as easier to learn, and, most important, spent more time studying the difficult stories than they did the easy stories. The poor students spent equal amounts of time studying the easy and hard stories.

When high school or college students serve as subjects, and ratings are made of the comprehensibility of stories that have been purposely garbled, learners apparently are sensitive to major distortions in the text, especially when information about the story's setting or its resolution are affected (Pratt, Luszcz, MacKenzie-Keating, & Manning, 1982). Thus it seems likely that as we mature intellectually we acquire metacognitive knowledge and skills that help us distinguish what is easy and hard to comprehend. It is important that we actually use them.

**THINK
about It**

**6.2**    Here's a chance to show off that mature intellect. Read the following story and at the choice points (*), identify (circle one) the version (A or B) that is most likely to aid comprehensibility and retention.

*1. (A) It happened that he had something and was carrying it someplace in it. (B) It happened that a dog had a piece of meat and was carrying it home in his mouth.

*2. A Now on the way there he had to cross something lying across it. (B) Now on the way home he had to cross a plank lying across a stream.

 3. As he crossed he looked down and saw his own shadow reflected in the water beneath.

 4. Thinking it was another dog with another piece of meat he made up his mind to have that also.

 5. So he made a snap at the shadow.

*6. A This meant he had to open his mouth, lean way out over the water, and bend down close to the surface. (B) This meant he had to open it, lean way out over there, and bend down close to it.

 7. The piece of meat fell out.

*8. (A) Both of them tumbled into there and were swept over it to those below and that was it for that one.  B Both the dog and the piece of meat tumbled into the water and were swept over a falls to the rocks below and that was the end of the dog.[2]

The correct answers are provided at the end of the chapter.

## Illusions of Knowing   ●

Much of what we know has been learned from reading books, magazines, newspapers, and so forth. We do so much reading that many of us would probably consider reading to be something that we do well, perhaps even expertly.

[2]Adapted from Table 1, p. 496, in "Thinking about stories: The story schema in metacognition," by M. W. Pratt, M. A. Luszcz, S. Mackenzie-Keating, and A. Manning. In *Journal of Verbal Learning and Verbal Behavior*, 1982, 21, 495–505. Copyright 1982 by Academic Press. Reprinted by permission of the author and publisher.

Of course, not everyone is a skilled reader, and many adults have difficulty reading because they lack sound educational experiences. But among middle-class high school students and college students we would expect to find mainly proficient readers. Thus the results of experiments by researchers at the University of Wisconsin are rather startling (Epstein, Glenberg, & Bradley, 1984; Glenberg, Wilkinson, & Epstein, 1982). They investigated students' reactions to passages such as the following:

### Media Politics

The political behavior of the American public is becoming increasingly unpredictable due to widespread uncertainty regarding salient issues, major national concerns, and candidate discriminability. Public opinion polls report unexplained vacillation in party affiliation, as well as frequent fluctuations in candidate preference. Feelings of ambiguity and confusion that discourage the American citizen from partaking in the political process may explain this stability in the opinions of the electorate.[3]

Both high school and college students were asked to read this paragraph under various experimental conditions. For example, sometimes the paragraph was the third of a three-paragraph passage and sometimes it was the only paragraph read. Students were always told, however, that they were to read the paragraph as if they were studying for a test and to note any contradictions that might be present. Surprisingly, many students failed under these instructions to detect the clearly contradictory information in the last sentence of the paragraph. (Did you spot the contradiction?) In fact, when students were asked to indicate how well they comprehended the paragraph after reading it, many reported that they understood it even though they had not detected the contradiction. A belief that comprehension has been attained when in fact comprehension has failed can be called an *illusion of knowing* (Glenberg et al., 1982). The proportion of students who were susceptible to the illusion of knowing varied with the experimental condition; for example, illusions were more frequent when this was the third paragraph read than when it was read alone. What was most amazing, however, was that in some conditions more than half the students failed to note the contradictory information.

As the researchers point out, illusions of knowing are not consistent with the idea that people carry on active, accurate, on-line monitoring of what they are reading (Glenberg et al., 1982). *Comprehension monitoring,* or what is sometimes called *critical reading,* is evaluation of what one comprehends as one progresses through a text (Collins & Smith, 1982; Jenkins & Pany, 1981). Comprehension monitoring entails monitoring ongoing processes for comprehension problems as well as taking appropriate remedial action when a comprehension problem is detected (Collins & Smith, 1982). An example of a remedial action is rereading when monitoring signals that something is not understood. The illusion of knowing is especially disturbing because when readers think they understand something but don't, they never recognize that they have a problem and need to take remedial action.

[3]From "The illusion of knowing: Failure in the self-assessment of comprehension," by A. M. Glenberg, A. C. Wilkinson, and W. Epstein. In *Memory and Cognition*, 1982, *10*, 597–602. Copyright 1982 by the Psychonomic Society, Inc. Reprinted by permission.

If we don't actively strive for comprehension, we may mistakenly believe that everything is understood.

What lies behind comprehension failure? One possibility is that many people operate according to a default assumption as they read (Glenberg et al., 1982). The *default assumption* is the assumption that one understands something unless one receives a signal to the contrary. That is, often people don't strive for comprehension but assume that they understand what it is they are reading (or listening to) unless something signals them otherwise (for example, obvious inconsistencies). The default assumption is illustrated by the joke about the man who falls from a high building and says as he drops past the tenth floor, "Well, so far, so good." Without actively striving for comprehension, people may suggest that their understanding of text material is good when it is not. The consequences can be serious.

The default assumption is an apparent example of what Ellen Langer of Harvard University calls mindlessness (Langer, 1989; Langer, Blank, & Chanowitz, 1978; Langer & Piper, 1987). *Mindlessness* is a tendency to process information without attention to details and in a rigid, even automatic fashion.

The opposite of mindlessness is *mindfulness,* which is characterized by active distinction making and differentiation. Interestingly, Langer initially arrived at these conclusions about the way people think on the basis of her observations of elderly people who entered certain kinds of nursing homes (Langer, 1989). Elderly residents of a nursing facility often are not encouraged to make decisions and are not given significant responsibilities. As a consequence, they become mindless rather than mindful in their thinking. Of course, Langer is suggesting that people of all ages are capable of mindlessness.

Mindlessness is evident when we make rigid use of information. Earlier experiences may leave us "set" to repond in a certain way. As Langer and her associates (1978) have suggested, "When the structure of a communication, be it oral or written, semantically sound or senseless, is congruent with one's past experience, it may occasion behavior mindless of relevant details" (p. 641). In some situations a set to respond in a particular way is advantageous, but too often mindless responses are far from helpful.

The illusion of knowing illustrates this mindless kind of information processing. Consider how an illusion of knowing might be produced. A title or the main headings in a passage provide cues as to what the passage is about. Perhaps at this point we think of what we already know about this material and even predict what it is that we will learn from the passage. Moreover, as we read, we develop expectations about what will follow. If our thinking about the contents of a passage sets us up to accept certain ideas or conclusions, we may fail to make active distinctions among the words and ideas which we encounter. In Langer's words, mindlessness occurs because we make a "premature cognitive commitment" to information, and then treat mindlessly information that is related to the information to which we have become commited (Langer & Piper, 1987). Consider the last sentence in the "Media Politics" passage. Given what we have read before coming to the contradictory statement (or even given what we knew before we read the passage), and perhaps given our expectation that the final sentence in a paragraph is often only a summary of what we have just read, we are likely to commit ourselves to the idea already expressed, that the American electorate is unpredictable and opinions are marked by vacillation. That is, we mindlessly accept what follows.

It is hypothesized that one reason people treat information mindlessly is that they are often encouraged to think absolutely rather than conditionally (Langer & Piper, 1987). For example, students often are educated in an absolute fashion. New ideas are expressed as members of a discrete category of things, and not as falling on a continuum. They are told that "X is this" and "Y is that." They aren't always taught to make distinctions—that is, to be mindful; they are told simply to accept X and Y as members of specific categories. Theirs not to reason why!

A clever series of experiments revealed that if people were shown novel objects under conditions that reinforced absolute thinking (this *is* an X), they would treat these objects mindlessly; whereas if the same objects were presented in a conditional form (this *could be* an X), people would treat the objects mindfully (Langer & Piper, 1987). Under the guise of a test of consumer behavior,

Harvard undergraduates were introduced to various objects, some familar and some not, in either an absolute or a conditional way. In one experiment the students were told that an unfamiliar piece of rubber "was a dog's chew toy" or "could be a dog's chew toy." The students were asked to estimate the prices of several objects, including the critical or target object. However, the real goal of the experiment was to see if college students would be more likely to suggest an unusual use for the critical object when it was presented conditionally than when it was presented absolutely. In the experiment with the piece of a dog's chew toy, the experimenter pretended to need an eraser when none was present. Across several experiments, results showed that students were more likely to think of an unusual use for a novel object (using a piece of a dog's chew toy as an eraser) when they had been shown the object in a conditional way than when they had been introduced to it in an absolute manner. These results imply that conditional instruction encourages creativity, which is part of mindfulness, and that mindlessness can be prevented by prompting people to think about ideas and objects conditionally.

Mindfulness, not mindlessness, is of course a goal of critical thinking. And while certain kinds of external prompts and cues may help prevent mindlessness (Glenberg et al., 1982), typically we are left on our own to think mindfully. Illusions of knowing, for example, will not be as likely to occur if we continually strive for comprehension rather than work by default. Mindlessness also may be prevented if we work to think conditionally rather than absolutely.

**THINK about It**

**6.3**   Indicate the degree of your agreement with each of the following statements about the educational setting. Use a 5-point scale, where 1 = do not agree at all and 5 = definitely agree, to rate your agreement with these statements.

1. If professors would stick more to the facts and do less theorizing one could get more out of college. Rating: ____
2. The best thing about science courses is that most problems have only one right answer. Rating: ____
3. It is annoying to listen to a lecturer who cannot seem to make up his mind as to what he really believes. Rating: ____
4. It is a waste of time to work on problems which have no possibility of coming out with a clear-cut and unambiguous answer. Rating: ____
5. Educators should know by now which is the best method, lectures or small discussion groups. Rating: ____
6. For most questions there is only one right answer once a person is able to get all the facts. Rating: ____
7. A good teacher's job is to keep his students from wandering from the right track. Rating: ____

Determine your average score by adding your ratings and then dividing by 7. My average score is: ____

The purpose of this test[4] is discussed at the end of the chapter.

● ● ● ● ● ● ● ● ● ● ● ● ● ● ● ● ● ● ● ● ● ● ● ● ● ● ● ● ● ● ● ● ● ● ● ● ● ● ● ● ● ● ● ● ● ● ● ● ● ● ● ●

One way to classify people's thinking about what is known is based on a distinction between dualism and relativism (Perry, 1970; Ryan, 1984a, 1984b). A _dualist_ is someone who views knowledge as a set of absolute truths or a discrete set of facts to be learned, whereas a *relativist* is said to see knowledge as the framework within which particular facts are interpreted (Ryan, 1984a, 1984b). This distinction has more than a passing resemblance to Langer's absolute versus conditional thinking.

Dualistic thinkers may not always engage in appropriate mindful activities. In a study investigating this possibility, students were classified as dualists or nondualists on the basis of their responses to the seven statements in TAI 6.3 (the more agreement, the higher the dualism score). Then the students were asked to spend 15 minutes writing responses to the following questions about comprehension-monitoring strategies:

> How do you determine (when you have completed a reading assignment or when you are reviewing the material) whether you have understood the material well enough? What specific information do you use to assess the degree to which you have understood the material you have read in a chapter? On what basis would you decide that you needed to go over the chapter again or to seek help in figuring it out? (Ryan, 1984b, p. 251)

Results revealed that dualists were more likely than relativists to be fact-oriented and to list such activities as:

Recall information from text in response to study guide questions.
Recall information from text as part of mental review.
Recall information from text in response to cues from headings or italicized words.
Recall information from text in response to cues in chapter summary.
Recall information from text while skimming chapter.
Recall information from text in response to others' questions.
Recall information from text in response to test questions.

The nondualists, in contrast, were more likely to be context-oriented and to identify such criteria as:

Determine the meaning of individual sentences.
Paraphrase the text.
Integrate different parts of text into a common framework.

[4]From "Monitoring text comprehension: Individual differences in epistemological standards," by M. P. Ryan. In *Journal of Educational Psychology,* 1984, 76, p. 250. Copyright 1984 by the American Psychological Association. Reprinted by permission of the author. Originally devised by Perry, 1968.

Devise examples of principles and concepts.
Determine author's plans or intentions.
Integrate text and lecture materials.
Determine relationship between each text section and its heading.
Assess amount of cognitive effort expended during reading.[5]

It was found that students who made use of the kinds of comprehension/application criteria associated with nondualistic thinking were almost twice as likely to earn A's or B's in an introductory psychology course as students who relied mainly on the knowledge standards illustrated by dualist thinking. It appears that an approach to knowledge that demands deep text processing is associated with better understanding and retention of text information as assessed by classroom examinations (Ryan, 1984b). Deep text processing is generally associated with mental activities that involve meaningful analysis of the material to be learned. Paraphrasing the material, determining the meaning of a sentence, integrating text and lecture material, seeking meaningful relationships, and other activities associated with nondualistic thinking illustrate this type of processing.

Research supports the idea that mindful activities associated with deep text processing produce better comprehension and retention than do less mindful activities (Zechmeister & Nyberg, 1982). What do you think? Do you tend toward dualism or relativisim? Do you need to modify your approach to study?

## Do We Know When We've Had Enough (Study, That Is)?

Once students move beyond the primary grades, a major task presented to them in nearly every academic course is this: Read the assigned material and be prepared to be tested on what you have read. A student frequently is left on her own to study in a way that prepares her adequately for a test. We've discussed some strategies to use when you study text material—thinking of related knowledge, organizing time and effort in relation to the difficulty of the material, actively striving for comprehension, and doing the kinds of things, such as making meaningful distinctions and attending to details, that are characteristic of mindfulness rather than mindlessness. But, given that we do these things, how do we know when to stop studying and go take the test? Although the obvious answer is "When we know it," this answer assumes that we know when we know it. As your own experiences may lead you to suspect, sometimes we think we know something but find out that we don't. What went wrong?

To examine the task we are describing, psychologists have used various kinds of material, ranging from simple facts to complex passages (Glenberg, Sanocki, Epstein, & Morris, 1987; King, Zechmeister, & Shaughnessy, 1980;

---

[5]From "Monitoring text comprehension: Individual differences in epistemological standards," by M. P. Ryan. In *Journal of Educational Psychology,* 1984, 76, p. 252. Copyright 1984 by the American Psychological Association. Reprinted by permission. Originally devised by Bloom et al., 1956.

Lovelace, 1984). The elements of the task, as studied in the psychology laboratory, are the same as those confronting a typical student (and the subjects in these experiments typically are college students). Material is presented to the students for them to learn in anticipation of a test. At some point the students are asked to predict whether they know the material well enough to perform successfully on the test. Then the students' predictions of what they know are compared with what they actually know as revealed by the test.

In one experiment of this type (King et al., 1980), college students were asked to learn associations between pairs of verbal items. The task was to study a pair so that when the first member of the pair was presented, the second member of the pair could be recalled. The task is analogous to learning to associate a name with a face or learning the definition of an unfamiliar word. Some of the subjects in this experiment simply studied the pairs several times. Other subjects alternated their study with test trials, in which the first member of the pair was presented and subjects had to recall the second member. After they had studied awhile in one of these two conditions, the presentation of items was stopped. At this point, the students were asked to predict whether they would recall the second member of each pair on a subsequent test trial. They were to ask themselves, "Do I know this well enough to recall it?" A rating scale was used to indicate how well each item was known.

Although students sometimes predicted accurately, they made many mistakes. That is, students sometimes predicted that they knew something but later found out they didn't. One thing was clear: those students who previously had experience with test trials did much better at predicting what they knew than those who did not have test trials. The lesson to be drawn from this experiment also is clear. When we think we know something, such as a particular fact that we are studying, we *may be* right; however, our accuracy at predicting what we know will be substantially better when we make that prediction after being explicitly tested on what we know. The implications for actual study should be obvious: study and then test yourself (and then study again what you failed on the test).

**THINK about It**

**?**

**6.4**   Read the following passage once, as if you were preparing for a classroom test. When you are finished reading, judge how well you would do on a test that examines your knowledge of possible inferences that may be drawn from the passage. This time use a 6-point scale, where 1 = not well, and 6 = very well.

### Control of Eating by Blood Sugar

For most animals hunger is virtually permanent as a result of difficulties in obtaining food; these animals eat whenever food is obtainable. However, for mammals with a plentiful food supply, hunger and consumption of food are regulated by the hunger and satiety eating control centers in the brain. These centers are sensitive to the level of glucose circulating in the blood. Increases in blood glucose stimulate the satiety center and thereby reduce eating; decreases in blood glucose stimulate the hunger center and thereby induce eating. Shortly after a meal, when the concentration of glucose in the blood is high, the satiety center signals a state of fullness prompting the animal to refuse food. Many hours after a meal, when the concentration of glucose in the blood is low, the hunger center responds and the animal is prompted to eat.[6]

How would you rate your knowledge of what you have learned? Do not look back at the passage. My rating is: ___
After making your rating, take the test at the end of the chapter.

• • • • • • • • • • • • • • • • • • • • • • • • • • • • • • • • • • • • • • • • • • • • • • • • • • • • • • • • •

When complex material (such as a prose paragraph) has been used as part of experiments investigating whether what we think we know is what we actually know, the results clearly demonstrate that predicting accurately what we know can be a very difficult task (Glenberg et al., 1987; Maki, Foley, Kajer, Thompson, & Willert, 1990). Thus students often place themselves at risk when they judge that they know what they are studying well enough to obtain a good score on a test of retention. Fortunately, research also has identified several strategies that can improve our accuracy in predicting what we know.

One strategy is directly analogous to a procedure we reviewed when we examined the prediction of fact recall. When students assess what they know about the contents of a passage, they are significantly more accurate when they are given a pretest consisting of items similar to the criterion or critical item (Glenberg et al., 1987). When students are given experience with test items similar to those found on the criterion test, they are better able to predict what they know and don't know. The pretest should tap knowledge of facts similar to those in the criterion item. Thus predictions of what we know, whether about our knowledge of simple facts or about our ability to recognize an inference drawn from a text, are more likely to be correct after explicit tests than without the benefit of prior testing.

Predictions of test performance also improve if students are prompted to answer questions about what they have read while they are studying (Walczyk & Hall, 1989). In other words, a pretest can be effective during the course of study as well as after study. This should not be surprising. After all, students who are asked to predict what they know after study that has included embedded questions have already been tested. Presumably, students have a better idea of what they know and don't know before the prediction task than do students who have not studied with embedded questions. Moreover, responding to questions while studying should aid comprehension because failure to answer an embedded question will signal immediately that a passage is not well understood. Students then have an opportunity to reread a passage in order to make sure that they understand the information before they move on.

[6]From "Enhancing calibration of comprehension," by A. M. Glenberg, T. Sanocki, W. Epstein, and C. Morris. In *Journal of Experimental Psychology: General, 1987, 116,* p. 133. Reprinted by permission of the author.

Of course, we don't have to rely on an experimenter or textbook writer to prepare questions that give us feedback about what we know and don't know. Active *self*-testing can contribute to effective comprehension monitoring, which works to combat the mindless kind of text processing that creates illusions of knowing. In fact, when text material is deliberately made more difficult to understand by deletion of letters from words in a prose passage, both retention and predictions of later retention are enhanced (Maki et al., 1990). Apparently the effort to decode the fragmented message requires more active processing of the passage's contents than does simply reading an intact passage. As a result, more is known about the information in the passage and more is known about what is known! We don't suggest that you consider erasing letters from words in your textbook, but we do suggest that you consider the benefits of active text processing. You may recall, for instance, that research reveals a link between course grades and active comprehension strategies associated with deep text processsing (Ryan, 1984b).

The student who says, "I thought I knew it" in the face of evidence to the contrary is likely to have fallen victim to a subjectively compelling feeling of familiarity based on exposure to the material in question. The student may have used the ease with which he recalled information immediately after he studied it to judge what he knew (Morris, 1990). This feeling may have little bearing on his ability to recall the information later, at the time of the test. We now see that this result is probably the consequence of studying without the mindful differentiation necessary for successful comprehension and retention, as well as for accurate predictions of what is known.

---

**THINK about It**

**6.5** From what we have learned about text comprehension and retention, we are in a position to organize what we know about the knowing process. Cognitive processes that are considered critical to our understanding (see Rusch, 1984) are:

*S*urveying what it is that we are to learn.
*P*rocessing the material to be learned in a meaningful way.
*A*sking questions about what we are learning while we are reading.
*R*eviewing by testing ourselves about what it is that we know.

For each major step of the SPAR method of study, identify how comprehension and retention, or knowing what we know, is aided. Go ahead; write down what you feel are the most important results of these cognitive activities.

*Surveying:* _____

_____

_____

_____

*Processing meaningfully:* _____

_____

_____

_____

*Asking questions:* _____

_____

_____

_____

*Reviewing:* _____

_____

_____

_____

**You might try to remember these steps the next time you are required to wrestle with (or even to spar with) text material! You can check your responses with the summary of the major benefits of the SPAR approach at the end of the chapter.**

## Deciding We Are Right

Another important metacognitive decision must be faced whenever we are asked to remember something that we learned earlier. When we are asked a trivia question, for example, or for that matter a question as part of a classroom exam, we first attempt some kind of retrieval process, trying to find the answer in our memory. If we come up with an answer, we must decide whether we are right given the question that was asked. Is the answer that I have selected the correct one?

Making the correct decision in this situation can be seen as important when we consider what happens when we make a mistake. What are the consequences of thinking that you have recalled a right answer but in truth have not? When you place undue confidence in a wrong answer, you will terminate your retrieval efforts. It doesn't make sense to continue to look in your memory for an answer that you believe you have already found. You will never know whether further search of your memory might have produced the correct answer. Another result of a mistaken belief that a question has been answered correctly is that you are likely to make future decisions on the basis of wrong information. No doubt at least once you have been with a person who thinks that he knows the correct way to get to an unfamiliar address, only to find out after many minutes or even hours of searching that he doesn't. Perhaps the consequence of this misthinking produced only a temporary delay, but it may have caused you to miss an important appointment or an airplane you were trying to catch. You can imagine many situations in which thinking we know something when we don't can cost us more than just time or some inconvenience.

Another consequence of believing in the correctness of a wrong answer is that your attempts to learn new information can be interfered with. As a simple example, think about those times when you were doing an arithmetic problem and got to a point where you could go no further because you discovered that an answer at an earlier step was wrong, though you had been sure it was right. On a more general level, consider how difficult and even frustrating it is to attempt to learn complex information when your assumptions about this information are incorrect. And, of course, your interactions with other people are likely to be affected by a belief about them that isn't true.

Consider the following general information questions. For each question there are two alternatives, one of which is the correct answer. For each question, first select what you believe to be the right answer. Then indicate how confident you are that the answer you have selected is correct. To indicate your degree of confidence use the following 6-point scale: 0.50, 0.60, 0.70, 0.80, 0.90, 1.00. A judgment of 0.50 indicates that you are not at all confident, and are just guessing. A judgment of 1.00 indicates that you are very confident; in fact, you are positive this is the right answer. The reason the scale begins at 0.50 is that you can consider your performance on this two-alternative task in relation to what you would do by chance—that is, if you had no idea what the correct answer was. Simply by guessing you would be expected to get 0.50, or 50 percent, of the answers correct when there are only two possibilities. On the other hand, if you answer every item correctly, your probability of being correct is 1.00 (100 percent). Therefore, consider this task as one of judging how likely it is that you have circled the correct answer by using the six proportions ranging from 0.50 through 1.00.

1. What was the last state to join the Union?
    a. Hawaii      b. Alaska
    Confidence: _____
2. What was the name of Batman's original sidekick?
    a. Kato      b. Robin
    Confidence: _____
3. What was the name of the zeppelin that exploded in Lakehurst, N.J., in 1937?
    a. Berlin      b. Hindenberg
    Confidence: _____
4. Who wrote *David Copperfield*?
    a. Jane Austen      b. Charles Dickens
    Confidence: _____

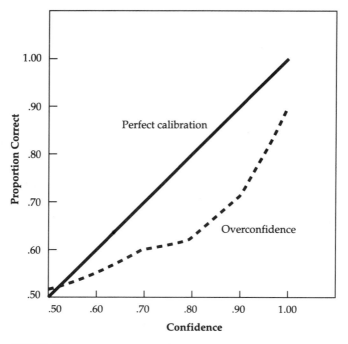

**Figure 6.1**

5. What is the last name of the man who showed that lightning is electricity?
   a.  Franklin        b.  Edison
   Confidence: _____

(The correct answers are given at the end of the next paragraph.)

    With many responses to such questions, it is possible to calibrate an individual's confidence. A calibration curve reveals the probability that a person is correct given a particular level of confidence. For example, we said earlier that if you were just guessing, you would get about 50 percent of the answers right; if you were right every time that you said you were positive (1.00) an answer was correct, then you would be 100 percent correct for that level of confidence. A calibration curve plots percent or proportion correct at each of the various levels of confidence. Good calibration is found when an individual's level of confidence matches the proportion of his or her correct answers. Results from a perfectly calibrated individual are shown by the straight line in Figure 6.1.

    (Answers to the five general information questions: 1. a; 2. b; 3. b; 4. b; 5. a.)

    It would be difficult to say how well calibrated you are after answering only five questions. The reason can be illustrated by the task confronting you should you want to find out if the prediction of the local TV weather forecaster is right. Suppose the prediction is 50 percent chance of rain. If it doesn't rain, can you tell if the weather forecaster made a good prediction? What if the prediction was 70 percent chance of rain? Now if it doesn't rain, should you stop believing in this weather forecaster? If the weather forecaster is a good predictor, you would expect the predicted probability of rain to match the actual probability of rain. However, you will know this only if you examine the accuracy of many, many of the forecaster's predictions. On any one occasion, it is impossible to say if the forecast is accurate. A 70 percent chance of rain means that there is a 30 percent chance of no rain.

Calibration curves assessing an individual's confidence in a correct answer are typically based on answers and confidence ratings for hundreds of questions (or, in the case of the weather forecaster, for hundreds of forecasts). In this manner information about prediction accuracy is obtained over the long run. For all questions answered with a 60 percent confidence that they are right, is the proportion correct for this category actually 0.60? The results from a host of studies calibrating people's confidence reveal an interesting if somewhat disturbing picture (Lichtenstein, Fischhoff, & Phillips, 1982). In general, most people are overconfident about what they know. This state of affairs is illustrated by the calibration curve drawn with dashed lines in Figure 6.1. As you can see, overconfidence occurs when the proportion of answers correct is less than the level of expressed confidence.

**THINK about It**

**6.6**    Once again, select an answer (circle one) to each of the following questions and rate your confidence using the same confidence scale we described earlier (0.50 through 1.00).

1. What is the name of the poker hand in which all of the cards are of the same suit?
    a.  Flush          b.  Straight

    Confidence: _____

2. In what country is the highest waterfall?
    a.  Venezuela          b.  Canada

    Confidence: _____

3. What is Paul McCartney's wife's first name?
    a.  Linda          b.  Yoko

    Confidence: _____

4. What is the last name of the criminal who was killed by FBI agents outside of a Chicago movie theater?
    a.  Capone          b.  Dillinger

    Confidence: _____

5. What airline once advertised that "we're ready when you are"?
    a.  Delta          b.  TWA

    Confidence: _____

6. What color is indigo?
    a.  Blue          b.  Red

    Confidence: _____

7. Who said, "Give me liberty or give me death"?
   a.  Patrick Henry        b.  John Paul Jones

   Confidence: _____
8. What country possesses the world's most extensive and richest iron ore deposits?
   a.  Brazil        b.  Russia

   Confidence: _____
9. Of what country is Budapest the capital?
   a.  India        b.  Hungary

   Confidence: _____
10. What is the name of the brightest star in the sky excluding the sun?
    a.  North Star        b.  Sirius

    Confidence: _____

Check your answers with those at the end of the chapter. Note whether any answers were wrong but were ones that you judged with a relatively high degree of confidence were right. If you find one or more, what do you think are some of the reasons for extreme confidence in wrong answers?

## Reasons for Overconfidence

The tendency for people to be wrong when they are confident that they are right does not disappear when lengthy instructions are provided so that there is no possibility of misunderstanding the nature of the task, or even when individuals' motivation is increased by an opportunity to bet real money (Fischhoff, Slovic, & Lichtenstein, 1977). What explains this unwarranted confidence in information retrieved from memory? One possibility is that people are generally unaware that memory retrieval involves processes of inference and reconstruction that can introduce error. One group of investigators suggests:

> People reach conclusions about what they have seen or what they remember by reconstructing their knowledge from fragments of information, much as a paleontologist infers the appearance of a dinosaur from fragments of bone. During reconstruction, a variety of cognitive, social, and motivational factors can introduce error and distortion into the output process. (Fischhoff et al., 1977, p. 563)

People, in other words, operate under the mistaken belief that what is produced from memory is a copy of an earlier experience. In fact, what is produced from memory may be inferred from other information in memory. Consider the following question:

Potatoes are native to what country?
   a.  Ireland        b.  Peru

How confident are you that the answer you selected is correct? The correct answer is Peru; however, many people answer Ireland and indicate with a high degree of confidence that they are right (Fischhoff et al., 1977). Thus such questions can be considered deceptive (as are the even-numbered questions in TAI 6.6). What makes a question deceptive?

It is likely that the correct answer to the above question, Peru, was never directly experienced. What possibly was experienced is information about the long-time association of the Irish and potatoes. Many people remember reading about the terrible potato famine of the mid–19th century, when nearly a million people died and another million emigrated from Ireland, mainly to the United States. Thus a choice of Ireland as the correct answer may mean that we are making an inference on the basis of easily available information about the association between Ireland and potatoes. (You may see an availability heuristic at work here, of the sort described in Chapter 5.)

Simply to be aware of the frequently inexact record of our memory is one step in the direction of being more realistic about the confidence that we assign to an answer. A second step is to become more critical about our inference processes. We frequently fail to ask important questions about what it is that we know, and we sometimes ignore relevant information. For example, we often consider only reasons why our answer may be right. This bias is evident when we consider the findings of researchers who examined confidence judgments after asking people to list reasons for the answers they selected (Koriat, Lichtenstein, & Fischhoff, 1980). Listing reasons that contradicted an answer had the most effect on the accuracy of confidence judgment. As a practical suggestion, therefore, while it is important to retrieve evidence from memory about an answer, we are likely to be in the best position to assess what we know if we examine reasons why we may be wrong, something we are not normally inclined to do (Koriat et al., 1980).

**THINK about It**

**6.7**   For each of the following questions, examine the answer and the confidence level that have been identified. The numbers are chosen from a 6-point scale, where 1 = guessing and 6 = positive. Thus low numbers indicate that the person has little confidence that he or she has selected the right answer. Higher numbers indicate increasing levels of confidence; a 6 means that the person is absolutely sure he or she has chosen the right answer. The answers that have been circled are always the right ones. For each question, assume that the person has chosen the right answer and exhibits a level of confidence corresponding to the number given.

After examining the answer and the level of confidence, look over the reasons that are given to support the correct choice. Select the reason (circle one) that best matches the confidence level. Do *not* select the reason that best explains why the answer is correct; rather, select a reason you think goes with the degree of confidence given. Remember, the answer that has been circled is in fact the right one. Your task is to circle the reason that best fits the level of confidence in that right answer.

1. What is the capital of New York?
   a. New York        (b.) Albany
   Confidence level: 3
   Reasons:
   > i. "I used to live in New York when I was younger and I know the capital is Albany."
   > ii. "I really have no idea but I picked Albany because it sounds like it would be the capital of a state."
   > iii. "I've never been to Albany, but I've been to New York City and I don't remember seeing a capital building or state legislature or anything like that. So it's probably not New York City."

2. Who said, "Speak softly and carry a big stick"?
   a. Woodrow Wilson        (b.) Theodore Roosevelt
   Confidence level: 5
   Reasons:
   > i. "I remember studying Roosevelt in a history class I took last semester and I'm pretty sure I remember reading that he had made that statement, but I'm really not positive. Besides, I'm fairly sure Wilson wouldn't have said that."
   > ii. "For some reason I associate that quotation with Theodore Roosevelt. I think I remember reading it somewhere."
   > iii. "My roommate did a history paper last semester and I think I remember her mentioning that quotation."

3. Who was the first black person ever elected to the U.S. Senate?
   (a.) Edward Brooke        b. Andrew Young
   Confidence level: 2
   Reasons:
   > i. "I remember an article in *Time* magazine on Brooke. Besides, I think Young was U.N. ambassador, not a senator."
   > ii. "I really had no idea; I just took a wild guess."
   > iii. "I think it's Brooke because there's some association in my mind with him being the first black senator, but I'm not sure where that association came from."

The particular reasons we feel are most appropriate given the reported levels of confidence are reported at the end of the chapter.

• • • • • • • • • • • • • • • • • • • • • • • • • • • • • • • • • • • • • • • • • • • • • • •

There is evidence that people can be trained to improve the accuracy of their confidence judgments by learning to be more critical of the processes of answering questions and judging confidence (Zechmeister, Rusch, & Markell, 1986). The elements of the training sessions emphasized several aspects of the confidence-judgment process that we have mentioned. For instance, after experience with an initial confidence-judgment task, students were given personal feedback regarding their calibration of confidence accuracy. They also experienced at firsthand the results of a brief test that included deceptive questions meant to illustrate how we sometimes are sure we are right when we are wrong. (We have duplicated this experience in TAI 6.6.) These procedures were motivated by the results of previous research showing that feedback can help to reduce overconfidence, but that the feedback most likely to be helpful was personal feedback, "whose relevance cannot be rejected with the claim 'I'm not like that'—as might confront a report that most people are overconfident" (Lichtenstein & Fischhoff, 1980, p. 170).

Another procedure used to train accuracy in judgment of confidence was a "reasons test." Ten general information questions were presented with the correct answer indicated, along with three possible reasons why someone might select the correct answer. A confidence rating was presented also. The students' task was to select a reason that best matched the confidence level indicated (as in TAI 6.7). The purpose of the test was to determine whether students could identify an appropriate reason for the degree of confidence expressed in the rating. For example, someone who has a particularly good reason for knowing that an answer is right should not be using a very low confidence level, indicating that he or she is guessing. Conversely, someone who has a very weak reason for believing the answer is right should not be using a confidence rating that indicates the answer is known for sure. As part of the training exercise, students were given feedback on their performance on the reasons test.

Also included as part of the training session was discussion of the need to be more critical when one examines evidence to support a belief that an answer may be right. The experimenter suggested that when students were thinking about the validity of their answers, they should put themselves in the position of a tough prosecuting attorney cross-examining a witness. It was emphasized that most people do not adequately cross-examine the evidence for an answer they have selected, often because they consider only evidence that supports their belief that an answer may be right and give less attention to reasons why an answer may be wrong.

The results of this research revealed that training resulted in greater accuracy in confidence judgment on a posttest in comparison with the judgments of a control group. However, when the results were examined as a function of the students' achievement (on the basis of grades in an introductory psychology course), two things stood out. First, it was clear that low achievers initially—that is, at the time of the pretest—were more in need of of training than were high achievers. Second, the effect of training was reflected mainly in the changes made by the low achievers from the pretest to the posttest. The researchers suggested that these results were due to the fact that high achievers are more likely than low achievers to engage spontaneously in those cognitive activities that are important when one judges what one knows. In other words, students who were doing well in their classes were least in need of training

●    We can reduce overconfidence by mentally cross-examining the evidence for our answers.

because they already were aware of the activities that were emphasized during the training sessions. Fortunately, the study's results showed that students who were in need of training (the low achievers) could be trained to improve the accuracy of their confidence judgments.

Two other results of this training project supported the conclusion that good students generally are better able than poor students to judge what they know and don't know. First, as part of the pretest (before training), some students were asked to give reasons to the experimenter why the answer they selected was the right one. Research has shown that informing students that they will have to explain to a group of their peers why they chose a particular answer serves to reduce overconfidence (Arkes, Christensen, Lai, & Blumer, 1987). The requirement to give reasons did reduce overconfidence, but only for low-achieving students. Second, when the results of the reasons test were evaluated, it was found that low achievers made significantly more mistakes than did high achievers, an indication that good students had a better idea of what level of confidence they should express given the evidence they possessed. Both of these findings suggest that a characteristic of a good student is a tendency spontaneously to examine in a critical way what is known about what is known. What do you think?

· · · · · · · · · ·
# Principles of Critical Thinking about Knowing What We Know: A Summary

1. Knowing what we know requires good metacognitive skills; that is, effective planning, monitoring, and evaluating of cognitive processes.

2. Illusions of knowing—that is, beliefs that comprehension has been attained when in fact comprehension has failed—apparently arise from a "default assumption" when one reads a text.

3. Effective comprehension monitoring is apparently related to thinking that is conditional rather than absolute, relativistic rather than dualistic. Generally speaking, comprehension and retention, as well as accuracy of judging what we know, are enhanced by cognitive effort aimed at producing meaningful elaborations and meaningful distinctions for the material to be learned.

4. An optimal strategy for judging whether we know what we know is to ask questions both during and after study.

5. An effective approach to the study of text material is the SPAR strategy: *Survey, Process* meaningfully, *Ask* questions, *Review.*

6. We sometimes assume that memory is a faithful record of the past and fail to recognize that what is "remembered" can include reconstructions based on incomplete retention and inferences.

7. People can reduce overconfidence regarding the correctness of their answers if they mentally cross-examine the evidence for their answers, and especially if they ask why their answers might be wrong.

· · · · · · · · ·
# Think about It: Discussion of Answers

**6.1**    The kinds of metacognitive knowledge that are relevant to studying for a test include answers to questions such as the following:

*Person:* Is this a topic I know a lot about or do I know only a little? Is this something that interests me?

*Task:* What kinds of questions about this material is the instructor likely to ask?

*Strategy:* Are there tricks (such as specific memory aids) that I can use to learn this type of material?

The regulatory component of metacognition for this task might include the answers to such questions as:

*Planning:* Does my past experience (knowledge component) indicate that I need to study this material a lot or a little? Should I study certain topics more than others?

*Monitoring:* When I study, do I find that I am understanding the concepts and ideas that are presented?

*Evaluating:* Can I devise a test of my knowledge of this material to find out what I actually know and don't know?

**6.2**    The passage is from research that was intended to illustrate those aspects of a story that are most critical to the development of the reader's organized knowledge. In this research, a garbled version of the story made use of 1A, 2A, 6B, and 8A. Results also showed that changes in the beginning, where the setting is described, and at the end, which describes the resolution, were most likely to affect judgments of story knowledge. You may remember that in Chapter 2 we discussed how stories are frequently understood in terms of cause and effect relations (rustlers steal cattle, sheriff chases rustlers, and so on). Certain kinds of knowledge are critical if these causal relationships are to be seen, and it is important that this knowledge be present in particular locations in the narrative. An ability to organize knowledge in such a way that the cause is seen to precede the effect should provide a cue as to whether a narrative will be easy or hard to understand.

**6.3**    These statements are aimed at identifying students who are dualists rather than relativists in their thinking (see Perry, 1970). The higher the score, the more dualistic the thinking. In a study conducted by Ryan (1984a), students who averaged 3 or greater were classified as dualists; those who scored less than 3 were considered to be relativists. Dualists are students who tend to appreciate external structures that define "rightness" (p. 1228). As we discuss in the text that follows this TAI, relativists tend to believe that "rightness" depends on the context. The implications of these types of thinking are also discussed in the text.

**6.4**    Is the following inference true or false?

Inference: Intravenous injections of insulin lower glucose concentrations in the blood. An intravenous injection of insulin will cause a mammal who is hungry to refuse food.[7]

Now check the passage in TAI 6.4 to determine whether the inference is true or false. How well did you predict your knowledge of the passage? Keep in mind that you had a 50:50 chance of being correct and that you were tested on only one passage. The task is considerably easier than any you would normally encounter in a classroom. Nevertheless, after attempting this task, you should be able to understand better the experimental situation in which students were placed when psychologists investigated what students thought they knew when they studied text material.

**6.5**    The SPAR method of studying will accomplish the following:

*Surveying* serves to activate relevant prior knowledge that will aid comprehension. Also, when we look over the material we are about to study before

---

[7]From "Enhancing calibration of comprehension," by A. M. Glenberg, T. Sanocki, W. Epstein, and C. Morris. In *Journal of Experimental Psychology: General, 1987, 116,* p. 133. Reprinted by permission of the author.

we actually do so, we can organize our study in the most efficient way—by spending more time on the material that is more difficult or less familiar, for example.

*Processing meaningfully* requires us to make the kinds of active differentiations and meaningful analyses that are associated with greater comprehension and retention. There also is evidence that active processing helps us to estimate more accurately how much we will know at a future time (at the time of the test) than does less active processing. A review of those characteristics of study associated with nondualistic thinking will provide examples of the kinds of meaningful processing that are important for study.

*Asking questions* during study serves both to provide a pretest of what we know and, most important, to direct our attention during study to material that we don't understand or are having difficulty remembering. Asking questions is, in other words, an effective form of cognitive monitoring.

*Reviewing* what we know by explicitly testing ourselves before a test has been shown to be an important strategy, because too often we are deceived about what it is that we really do know. It is recommended that the material should be reviewed *not* immediately after study, but after an interval of time has passed (perhaps three to four hours). This strategy allows us to find out what we know when the conditions of testing are most similar to those at the time of a final test.

**6.6**    The correct answers are: 1. a; 2. a; 3. a; 4. b; 5. a; 6. a; 7. a; 8. a; 9. b; 10. b. Did you find that one or more of your answers were wrong but that you expressed a high degree of certainty that you were right? We hope so. The questions were planned this way, as you will see in the text that follows this TAI.

**6.7**    We suggest that the most appropriate reasons are: 1. iii; 2. i; 3.iii. Our analysis is in the text following this TAI.

# • • • • • • • • •
# Recommended Readings

At the top of our list is the stimulating, instructive book *Mindfulness* (1989), by Ellen Langer. She illustrates both the roots of mindlessness and its consequences, and shows how the opposite kind of thinking, mindfulness, can improve our lives in everyday situations ranging from caring for the elderly to working at our job. Robert Sternberg describes his triarchic theory of intelligence in *Intelligence Applied* (1986b). He emphasizes the role of "metacomponents" (planning, selecting, monitoring) in intelligent thinking. John Flavell's (1979) article "Metacognition and cognitive monitoring" is a good introduction to the general topic of metacognition. At a somewhat more advanced level, we can reveal our biases again and recommend Chapter 11, "Metamemory: Knowing about Knowing," in Eugene B. Zechmeister and Stanley Nyberg's *Human Memory* (1982). Robert Kail discusses the development of metamemory skills in *The Development of Memory in Children* (1990).

# SOLVING PROBLEMS, MAKING DECISIONS, AND CONVINCING OTHERS

# Solving Problems

**Who understands ill, answers ill.**
**Arrows are made of all sorts of wood.**
**A wise delay makes the road safe.**
**He thinks not well that thinks not again.**

Principles of effective problem solving articulated in proverbs
(Polya, 1971)

• • • • • • • • • • • • • • • • • • • • • • • • • • • • • • • • • • • • • • • • • • • • • • •

Much of our everyday thinking is about solving problems. Some problems are quite simple, even trivial, such as finding a way to cross a busy street; others are anything but simple and trivial, such as finding a job or helping the homeless in our community. Nevertheless, all problems share certain basic characteristics, and the steps necessary to solve a problem are frequently the same no matter what the nature of the problem. The reasons why we fail to solve a problem also frequently are similar no matter what the problem. In this chapter, the nature of problems, the steps necessary to solve them, and some of the ways we can make our problem solving efforts more successful, are examined. For the most part, the emphasis is on problems with clear goals and for which there is only one "right" answer. Many everyday problems however, have more than one possible solution or answer, and we must decide on the "best" one given the circumstances. In Chapter 8, ways to make such decisions are discussed. First, however, the problem of problem solving is discussed.

## • • • • • • • • • •
# Introduction

RUSSIAN LEADER WRESTLES WITH PROBLEMS OF DEMOCRATIC REFORM

LEGISLATORS DEBATE PROBLEMS OF URBAN RENEWAL

WOMEN FACE PROBLEM OF DISCRIMINATION

NASA WORKS ON PROBLEM WITH SPACE SHUTTLE

CITY SCHOOLS HAVE PROBLEM WITH DROPOUTS

No doubt you have seen headlines like these in newspapers or in news magazines, such as *Time* and *Newsweek*. Life is full of problems, both large and small. We simply can't avoid them. Thus a measure of how successful we are in life is how well we deal with life's problems. On a personal level, to be happy and productive is to deal successfully with problems of interpersonal relationships, feelings of despair, academic demands, and many other problems. In society at large, we must find appropriate solutions to such problems as drug abuse, toxic waste, illiteracy, and unemployment to ensure happiness and prosperity to millions of people.

As the mathematician George Polya (1971) points out, problem solving occupies a significant part of our conscious thinking. Reflect for a moment on what you have been thinking about during the last 24 hours. What have been some of your major concerns? It is likely that much of the time you have been thinking about some end or goal and the means by which you may achieve it. In this chapter, we discuss ways to think critically about problem solving. You will learn what cognitive psychologists, educators, and others have discovered about the problem-solving process, and we hope that along the way you will learn how to become a better problem solver.

## • • • • • • • • •
# Characteristics of Problems

Most people would not find it hard to define a problem. A problem exists when something that we want is (temporarily?) unobtainable. Crossing the street without getting injured in traffic can be a problem. Although the goal may be simply to get to the other side, speeding cars may prevent us from doing so safely. Fixing a leaky faucet is a minor problem familiar to most homeowners. Finding the right person to marry can be a personal problem of considerable magnitude, and housing the country's homeless puts leaky faucets in perspective. All problems have certain identifiable characteristics, and whether you are working on the kitchen plumbing or negotiating better living conditions for displaced persons, these same characteristics are present.

A problem can be viewed as having four basic components (Glass & Holyoak, 1986, p. 366):

1. A goal, or a description of what would be accepted as a solution to the problem.
2. Objects, tools, materials, or other resources available to help achieve the goal.
3. A set of operations or actions that can be taken.
4. A set of constraints (rules) that cannot be violated during problem solving.

Although these components are part of any problem, they are not necessarily present in all problems to the same degree.

A distinction is sometimes made between well-defined (or well-structured) and ill-defined (ill-structured) problems (Simon, 1973). A *well-defined problem* is one in which the goal is clearly identified, as is the path to that goal. The objects or tools needed to solve a well-defined problem are usually easily obtainable. Fixing a leaky faucet and crossing the street are typically well-defined problems. Some of the problems we will use in this chapter to illustrate important problem-solving strategies fall in this category, because most of the problems that cognitive psychologists have used to study thinking processes have been well-defined ones.

An *ill-defined problem* is one in which the goal is not clearly defined (there even may be more than one potential goal) and there are likely to be many paths to the goal. Because a goal may not be clearly defined, it is often difficult to evaluate the extent to which a solution moves one toward the goal. The specific tools required to solve an ill-defined problem also are not necessarily obvious. Housing the country's homeless is an ill-defined problem. So are writing a novel, choosing a spouse, and finding the right job. It turns out that most of life's problems are ill defined.

The boundary between well-defined and ill-defined problems is necessarily vague (see Simon, 1973). Consider a game of chess. Although any particular move appears to involve a well-defined problem (that is, to determine the move most likely to win the game), when the whole course of the game is considered, we see that it is a dynamic process. An unexpected move by an opponent or an unusual board situation that develops requires the player to make new calculations and to use new information. We might apply the same analysis to a problem of crossing the street. Changes in traffic flow or weather conditions may require us constantly to change our approach to this relatively straightforward problem. The Nobel Prize–winning scientist Herbert Simon argues that well-structured problems are something of an illusion (Simon, 1973). Nevertheless, he also argues that the thinking processes associated with so-called well-structured problems are similar to those used to solve problems that are clearly more ill structured. Thus we are able to learn much about the cognitive processes involved in problem solving in general by studying how people approach relatively well-structured problems.

One aspect of the problem-solving process is not always captured in the study of more or less well-defined problems. When we are confronted with a well-defined problem, the major issue often is how to arrive at a strategy that will effectively lead to the right answer. When we are confronted with more ill-defined problems, a major issue can be how to deal with the uncertainty created by the fact that there is no single right answer. In other words, many problems, especially those that are part of everyday living, have many possible solutions. Moreover, these alternative solutions are apt to vary in their consequences, and some consequences are more serious than others. How do we decide what is the "right" answer to the problem? How do we anticipate and deal with the consequences of the answer we have chosen? This important aspect of human problem solving will be discussed more fully in Chapter 8. For now, the emphasis is on more fundamental aspects of problem solving, the ones that are found in nearly every problem situation.

**THINK about It**

**7.1**    Below are listed some typical everyday problems:

1. Losing weight.
2. Solving for the unknown in $4X + 3X = 14$.
3. Breaking a date with someone.
4. Earning an A on a history test.
5. Getting your car out of a ditch.
    a. Consider problem 5: getting your car out of a ditch. How would you describe this problem in terms of the four major components of a problem?
    b. Can you rank-order all these problems, from most well defined to most ill defined? What considerations went into your ranking?

To help you with this exercise, let us illustrate how you might analyze one of the problems other than 5. Consider problem 3: breaking a date with someone. To make things interesting, let's assume that the date was made with someone whom you would like to be romantically involved with (but are not yet). Perhaps you have encountered such a problem. The four basic components of the problem might look like this:

*Goal:* Informing someone that you can't make a promised date without upsetting that person or having him or her think less of you.
*Objects/tools:* Telephone, telegraph, mail, hand-delivered note, skywriting, humorous card, presents (candy, balloons, whatever), delivery vehicles, and so forth.
*Operations:* Personal contact, message delivery through third party, including present with message, leave message on answering machine, tack note to door, hire pilot and airplane for skywriting task, and so forth.
*Constraints:* Information must reach person before time of date, message must convey appropriate regret, excuse must be good, and so forth, given your circumstances (for example, an emergency trip to the hospital may leave you unable to deliver a message personally).

Now, it's your turn.

● a. How would you analyze problem 5 in terms of:

   Goal: _____

   Objects/tools: _____

   Operations: _____

   Constraints: _____

● b. How would you rank-order the five problems, from most well defined to most ill defined? My rank ordering is: _____

   Our analysis and ranking are at the end of the chapter.

● ● ● ● ● ● ● ● ● ● ● ● ● ● ● ● ● ● ● ● ● ● ● ● ● ● ● ● ● ● ● ● ● ● ● ● ● ● ● ● ● ● ● ● ● ● ● ● ● ●

## Approaches to Effective Problem Solving

● Polya (1971) calls attention to the fact that effective strategies for solving problems have been recorded informally by writers and poets for centuries. He suggests that many of these classic problem-solving strategies can be grouped under four general principles:

Be sure to understand the nature of the problem.
Make a plan to achieve the goal.
Try out the plan.
Monitor the outcome of the plan.

These principles are similar to those identified by the philosopher and educator John Dewey (1933) as principal components of a general theory of "good thinking" (Baron, 1981). Before the first principle in the list we would add "Recognize the problem" (see Bransford & Stein, 1984). Too often we fail to work on a problem simply because we fail to recognize that we have one. For instance, mindlessly doing what we have always done in a situation is one way we fail to recognize that a problem exists. (You should remember our discussion of mindlessness in Chapter 6.)

As you perhaps have come to appreciate, the problem of learning to think critically is not simply a matter of discovering important strategies or principles to use in a given situation. Often these strategies are not difficult to identify. For example, the principles that we just listed, which are based on Polya's and Dewey's analyses of thinking, are the basis of many contemporary approaches to teaching effective problem solving (such as Bransford & Stein, 1984). What we are supposed to do, in other words, is clear. Our task is to learn these strategies well enough so that they are incorporated into our everyday problem-solving activities. A disposition to consider problems in a thoughtful and perceptive manner, which is a defining characteristic of a critical thinker (as we saw

Often there are many ways, or operations, to solve a problem.

in Chapter 1), is of paramount importance. Unless we are disposed to approach everyday problems in a thoughtful way, the strategies we learn will be unused knowledge in a mindless warehouse.

## Understanding the Nature of a Problem

### Reviewing Givens and Assumptions

A given is something that is specified or stated. Unless we have reason to doubt the source, we typically accept a given as true, as fact. An assumption, on the other hand, is something we take for granted but that is not necessarily true. Assumptions are based on inferences that we make. When we are told that someone is "flying to Boston" we may assume (infer) that this person is taking a commercial airplane.

All problems have both givens and assumptions. Givens typically are part of the problem description (for example, "It cannot be more than three feet tall."). They are just what the name implies: information that is given to us as facts to be considered as we work on a problem. Assumptions are what we bring to the problem. Although we may not be told that someone is using an airplane to "fly to Boston," it would be understandable if we made that assumption. It is important to remember, however, that an assumption is something we infer, and that while we may take it for granted (for example, that a commercial airplane is involved), it may or may not be true (our traveler could be flying in a private airplane or even in a hot-air balloon).

In order to understand the nature of a problem, we need both to understand exactly what is or is not given to us (that is, what are the facts) and to make correct assumptions about the problem. Failure to solve a problem frequently is due to one of two states of knowledge (or both) regarding the givens and assumptions of the problem: (1) the givens are not known or understood; (2) our assumptions about the components of the problem are incorrect. (It is also possible that we lack the necessary skills to solve the problem. For example, we may need to know how to use a plumber's wrench in order to repair a leaky faucet, or know how to use a typewriter or word processor in order to write a novel. For now, however, let us consider these how-to skills as part of the givens of a problem.)

We may not know or understand a given because we did not pay attention to everything that was explained to us, because the problem specification lacked critical information (not necessarily our fault), or perhaps because we did not fully comprehend what was presented to us. For instance, a serious obstacle to successful problem solving is the fact that we can attend to only so much information at one time. In other words, we are only human (and not, for example, computers). Our information-processing capacities have serious limitations that must be taken into account whenever we analyze problem-solving performance (Simon, 1981). For instance, when a problem description contains large amounts of information, we may find it difficult to keep it all in mind. Critical information about the problem in this case may never be well learned, or if it is learned, it may soon be forgotten because our information-processing system is overloaded.

**THINK about It**

**7.2**   A classic problem in cognitive psychology is the nine-dot problem. Nine dots are arranged like this:

```
o    o    o

o    o    o

o    o    o
```

The goal is to draw four straight lines that connect all nine dots without lifting your pen or pencil from the paper once you begin. Try it. We give the answer at the end of the chapter, but if you don't solve the problem in a short time, please read further in the text before looking at the solution.

Remember that the components of a problem include the goal, the tools or materials available to reach the goal, a set of permissible operations, and any rules or constraints. An incorrect assumption about any of these components can lead to difficulties in problem solving. For instance, when we have a household problem such as fixing a broken chair, we may make an incorrect assumption that a solution has to be produced from the same material that is in the chair. That is, we falsely assume that only certain materials can be used. We fail, in other words, to realize that, as the proverb says, "arrows are made of all sorts of wood."

A well-defined problem often used by psychologists to illustrate how our assumptions about a problem can interfere with finding a solution is the classic nine-dot problem, which was described in TAI 7.2. Most people have a great deal of difficulty with this problem. To discover why, let's consider both the givens in the problem description and the assumptions people often make about the problem. The givens are: a stated goal of connecting nine dots with four straight lines; tools are a pen or pencil; operations consist of drawing lines; constraints are that the solution must involve four straight lines and the marking instrument cannot be lifted off the paper once the task is begun.

Although these givens may appear clear, think about what is not stated and what a problem solver might assume. What assumptions, in other words, are likely to be made concerning this problem? Some assumptions will no doubt be unique to each problem solver. For example, some people might assume that it's a trick problem, or that it's a test of intelligence. Either or both assumptions can produce unnecessary anxiety, which may interfere with successful solving of the problem. That there is a trick to this problem is arguably a better assumption than that the problem is an intelligence test. Other assumptions people are likely to make are that the dots must be spaced exactly as they are shown, that only one pencil or pen can be used, that a regular-sized pen or pencil must be used, that the lines to be drawn cannot go outside the configuration. None of these assumptions is necessarily true. Within limits the arrangement of dots can be larger or take on a different form—a rectangle, for example. Nevertheless, a false assumption about the size or shape of the configuration is not typically going to interfere with obtaining the solution. Believing that only a regular-size pen or pencil can be used is an incorrect assumption only if that assumption was not made by the problem maker. It is conceivable that someone might create a problem like the nine-dot problem but suggest as a solution that you use a writing instrument with a one-inch-wide "point," thereby covering more than one row or column of dots with one stroke. However, if this were the nature of the problem, you would probably feel cheated because the obvious assumption is that instruments of normal size will be used.

As you may have realized, holding the false assumption that the four lines to be drawn must stay within the apparent borders of the figure can prove seriously troublesome. Note that the problem description does not say that your lines must stay within the "borders." If you have not yet discovered a solution, take a look at the problem again without making the assumption that the pencil lines must stay within the figure's apparent borders. (It still may not be easy; see Weisberg, 1986.)

. . . . . . . . . . . . . . . . . . . . . . . . . . . . . . . . . . . . . . . . . . . . .

**THINK about It**

**7.3**    Consider the following problem:

John is driving on a freeway when his car engine sputters and stops running. He manages to coast without power to the side of the road. Traffic is heavy and moving very fast on the freeway.

Identify the givens, which are provided in the problem description, and possible assumptions that someone in John's position might make as he tries to get out of his predicament. For the assumptions that you identify, indicate both ones that are likely to interfere with successful problem solving and those that could solve the problem.

*Givens:* _____

_____

_____

*Assumptions that could interfere:* _____

_____

_____

_____

*Assumptions that could solve the problem:* _____

_____

_____

_____

We identify givens and possible assumptions at the end of the chapter.

. . . . . . . . . . . . . . . . . . . . . . . . . . . . . . . . . . . . . . . . . . . . .

## Representing a Problem

Limitations on our information-processing capabilities, such as an ability to remember only so much information presented at one time, suggest that we learn to write down the components of a problem whenever we can (Wickelgren, 1974). Many problems can be solved more easily if we take the time to make a list or table or to draw a map or figure to represent various features of the problem. Constructing a complete list of the givens, for example, will help you to focus on what is known and help to ensure that you haven't forgotten a critical element. When many possible alternative solutions are available, making a list of them gives you an opportunity to weigh each option in relation to the others. You might even consider ranking options according to the perceived likelihood of their success. When you attempt spatial problems, such as finding a new route to a distant location, or math problems, especially those in geometry, some form of diagram or figure is always recommended (Polya, 1971; Schoenfield, 1983). But nonspatial problems can be aided as well.

It is not difficult to demonstrate the effectiveness of paper-and-pencil representation in problem solving (see Sternberg, 1986b). Consider a traditional ordering problem such as the following:

Tom is taller than Mike.
Sue is shorter than Tom.
Sue is taller than Alice.
Mike is taller than Sue.

Who is the shortest?

For most people the problem seems to highlight our limited information-processing capabilities. We find ourselves having difficulty processing all the information that was given to us. Although you probably can solve the problem mentally by rereading carefully the givens of the problem, a solution appears easily when you take paper and pencil and construct an array of the facts. Try it. By listing the names of the people identified in the problem in order of height, or by drawing stick figures depicting the height of each person, the answer (Alice) emerges easily.

Although the benefits of paper-and-pencil representation seem to be obvious, many people rely exclusively on internal representation. Why? Several major factors appear to contribute to the common reluctance to use paper and pencil to represent a problem's components. First, to put it bluntly, we are lazy. Taking the time to make a list of givens, to draw a diagram revealing possible moves, or to construct a picture model of a problem situation requires more effort and conscious involvement than people often are willing to put into the task. Critical thinking, let us remind you again, is hard work.

Many people also seem to have the impression that using a paper and pencil to help them solve problems indicates that they aren't as smart as someone who does it mentally. Paper-and-pencil methods, in other words, are seen as a crutch for those who can't get along on their own. The source of this silly belief isn't clear, but perhaps it has something to do with the general awe that people have for those who can solve difficult problems quickly without benefit of external devices. What may not be appreciated, however, is that these "experts" often come by their abilities only after much practice or as the result of experiences that others have not had.

Constructing external representations of problem components also takes time. Someone may not want to take the time because she has never disciplined herself to work systematically on problems, or perhaps because she associates time to solve a problem with intelligence. Taking time to work on a problem is perhaps viewed in the same way as using paper and pencil: it isn't something that so-called smart people do. In the next section, however, we will demonstrate that taking time is exactly what smart people frequently do.

**THINK about It**

**7.4** In the next two minutes, write down as many words as you can that begin with a particular letter of the alphabet. To do this task yourself, you need a watch that indicates minutes clearly. You also need to select at random one of the consonants of the alphabet. You can approximate a random selection procedure by closing your eyes and placing a fingertip on a page of this book. Immediately perform the task with the consonant that appears closest to the right of your fingertip. Or simply ask a friend to do this task, say with the letter *y.* Observe your own behavior or that of your subject when either of you performs the task.

The letter is: _____

Words beginning with this letter are: _____

_____

_____

_____

_____

_____

_____

_____

We provide some observations at the end of the chapter, and in the text following this TAI.

## Making a Plan

### Allocating Resources

Some years ago one of the authors read about a successful behavioral intervention aimed at helping impulsive children solve various kinds of problems that required them to use their hands. One task was to arrange wooden pieces of various shapes to match a pattern in a picture shown to the children. The impulsive children initially had great difficulty with this kind of task. When shown the picture, they quickly set about trying to put the pieces into the appropriate pattern, but more times than not were unsuccessful. The behavioral intervention required the children, after seeing the picture but before touching the pieces of wood, to sit on their hands and count to five. This simple strategy significantly improved their ability to complete the task successfully. Once they were restricted from impulsively jumping right in, they became more proficient problem solvers. Apparently, acting impulsively interfered with successful problem solving by not permitting them an initial period of time to think about possible approaches to the problem. As you will see, successful problem solving in general requires one to be reflective rather than impulsive ("Look before you leap," as the proverb says).

Robert Sternberg, a cognitive psychologist at Yale University, has probably written more about the topic of human intelligence than any other individual in the last twenty years (e.g., Sternberg, 1977, 1984, 1986a, 1986b). A major difference between Sternberg's view of intelligence and more traditional views is his emphasis on metacognitive processes (Sternberg, 1986a, 1986b). (You should remember that metacognition was discussed at length in Chapter 6.) As Sternberg points out, many people, both nonscientists and scientists, confuse intelligence with speed of mental processing. We tend to classify "smart people" as quick thinkers. In fact, most standard intelligence tests are timed, and so they place a premium on speed of response. Sternberg argues that while rapid execution is a good index of intelligence in some people and in some situations, speed of mental functioning often is not an appropriate measure of intelligence. In his view, what is most appropriate is the metacognitive processes involved in speed selection—that is, knowing when to work fast and when to work slowly. Metacognition, in other words, is involved in the allocation of resources—such as time, which we must decide how to use when we work on a problem. Sternberg suggests that metacognitive processes involved in effective allocation of resources are a central feature of general intelligence. So it is understandable that appropriate resource allocation is associated with intelligent problem-solving behavior. Smart people, in other words, often are reflective, taking time to make a plan before beginning.

Although the everyday problems we encounter are not usually timed in the same way as problems found on standardized tests, time is nearly always important when we solve problems. The nature of the problem itself frequently dictates that we find a solution in a given period of time. We may not be in a particular rush to cross a busy street, but failure to cross within a reasonable amount of time is likely to produce a whole new set of problems if we miss appointments or fail to accomplish a task we set out to do. Similarly, not finding a job may initially inconvenience us only slightly, but after a while being without a job can have serious consequences. Time is also important simply because we often have only a limited amount available to deal with problems. We do, after all, have to sleep, eat, and leave time for family as well as other important obligations. Because life presents us with many problems, none of us can afford to spend all our available time on just one problem.

Because time is such a valuable resource, finding a solution to a problem often has a certain sense of urgency; sometimes we may even experience feelings of panic when we judge that solving a problem will take more time than we have available. These feelings may suggest that in order to be successful we must begin work immediately and continue as fast as possible. However, a particularly important problem-solving strategy is to resist the temptation to jump right in, and instead allocate time for an initial period of planning and preparation. ("A wise delay makes the road safe," says the proverb.) During this period we can examine the materials or tools available and the options open to us. Then we can make important decisions about the best way to proceed given the resources that we have, including the time remaining. Time spent in a planning stage may save time in the long run. He who hesitates is *not* always lost, and often is on the way to a better solution.

Consider a common measure of verbal fluency found on standardized tests of intelligence. The task is to write down in a fixed period of time as many words as you can that begin with a certain letter, say *y*. (You encountered this task in TAI 7.4.) As Sternberg (1986b) notes, many people approach this task by quickly beginning to write down words as they come to mind—that is, in no particular order. We can improve our performance on this test of verbal intelligence, however, by first spending time planning a systematic strategy. One systematic strategy is to list the vowels mentally and write down as many words as possible that have a particular vowel in the second position. No doubt there are other strategies as well.

**THINK about It**

**7.5**  Examine the following problems and describe how time spent planning a systematic strategy could help the problem solver find a solution and how failure to allocate time for planning might hinder successful problem solving.

1. Finding a particular restaurant in an unfamiliar city.
   a. Planning will facilitate problem solving by: _____

   _____

   _____

   _____

   b. Without planning, solving the problem might be hindered by: ____

   _____

   _____

   _____

2. Deciding what courses to choose to fulfill your graduation requirements.
   a. Planning will help by: _____

   _____

   _____

   _____

b. Without planning, I am likely to: _____

_____

_____

_____

3. Making it through a job interview in order to get a job.
   a. Planning will help by: _____

_____

_____

_____

b. Without planning, the result may be: _____

_____

_____

_____

Our analysis is at the end of the chapter.

## Accessing Relevant Knowledge

Sometimes solving a problem is simply a matter of applying previously acquired knowledge. A chess grandmaster, for example, can look at a chessboard and quickly decide what options are available to checkmate an opponent. As a novice chess player we probably would not be surprised if a grandmaster quickly finished us off with a few well-chosen moves. After all, a grandmaster has played thousands more games than a novice has. Through years of practice, the grandmaster has acquired considerable knowledge about the domain of chess that is relevant to defeating an opponent.

Of course, there are many other situations in which successful problem solving depends on the application of knowledge relevant to the domain in question. Most of us would have trouble trying to solve a complex math problem or fix a broken computer without relevant background knowledge in these domains. It is important to be able to recognize when we have the relevant domain-specific knowledge to deal with a problem and when we need to acquire it before proceeding. Few of us would tackle open-heart surgery or even an appendectomy without first obtaining training in medicine and surgery. To be a proficient problem solver in a particular domain, whether it be surgery, plumbing, law, or business, we must acquire a certain amount of domain-specific knowledge.

When we possess relevant domain-specific knowledge, a solution to a problem sometimes will arise naturally, even automatically (Bransford et al., 1986).

Consider a problem of categorization. How would you arrange the following words into two meaningful categories: cat, pencil, brush, turkey, horse, crayon. Two obvious categories are "animals" and "things to make marks on paper." You might say that such a problem is trivial, and you are right. Note, however, that the problem is made trivial because as English-speaking adults you have acquired considerable knowledge about common English words and their meanings. A solution comes to mind quite naturally under these circumstances.

On some occasions, domain-relevant knowledge is available to facilitate problem solving but it is not retrieved by the problem solver. This type of (un-used) knowledge is sometimes referred to as inert knowledge (Bransford et al., 1986). *Inert knowledge* is knowledge that is accessed only in some contexts even though it is applicable to other contexts as well. Knowledge will remain inert if we fail to recognize that it is relevant to a problem or task at hand. Consider the problem of calculating the area of a parallelogram, such as this one:

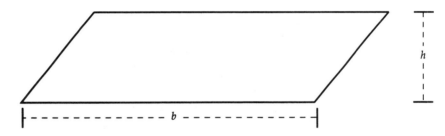

Most of us were introduced to problems like this in junior high school. Typically we were asked to calculate the area of a parallelogram after we had learned how to calculate the area of a rectangle. In fact, as you perhaps remember, the two formulas are very similar: the area of a parallelogram equals base times height ($b$ times $h$, above), whereas that of a rectangle is width times height. The parallelogram calculation is easy to understand when you access the relevant knowledge about the area of a rectangle. When a parallelogram problem is first introduced, some students recognize right away the relevance of the information that they learned about calculating the area of a rectangle. Other students need to be prompted to retrieve that information. To facilitate access to this knowledge, a math teacher may show students that the parallelogram can be made into a rectangle if one side is lopped off and pasted on the other side (so that the parallelogram becomes a rectangle). We need to search constantly for ways to facilitate the use of domain-relevant knowledge whenever we try to solve a problem. One strategy for activating potentially relevant knowledge is to use analogical thinking.

## Analogical Thinking

At one time or another, you probably have heard yourself say to someone, "This is just like . . ." or perhaps more formally, "This is analogous to . . ." At those times you probably were thinking analogically. We form analogies by identifying

Thinking analogically may help us access relevant knowledge.

abstract similarities between concepts or entities (Holland, Holyoak, Nisbett, & Thagard, 1986; Wickelgren, 1974). We use analogical thinking to understand new concepts ("The brain is analogous to a computer"), to learn new skills ("Riding a horse is like riding a bike"), and to solve problems ("Finding the area of a parallelogram is similar to finding the area of a rectangle"). Children as young as 3 to 5 years old are observed to use analogies when they think about new situations (Siegler, 1989). Constructing analogies is very much a part of everyday thinking, but because you have been doing it for so long, you may not recognize its importance. However, thinking analogically is one of the most effective cognitive tools we possess.

Consider the analogy between riding a horse and riding a bicycle. The analogy works when we recognize important similarities between these two activities. For instance, consider the act of getting on a bicycle and that of mounting a horse. It is not important that horses do not have pedals or that bicycles do not have stirrups. We are able to recognize a certain abstract similarity in the act of mounting in both cases. Perhaps we also recognize that both activities require a rider to conquer a fear of falling off. No doubt you can see other important similarities.

Riding a bicycle and riding a horse have certain physical features in common. We may even have been led to think of an analogy between these activities because the physical act of mounting a horse reminded us of the physical act of swinging a leg over a bicycle frame to get seated. Similarly, we may consider the heart as analogous to a pump because we notice a physical similarity between the heart's muscle activity and the action of a mechanical pump. On the other hand, an analogy can exist between two concepts or entities that are quite different physically. Waging war and playing chess obviously differ physically, yet they have common abstract properties, such as the need to plan an attack and protect an important leader (a king or queen). When we say the brain is like a computer, we do not mean that a brain has silicon chips or that it can be directed by instructions from a keyboard. Rather, such an analogy may help us to recognize important similarities between these entities in the abstract processes of registering, storing, and retrieving information, or in the requirements for "hardware" and "software."

**THINK about It**

**?**

**7.6**  Try to form analogies with the following pairs of concepts. Describe how the analogy works; that is, point to important similarities between these concepts.

1. A job interview :: a blind date

   Analogy: _____

   _____

   _____

   _____

2. A dictionary :: a library

   Analogy: _____

   _____

   _____

   _____

3. Playing basketball :: working for a small business firm

   Analogy: _____

   _____

   _____

   _____

Our efforts in this regard appear at the end of the chapter.

Analogical thinking often involves the transfer of knowledge from a well-known domain to a lesser-known domain. From the well-known domain we obtain what is called the source analog. Knowledge from the source analog is then transferred to a target in the lesser-known domain (Holyoak & Koh, 1987).

Should you first learn to ride a bicycle and then face the task of learning to ride a horse, bicycle riding can function as a source analog for the new task of horseback riding. We appreciate the fact that finding the area of a parallelogram is analogous to finding the area of a rectangle because knowledge from the source analog (rectangle problem) transfers to the target (parallelogram problem).

Analogical transfer is said to have played a role in producing some of the world's greatest discoveries. The German chemist August Kekule supposedly discovered the molecular structure of benzene when he dreamed of a dancing snake biting its own tail (Sternberg, 1986a). Kekule apparently recognized an important similarity between the circular properties of the dancing snake and the hexagonal structure of the benzene molecule. Sir March Isambard Brunel, a British engineer and the first person to build an underwater tunnel, reportedly solved the problem of underwater construction by watching a shipworm tunneling into timber. The worm constructed a tube for itself as it moved forward into the wood (Gordon, 1961). Weisberg (1986) writes that Johannes Gutenberg apparently invented the first printing press by thinking about the operation of a winepress. Gutenberg had first considered the problem of printing as analogous to that of using seals to press letters into wax. However, he was stumped as to how a large number of letters could be pressed at one time. While watching the operation of a winepress, which is capable of applying a uniform force over a wide, flat surface, Gutenberg solved the problem of pressing many letters onto paper at one time.

It is not clear whether these particular accounts of scientific discovery arising from analogical thinking are completely factual (Weisberg, 1986); nevertheless, analogical thinking does play an important role in scientific reasoning in general. This is seen in the results of a study in which ten experienced scientists, including one Nobel laureate, were asked to generate solutions to a difficult physics problem involving two wire springs (Clement, 1988). The problem was to decide which of two springs of different sizes would stretch the farthest. The experts were asked to "think aloud" (that is, verbalize their thoughts to the interviewer) while attempting to solve the problem. Transcripts were made of the experts' thinking processes and later examined for evidence of analogical thinking. The experts spontaneously generated a wide variety of analogies during the time they worked on the problem. One scientist thought of diving boards of different lengths and imagined a diver getting ready to jump from the boards; longer diving boards bend more than shorter diving boards. Thus there is clear evidence that scientists do look for analogies when they attempt to solve scientific problems. Perhaps we should not question the idea that a snake, a worm, and winemaking had something to do with some of the world's greatest scientific discoveries.

Scientists aren't the only ones to reason analogically when they are confronted by a problem; college students asked to solve laboratory problems as part of various psychology experiments can be observed to do so as well (Holyoak & Koh, 1987; Spencer & Weisberg, 1986). In one such experiment, the researchers studied students' attempts to solve a classic problem in cognitive psychology, Karl Duncker's (1926, 1945) radiation problem (Holyoak & Koh, 1987). The problem is this:

> You are a doctor faced with a patient who has a malignant tumor in his stomach. To operate on the patient is impossible, but unless the tumor is destroyed, the patient will die. A kind of ray can be used to destroy the tumor. If the rays reach the tumor all at once at a sufficiently high intensity the tumor will be destroyed. Unfortunately, at this intensity the healthy tissue that the rays pass through on the way to the tumor will also be destroyed. At lower intensities the rays are harmless to the healthy tissue but will not affect the tumor either. How can the rays be used to destroy the tumor without injuring the healthy tissue? (Gick & Holyoak, 1983, p. 3)

What solutions would you suggest to save the patient?

Don't be frustrated if you aren't able to solve this problem quickly. Few college students spontaneously produce an acceptable solution (Gick & Holyoak, 1983; Spencer & Weisberg, 1986). Students in one experiment, however, were more likely to be successful if a few minutes before they saw the ray problem they read the following story:

> In a physics lab at a major university, a very expensive lightbulb which would emit precisely controlled quantities of light was being used in some experiments. Ruth was the research assistant responsible for operating the sensitive lightbulb. One morning she came into the lab and found to her dismay that the lightbulb no longer worked. She realized that she had forgotten to turn it off the previous night. As a result the lightbulb overheated, and the two wires in the filament inside the bulb had broken into two parts. The surrounding glass bulb was completely sealed, so there was no way to open it. Ruth knew that the lightbulb could be repaired if a brief, high-intensity laser beam could be used to fuse the two parts of the filament into one. Furthermore, the lab had the necessary equipment to do the job.
>
> However, a high-intensity laser beam would also break the fragile glass surrounding the filament. At lower intensities the laser would not break the glass, but neither would it fuse the filament. So it seemed that the lightbulb could not be repaired, and a costly replacement would be required.
>
> Ruth was about to give up when she had an idea. She placed several lasers in a circle around the lightbulb, and administered low-intensity laser beams from several directions all at once. The beams all converged on the filament, where their combined effect was enough to fuse it. Since each spot on the surrounding glass received only a low-intensity beam from one laser, the glass was left intact. Ruth was greatly relieved that the lightbulb was repaired, and she then went on to successfully complete the experiment.[1]

The lightbulb story functioned as a source analog for many students, who ably transferred the knowledge gained from reading this story to the novel ray problem. An acceptable solution to the ray problem is called the convergence solution. This solution suggests that the doctor use more than one ray of low intensity and focus the rays on the tumor, thus protecting the healthy tissue but destroying the tumor by converging the energy of the multiple rays. You can see that this solution is analogous to the solution employed by Ruth to fix the broken filaments in the lightbulb.

[1]From "Surface and structural similarity in analogical transfer," by K. J. Holyoak and K. Koh. In *Memory and Cognition*, 1984, *15*, 332–340. Copyright 1987 by the Psychnomic Society, Inc. Reprinted by permission of the author.

Although these results show that students use analogical transfer to solve problems, not all the news is good. Even slight variations in the lightbulb story led many fewer students to transfer knowledge from the story to the ray problem (Holyoak & Koh, 1987). Moreover, if students first read a very different analogous story, one about a general planning an attack who has to use multiple roads to converge his forces on a fortress, they often were no better at solving the ray problem than were students who did not read any previous stories (Spencer & Weisberg, 1986). On the other hand, students were aided in their problem-solving efforts when the experimenter hinted that they might use information gleaned from the earlier stories (Holyoak & Koh, 1987). It appears that sometimes a source analog is available but we fail to use it; sometimes, that is, useful knowledge remains inert.

How might you learn to generate effective analogies during the problem-solving process? Perhaps one way is to attempt to model your thought processes on those of the scientists described earlier. The "thinking aloud" transcripts revealed two primary ways in which the scientists generated analogies: (1) through a transformation, and (2) through an association (Clement, 1988).

We generate an analogy through a transformation when we produce an analogous situation by transforming the original situation in some way. William Gordon (1961, p. 34) says this process can involve "making the familiar strange." We transform a situation by distorting, inserting, transposing, or otherwise changing one or more of its features. Thus something that was previously assumed to be fixed might be moved or altered in some way. One of the scientists who worked on the wire-spring problem wondered how it would look if a spring were twice as long (Clement, 1988).

Analogies are generated through associations when some feature of the present problem reminds us of an analogous situation. This process is not necessarily equivalent to simply letting one's mind wander, as we might do when we free-associate. Rather, effective associations tend to be constrained by features of the problem. One scientist, after spending some time thinking about the wire springs, asked himself, "What else stretches?" This question led him to think about rubber bands and other stretchable material. Another subject reported that the wire springs reminded him of roads winding up a mountain. These associations based on specific features of the problem led subjects to generate possible source analogs (Clement, 1988).

- - - - - - - - - - - - - - - - - - - - - - - - - - - - - - - - - - - - - - - - - - - - - - - - - - - -

**THINK about It**

**7.7**  For each of the problems listed below, try to think of one or more analogous situations that might provide clues to help solve the problem. By way of example, consider a problem involving a couple who are having difficulty defining their roles in a romantic relationship. Can you see how such a relationship might be viewed as analogous to performing as a trapeze team? That is, consider how members of a trapeze team might behave and how this behavior is relevant to making a relationship work. From our point of view here on the ground, it seems that the flying partners must understand that they are successful only when they work in harmony. To do so they must anticipate each other's moves, inspire confidence in each other, and reach out to each other at the right time. We suggest that analogous behavior is necessary if a romantic relationship is going to be successful.

Try to identify possible analogous situations that might enhance your thinking about a solution to the following problems.

1. Getting to hear a concert when all the tickets have been sold.

   An analogous situation is: _____

   _____

2. Motivating a young child to work on a difficult school task.

   An analogous situation is: _____

   _____

3. Improving a grade in a biology class.

   An analogous situation is: _____

   _____

Analyze the analogies you produced and determine whether they were produced through association or through transformation.

We provide examples of analogical thinking through both association and transformation at the end of the chapter.

• • • • • • • • • • • • • • • • • • • • • • • • • • • • • • • • • • • • • • • • • • • • • • • • • • • •

## ● Setting Subgoals

*NOTE*

Psychologists who take an information-processing approach to the study of thinking analyze problem-solving activities in terms of the system (the problem solver), the task environment (the givens of the problem), and the problem space (the way the problem solver views the problem) (Simon, 1978). We mentioned earlier that a problem may be difficult because of information overload: too much information is given to us at one time. That analysis of a problem was in terms of the limitations of our information- processing system. The givens of a problem—that is, the description of the goal and the resources and operations available to reach that goal—define the task environment.

A problem space is the problem solver's representation of the problem (Simon, 1978). In other words, how does the problem solver "see" the problem? The assumptions the problem solver makes about the problem influence the way the problem will be viewed. As you have seen, incorrect assumptions can produce difficulties. Moreover, our knowledge about a problem will change as we try out various plans to solve it and gain experience with the tools and operations related to the task. These activities will affect our representation of the problem. We may even change some of our assumptions about the nature of a task as we work at it. Someone working on the nine-dot problem, for instance, may incorrectly assume that the lines must stay within the artificial borders but later may realize that drawing a line outside the dot configuration is not ruled out. This information will immediately alter the problem solver's knowledge state (although, as we noted, it does not make the problem immediately easy). Given this new knowledge, the individual's problem space is different from what it was before. One way to think about problem solving is to think of a problem solver moving from one knowledge state to another (Simon, 1978).

An important question is: What is the best way to move from one knowledge state to another to reach the goal? Let's consider some possible strategies. First, we might simply work on a trial-and-error basis. Although all of us at one time or another have approached a problem in this way, perhaps when we have been under stress (see Mayer, 1983), a trial-and-error strategy clearly goes against the idea that effective problem solving should be planful. As we have indicated, allocating time to make a systematic plan to solve a problem is likely to be a better approach than "let's see what works." Simon (1978) points out that humans, even when they do try trial and error, are not likely to keep it up very long.

An important strategy for moving through a problem space is that of subgoal analysis (Newell & Simon, 1972). Basically, in subgoal analysis we break a problem into parts (subproblems) and then work on each of the parts. Thus we see a problem not as one large problem but as a series of smaller problems, the solutions to which carry us toward a goal. This particular approach to problem solving has considerable applicability, and is typical of much of human problem-solving activity (Nickerson, Perkins, & Smith, 1985). Analyzing a problem in terms of subgoals is an important technique to learn and to model when teaching problem solving activities to others (Simon, 1980).

Subgoal analysis, or what is also called means–end analysis (Simon, 1981), has several stages. In the first stage, we compare our present situation with a goal state and list the differences. We then select one or at most a few of the differences to work on in order to reduce the number of differences between where we are and the goal state. We then look for the tools and operations necessary to work on these differences, and when we find them, we use them to reduce the differences. When the subproblem is completed, we compare where we are now with the goal and then begin the process all over again. In this manner we move closer and closer to a goal by successfully solving subproblems that reduce the differences between where we are and where we want to be.

Anyone who has planned a trip by car between two widely separated locations no doubt has used some sort of subgoal analysis. Obviously, before we start out on a trip we are not where we want to be. To get to our goal, in this case a distant location, we typically first break the trip into parts. We set up, in other words, subproblems to be solved. To get to the West Coast from Chicago we might plan to drive to Kansas City the first day, drive to Denver the next day, and so on. After each day's driving we can compare our present location with the final destination. Anyone who has driven long distances with small children in the car will recognize that young children often have difficulty with this type of problem analysis. They are not able on their own to note the differences between a present state and a goal state and must continually ask: "Are we there yet?"

Subgoal analysis has several important benefits as a problem-solving strategy:

1. By carrying out subgoal analysis you can reduce considerably the number of routes to a goal in comparison with the number that would have to be explored by trial and error. Suppose a solution to a problem can be reached by 100 possible paths. You might think of this as 100 ways to begin a trip to Los Angeles by car from Chicago. One path might take you (in the wrong direction) toward New York. Or you could head south before you head west. Just to keep things simple, assume further that there are 25 ways to start out on the trip in each of the four directions: east, west, north, south. Remember, we are talking about *possible* ways that would have to be tried out if all we relied on was trial and error. Now suppose you can define a subgoal that you know is in the general direction of Los Angeles. You might simply break the problem down into the subproblem of "moving west from Chicago." Immediately, by focusing your attention on a subproblem that you know to be in the right direction, you have reduced the number of routes you need to try from 100 to 25—a reduction of three-fourths! When you consider that for many problems the number of initial ways to begin is often quite large, you should be able to see the advantages of subgoal analysis over a trial-and-error approach to problem solving. (Wickelgren, 1974, provides a mathematical analysis of path reduction in subgoal analysis.)

2. Another important benefit of subgoal analysis is that its effect is often to replace a single difficult problem with two or more simpler ones (Wickelgren, 1974). What initially looks like an impossible leap may look possible when it is viewed as a series of small steps. How many times have you put off starting a problem because it was "too difficult"? When we look at a difficult and apparently unmanageable problem as a series of easier and more manageable problems, we lose an excuse for not getting started. Moreover, by taking relatively simple steps that we can accomplish quickly and easily, we are likely to be reinforced by our successes and to be motivated to continue working on the problem (Sternberg, 1986b).

3. Subgoal analysis also helps to diagnose the source of a problem's difficulty. Many problems are complex in that they require a series of steps for their solution. When we first begin working on a problem, it is often difficult to anticipate everything that will be required to solve it. For example, a problem may require many operations, some of which we are capable of performing and others that we are not. Many tools may be required, some of which we will have available and others that we won't. By breaking a problem into parts we can see exactly what particular operation or tool we need to make progress. Thus, when you perform subgoal analysis you are in a position to identify obstacles and make adjustments to overcome them (Mayer, 1983).

Consider an ill-defined problem of writing a good term paper. No doubt you are better at some components of the problem than at others. For example, you may be good at finding references but less expert at composing a coherent paragraph. By breaking the problem into parts, you can identify specific obstacles that are in your way and concentrate on overcoming them. Such an approach keeps you from making demoralizing statements such as "I can't write a term paper." On the other hand, you may have to admit, at least initially, that "I can't compose a good paragraph." Subgoal analysis permits you to focus on a specific obstacle that is in your path.

**THINK about It**

**7.8**   Switching from using a typewriter to using a word processor to prepare written documents can be a problem for many people. Basically, a word processor is a software system that allows you (with the aid of a computer, printer, and video monitor) to write, edit, store, and retrieve written material. The final document does not have to be printed until you have completed editing it, and you can save documents on disks for future reference.

Break the problem of learning to use a word processor into at least four subgoals. Perhaps you are familiar with word processors; in this case, you can use your own experiences with learning to use them to help you to analyze this problem. You might consider how you would teach someone who is unfamiliar with word processors to use them. If you are unfamiliar with word processors, or even with computers in general, do your best to analyze the problem as you see it into subgoals.

Four subgoals that are important when one learns to use a word processor are:

1. _____
   _____

2. _____
   _____

3. _____
   _____

4. _____
   _____

Describe how, without subgoal analysis, the problem may appear to someone to be difficult or even impossible. If you have never used a word processor, then this someone could be you.

_____
_____
_____
_____

We describe four possible subgoals in our analysis of the probler end of the chapter. These particular subgoals are ones that we have found ...., when we introduce students, particularly ones who exhibit some degree of computer phobia, to the world of word processors. Do we think alike?

FIELD EXPER.

## Trying Out a Plan and Monitoring Its Effectiveness
### Solution Monitoring

A friend of one of the authors is an architect by profession. As an architect, he designs buildings and draws exact plans for their construction. His job, though, is not over when a building plan is completed. He frequently visits the building site during construction to monitor the progress of the contractors and workers who are attempting to follow his plans. While on the site he determines whether his plan is working as he imagined it when he put it down on paper and checks to see whether any unforeseen obstacles have arisen. If shortages arise in certain materials, for example, or if the composition of the soil at the building site causes unanticipated problems with laying a strong foundation, he may have to alter the plan.

Even the best plans have to be monitored continually for their effectiveness. *Solution monitoring* is the process of evaluating progress toward the solution to a problem. Just like the architect, once we have made a plan, we must be constantly aware of how our plan is working. ("He thinks not well that thinks not again," says the proverb.) Solution monitoring is necessary if we are to avoid pitfalls, to make adjustments when we encounter obstacles, to remove us from blind alleys and loops, and to signal when we have reached a solution.

Approaching a problem by breaking it into subgoals lends itself well to solution monitoring. The basis of subgoal analysis is a comparison process. As you work on a problem you want to keep asking such questions as: "Where am I now?" "What differences still exist between my present condition and the goal?" "What is necessary to reduce the differences?" Effective subgoal analysis calls for constant monitoring. Also, because you are constantly comparing your present state with a goal state, you are in a position to recognize when you have achieved an acceptable solution. A solution has been reached when you no longer see differences between your present state and the final goal state.

Neverthelesss, subgoal analysis as a problem-solving strategy can lead to difficulties. Subgoal analysis focuses our problem-solving efforts on a goal state and the differences that exist between our present state and the goal state. We must constantly keep in mind that although we are working toward a final goal, subgoal analysis is based on reducing the difference between a present state and some immediate subgoal. There is a natural tendency to look ahead to the final goal, a behavior that can create difficulties when we attempt to solve a problem that requires some sort of detour or even requires us to move backward. Consider once again the problem of driving to a distant city. If you focused on your final destination, you might consider only routes that always moved you closer to the desired destination. However, careful monitoring of this particular solution strategy (in terms of time, amount of traffic, and rest stops) could reveal that other routes might be faster, safer, or more pleasant. This strategy might take you on a road that temporarily leads away from the direction you want to go. You might have to go out of your way in order to intersect a freeway or other highway that would allow you to travel faster and more comfortably.

A classic, well-defined problem involves moving two sets of three individuals across a river. The individuals can be described in various ways, but, as you will see, an important consideration is that members of one group cannot outnumber members of the other group on one side of the river. Perhaps you have heard someone describe this famous problem. One of the authors first heard a version of it described when in junior high school. Our version of the problem is this:

> Three cats and three rats are on one side of a river. A rowboat is available to transport them across, and both cats and rats are capable of rowing the boat. However, the boat can carry only two individuals at one time, and of course someone must row the boat to get it from one side to the other. Moreover, cats cannot outnumber rats on either side of the river or the cats will give in to temptation and eat the rats. Neither cats nor rats can swim the river. Devise a plan that will transport all six travelers across the river in the rowboat.

Take a few minutes to try to solve it. The problem can be solved in about 11 or 12 steps (see Figure 7.1 for one solution).

A difficult step, one that prevents many people from solving the problem, follows step 6 in the solution shown in Figure 7.1 (see Glass & Holyoak, 1986). At this point a change in strategy is required. While previous steps lead to a gradual reduction in the difference between a present state and the final goal state, step 7, which must be taken if the problem is to be solved requires a move away from the final goal state. At step 7 the problem solver is required to take a rat and a cat back to the other side, thus *increasing* the difference between the present state and the final goal state. Appropriate solution monitoring is necessary if we are to recognize when a step backward will lead us (eventually) forward.

---

**THINK about It**

**7.9**    Can you think of one or more problems you have encountered that required you to go backward in order to go forward? Consider a problem with which you are probably familiar, that of choosing a major and successfully completing the requirements for a degree. Provide an example of how you might need to go backward in order to go forward and get that degree.

When I change my major, I may need to go backward (in order to go forward) by: _____

_____

_____

At the end of the chapter we give an example based on our observations of students who have experienced this problem.

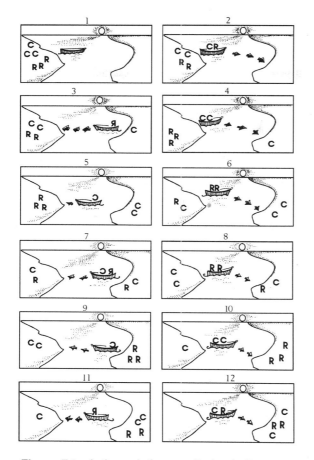

**Figure 7.1**  Active solution monitoring helps us recognize when a step backward will lead us forward (see steps 6 and 7).

## Problem-Solving Fixation or Set

Active solution monitoring should have a troubleshooting component. That is, we must be alert to deficiencies in our attempts at a solution and be ready to make detours, take a step backward, or review our initial assumptions. Sometimes we unintentionally fixate on a specific idea or way of doing things and so fail to see alternatives. One type of problem-solving fixation is called *functional fixedness*. This is a tendency to perceive an object as functioning in a way that we have seen it do in the past without considering alternative functions. Functional fixedness can be illustrated by subjects' attempts to solve a variation of Duncker's (1945) famous candle problem.

The objects used in the problem are shown in Figure 7.2. As you can see, they include a candle, a book of matches, and a box of tacks. The objects are on a table next to a wall. The problem is to fix the candle on the wall so that it will burn properly. (You might consider possible solutions before reading the next paragraph.)

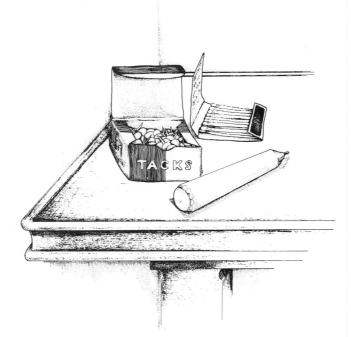

**Figure 7.2**   Duncker's candle problem. *Source:* Adapted from Figure 1.1, p. 7, in *Creativity: Genius and other myths,* by R. W. Weisberg, 1986. Copyright 1986 by W. H. Freeman and Company. Reprinted by permission.

A successful solution to the problem requires that the box be used in a novel way. The box must be seen as having a function other than that of a container. The classic solution is to take the box, empty it of tacks, then turn it upside down and put a tack through the edge of the box in order to fix the box to the wall. You then light the candle with one of the matches, drip hot wax from the candle on the box surface, press the bottom of the candle into the soft wax, and hold it there till the wax hardens and the candle is fixed to the surface of the box. Unless you recognize the rather unusual function of the box as a platform on which to set the candle, your problem-solving efforts are likely to be in vain.

Not everyone will have had experiences with objects or materials that are relevant to solving a particular problem. The phenomenon of functional fixedness should alert you to the fact that your success at solving a problem can depend on your past experience with objects or tools. Consider how two people whose experiences with an object have differed might think differently about that object. Then consider how this differential history of experience could produce differences in problem-solving performance. Let us relate one example.

The two-string problem (Maier, 1931) frequently has been used to investigate how successful problem solving is affected by the way we think about the tools or objects available to help solve a problem. In this task, two strings hang from the ceiling of a large room, too far apart for someone to reach one string while holding on to the end of the other. The challenge is to tie the ends together without detaching the strings from the ceiling. One or more objects in the room can be used in solving the problem. A classic solution is to use one of the objects as a weight, which can be tied to a string and swung like a pendulum. The problem solver holds one string and catches the swinging string when it approaches. Nevertheless, how people solve the two-string problem varies with the nature of the available objects (Maier & Janzen, 1968). Consider the fact that males find the pendulum solution to the two-string problem fairly quickly when the available object is a pair of pliers; however, they are significantly slower when the strings are satin ribbons and the available object is a pair of scissors (Duncan, 1961).

**THINK about It**

**7.10**  Consider the following problem from the perspective of functional fixedness.

Two individuals are preparing to go on a difficult canoe trip that involves camping overnight. The trip is difficult because the river contains many rapids and the campers will have to carry the canoe several times around obstacles in the river on which they will be traveling. One camper is very experienced, while the other is clearly a tenderfoot. The tenderfoot packs, among other things, a hammer to drive in tent stakes, a frying pan to cook fish, a saucepan to cook vegetables, a towel to dry oneself after swimming, a life jacket, an anchor for the canoe, nylon rope, a pillow, an ax to chop firewood, and potholders.

The expert camper takes one look at the pile of objects and tells the tenderfoot that there is no way they will be able to carry all those things in the canoe. Fortunately, the expert camper also is able to solve the problem by pointing out that the tenderfoot is fixating on only one use for some of these objects. What do you think the expert camper might suggest?

_____

_____

_____

_____

_____

_____

We offer suggestions at the end of the chapter.

Another form of problem-solving fixation can arise once we have discovered an effective problem-solving strategy. We all have a tendency to do something in a way that worked for us in the past. We often develop a *set*, in other words, to use a strategy in situations that are similar to those in which our strategy was successful earlier. There is nothing inherently bad about relying on a previously successful strategy; at least we have learned from our past experience how to solve a problem. The trouble arises when we repeat a strategy, perhaps simply out of habit, without questioning its effectiveness (a kind of mindlessness).

Two specific negative consequences of problem-solving set are illustrated by attempts to solve the Luchins water-jar problem.[2] The problem involves three jars of different sizes and an unlimited supply of water. The problem is to use the three jars in combination to produce a specified amount of water. For example, suppose you were given three jars $(A,B,C)$ that are capable of holding the following amounts (quarts) of water:

$$A = 20 \quad B = 49 \quad C = 4$$

How might you use the jars to come up with one quart of water? It is not permitted to estimate the amount of water in a jar; rather you must fill each jar to capacity to determine an amount. Of course you may throw out as much water as you want.

How about first filling jar $B$, then filling jar $A$ twice from the water in jar $B$ (that is, tossing out water after the first fill of $A$), leaving nine quarts in jar $B$, and then filling jar $C$ twice from the contents of jar $B$, leaving 1 quart in jar $B$. The solution can be diagrammed as:

$$B - A - A - C - C = 1$$

Now try the following seven problems.[3] Write down your solution to each problem in the form outlined above.

|   | | A | B | C | |
|---|---|---|---|---|---|
| 1. | Given | 21 | 127 | 3 | Find: 100 |
|   | Solution: _____ | | | | |
| 2. | Given | 14 | 163 | 25 | Find: 99 |
|   | Solution: _____ | | | | |
| 3. | Given | 18 | 43 | 10 | Find: 5 |
|   | Solution: _____ | | | | |
| 4. | Given | 9 | 42 | 6 | Find: 21 |
|   | Solution: _____ | | | | |

[2] From "New experimental attempts at preventing mechanization in problem solving," by A. S. Luchins and E. H. Luchins. In *Journal of General Psychology*, 1950, 42,279–297. Copyright 1950 by Heldref Publications. Reprinted by permission.

[3] From *Cognition*, 2nd ed., by A. L. Glass and K. J. Holyoak. Copyright 1986 by Newberry Award Records, Inc., a division of Random House. Reprinted by permission.

|  | A | B | C |  |
|---|---|---|---|---|
| 5. Given | 20 | 59 | 4 | Find: 31 |
| Solution: _____ | | | | |
| 6. Given | 23 | 49 | 3 | Find: 20 |
| Solution: _____ | | | | |
| 7. Given | 28 | 76 | 3 | Find: 25 |
| Solution: _____ | | | | |

When this series of problems is presented to people in this way, their calculations often reveal the effect of a problem-solving set. Consider the fact that problems 1 through 5 can be solved by the operations $B - A - C - C$. In fact, problem 6 also can be solved by this procedure. Problem 6, however, also can be solved by a much simpler procedure: $A - C$. Many people who work on this series of problems develop a set to use what worked in the past ($B - A - C - C$) and fail to see that a much simpler strategy is available for problem 6. Moreover, many people experience difficulty when they come to problem 7 because the previously successful strategy does not work. Problem 7 requires an $A - C$ solution. This difficulty is apt to be only temporary but can result in a significantly longer solution time than that of problem solvers who did not experience the same series of previous problems (Luchins & Luchins, 1950).

The effect of developing a problem-solving set, of relying merely on what worked in the past, potentially is twofold: (1) it may cause you to employ a more difficult or complicated method of solving a problem when an easier or simpler way to solve it is available; (2) it can interfere with successful problem solving when a previously successful method is no longer appropriate. Only by constantly monitoring your problem-solving efforts, by being alert to the possibility that other alternatives might work as well or better in a particular situation, can you avoid the negative consequences of problem solving set or fixation.

**THINK about It**

**7.11** Consider the problem of making the adjustments necessary to be successful in college after attending high school.

How might a set to respond in only one way (which was acquired in high school) interfere with successful solution at a later time (in college)? That is, speculate on how a particular problem-solving strategy that has worked in the past could eventually become undesirable either because it is no longer efficient or because it is now inappropriate.

_____

_____

_____

_____

_____

_____

We speculate on this problem as well at the end of the chapter.

• • • • • • • • • • • • • • • • • • • • • • • • • • • • • • • • • • • • • • • • • • • • •

*FIELD EXPER.*

• • • • • • • • •
## Critical Principles for Effective Problem Solving: A Summary

1. Strive for a complete understanding of the problem by carefully reviewing both its givens and your assumptions about it.

2. Learn to use external representations of a problem, as by using paper and pencil to make notes or drawings.

3. Be reflective, not impulsive, and allocate part of your problem-solving time to planning.

4. Don't continue to work on a problem for which you do not have adequate task-specific knowledge.

5. Search your past experience for relevant information, including information that you might discover by thinking analogically.

6. Approach complex problems by creating subproblems that lead in stages to a final goal.

7. When you attempt to solve a problem, monitor your efforts in an attempt to avoid relying on previously successful but now inappropriate procedures, or on habitual and familiar ways of doing things that hinder you from seeing alternative uses for objects.

• • • • • • • • •
## Think about It: Discussion of Answers

**7.1**   a.

*Goal:* To get the car back on the road in a position to drive.

*Objects/tools:* A vehicle powerful enough to pull the car from the ditch; chain and hook to connect the vehicles; someone to connect the vehicles and to operate the pulling vehicle.

*Operations:* May vary with weather conditions, the position of the vehicle, and so on, but would typically involve hooking the chain in appropriate locations and operating the pulling vehicle.

*Constraints:* Connect only at points strong enough to maintain the connection; pull car in one direction; pull with a steady motion; pull until the car is in a position to be driven.

b. Although other orders certainly could be defended, we suggest that one likely rank ordering, from most well-defined to least well-defined problems, would be: 2, 5, 4, 3, 1. (No wonder we have trouble losing weight!) It is not important that your rank ordering match ours perfectly; we hope, however, that you can see some general agreement.

**7.2**    If you successfully solved this problem without help, you belong to a very elite club. Rather than draw the lines for you, we describe the solution in terms of the letters in the nine-letter array. (We give the solution this way so that you won't accidentally see the correct answer when you consult the answer to TAI 7.1. An inadvertent peek might spoil your fun!) To solve the nine-dot problem, begin at $a$ and draw a line through $d$ and $g$, continuing your straight line past $g$ until you are lined up with $h$ and $f$ (that's right; go outside the configuration); then draw a straight line from that point through $h$ and $f$, stopping in line with $c$; then draw a straight line from your point through $c$ and $b$ to $a$, stopping where you started; finally, draw your fourth line from $a$ through $e$ to $i$. You've done it with only four straight lines and you haven't lifted your pencil or pen!

a    b    c

d    e    f

g    h    i

**7.3**

*Givens:* the car makes a sputtering noise and the engine stops; John coasts (without engine power) to the side of the busy freeway.

*Assumptions that could interfere:* the engine will not start without new parts; an expert mechanic is necessary to repair it; no one will stop to help; the nearest service station is miles away.

*Assumptions that could solve the problem:* after the engine cools down, it will start again; by opening the hood and looking at the engine, John can discover the problem (as by finding and reconnecting a critical wire that has come loose); a service station (or a telephone) is close by; the raised hood may alert a passing highway patrol to the need for help.

**7.4**    As we note in the text after this TAI, this problem is best approached planfully. When you attempted this task, did you (or your subject, if you asked a friend to do it) jump right in and begin writing down words, or was there evidence of a plan? As we indicated in the text, this task usually can be accomplished most efficiently if you take a few seconds to devise a systematic strategy, such as working through a list of vowels in the second position of the words.

**7.5**    1. Finding a particular restaurant in an unfamiliar city is something the authors have had occasion to do when we have visited a strange town on business. More times than we would like to admit, we have fallen into a group that sets out to find a restaurant when all that is known is that "it's just a couple of blocks up," or when some other equally vague information is known. As you might expect, without a plan to ask a native of the city or to consult a map, the restaurant is not always found quickly, or at all. A brief time spent on devising a plan to locate the restaurant is likely to keep our stomach off empty.

2. Without a deliberate strategy to help decide what courses to choose to fulfill your graduation requirements, you are likely to experience more than an empty stomach. Too often students take more courses than they need, or take the wrong courses, because they fail to sit down early in their college career and outline (perhaps with the help of a knowledgeable college counselor) a four-year plan. The absence of a plan can produce frustration and perhaps additional expenses and unnecessary time spent in college.

3. Making it through a job interview successfully calls for a deliberate strategy. The last thing you should do is wing it. Job-placement counselors with whom we have spoken suggest researching the firm or company where you are interviewing (not only so that you are knowledgeable about what you might be getting into but, importantly, so that you can provide evidence of your interest in this company by your responses to questions and by the questions you ask), paying close attention to clothes and appearance, and practicing speaking in a clear and articulate way to someone about why you want this particular job (that is, actually rehearsing for the interview). We heard about a person who during a job interview was asked why he wanted to work in the candy business. His reply was, "I didn't know you people made candy." Needless to say, he did not get the job. A company is not likely to hire you if you haven't made an attempt to learn about their business.

**7.6**    1. a job interview :: a blind date. Both require a good first impression and all that it takes to create one, such as attention to our appearance and a considerate manner. It seems likely that our levels of anxiety before the two events will be similar.

2. a dictionary :: a library. The library, like the dictionary, permits efficient search by use of the alphabet.

3. playing basketball :: working for a small business firm. It's teamwork, of course, that makes both a small business and a baskeball team successful. In both situations we must keep our eyes on the goal and cooperate when necessary, as by "handing off" when we get in trouble, so that a teammate (co-worker) can get the job done. A successful company, like a successful basketball team, is likely to have a winning spirit.

**7.7**    We suggest that you think about the following analogous situations to help your thinking about a solution to these problems. We'll let you develop the analogies more fully. These are only suggestions; obviously, others are possible and many no doubt will be more appropriate than those we have suggested.

1. Getting to hear a concert when all the tickets have been sold. *Analogy:* Getting into a World Series baseball game.

2. Motivating a young child to learn to work on a difficult school task. *Analogy:* Playing a difficult game.

3. Improving a grade in a biology class. *Analogy:* Climbing a rugged and steep mountain.

Our analogies were produced both through association and through transformation. Thinking about getting into a concert for which all the tickets have been sold reminded us (an association) of people standing outside a baseball stadium when a World Series or other crucial game is sold out. We have observed scalpers prowling around, and we have seen people with signs asking (begging) for an extra ticket. One solution suggested by this analogy might be to stand outside the concert hall looking clean cut, and holding a sign indicating our situation, with the hope that someone with a kind heart and an extra ticket will help us out.

When we thought about getting a young child to cooperate in learning a difficult task at school, we considered ways to transform this situation into one in which the child would want to cooperate. One possibility is to think of this situation as analogous to a difficult game that would allow the child to win a prize. In other words, the analogy is based on transforming the situation into a game. What might happen if the task were a game and not schoolwork? If you transform the situation in this way, you just might motivate the child to do the things he or she needs to do to learn the school task.

Finally, improving a grade in a course is often analogous (in our view) to climbing a mountain. We see an association between the effort and ability required to climb a mountain with the effort and ingenuity necessary to improve a grade. When you climb a mountain, it is important to set your sights on making it to the top, and to work persistently while you keep the final goal in sight. The problem of improving a grade might be solved in an analogous fashion.

**7.8**    This problem is particularly interesting because we see many students wrestling with it. It seems to us that many people often fear anything to do with computers because they make many unnecessary assumptions about them. One response we have heard is: "I can't possibly learn how to program a computer!" Of course, to use a word processor you don't have to know how to program a computer (it does help to know how to use a typewriter). We have attempted to help students get started on word processing by setting the following subgoals: (1) Learning to turn on the computer and boot a system disk; (2) learning how to write one sentence on the typewriter keyboard and print it on paper; (3) learning to save the single sentence on a storage disk; (4) learning to retrieve the single sentence that was saved. All these steps are supported by clear written instructions and troubleshooting advice, so there is little chance of failure at each step. After accomplishing subgoal 4, students are not yet capable, of course, of doing everything on a word processor, but we have found that at this point their inhibitions often are reduced, and their interest and motivation are increased to the point where they can take it from there. Note that each subgoal involves a relatively easy step. For example, to accomplish subgoal 1 all that is required is that the student insert a disk in the proper slot and turn on a switch. This isn't much different from toasting a slice of bread in a toaster!

**7.9**    Choosing a major and a career path that are compatible with your interests as well as your aptitudes is not always easy. Sometimes students find that their aptitudes do not match their interests. A student who is interested in becoming a physician, for example, may find that he does not have an aptitude for science courses. Another student who does have an aptitude for science and an interest in becoming a physician may find, during an initial experience with a course, that science and a career in medicine do not interest her as they once did. Once a student has begun a particular course of studies, the realization that his or her interests and aptitudes are not what they were thought to be may lead the student to change majors as well as career aspirations. Such a student may very well have to go backward in order to go forward. The junior chemistry major who decides to pursue a degree leading to a career in clinical psychology, for instance, may find that it is necessary to enroll in Psychology 101 with the freshmen if the requirements for a psychology major are to be completed and a degree obtained in that field.

**7.10**    The tenderfoot packed, among other things, a hammer to drive in tent stakes, a frying pan to cook fish, a saucepan to cook vegetables, a towel to dry oneself after swimming, a life jacket, an anchor for the canoe, nylon rope, a pillow, an ax to chop firewood, and potholders. The expert camper might very well suggest that while a life jacket, frying pan, towel, and nylon rope are reasonable, the functions associated with the remaining objects also can be served by these four objects. The pan that serves to fry the fish can also function as a saucepan (and even as a dinner plate). An ax with a broad head might substitute for the hammer, but neither tool may be necessary when one considers that rocks found along the riverbank can be used to pound tent stakes and even to break wood (if one's foot doesn't work). A rock may serve, too, as an anchor when it's tied to the nylon rope. Finally, a towel can function as a potholder and, when rolled up (perhaps with the life jacket), serve as a pillow. Campers more experienced than we are may be able to make even better suggestions. What do you think?

**7.11**    Depending on your age and experience, you may be in a better position than we are to discuss this issue. It's been awhile since we made the switch from high school to college. However, observations of students in our freshman-level classes have led us to identify three particular ways of approaching schoolwork that apparently worked well at one time for some of our students but are no longer appropriate, or at least no longer efficient: (1) spending only the minimum time necessary on a homework assignment (as a consequence, learning material only superficially); (2) not setting priorities; that is, not practicing time management (and as a result spending too much time on extracurricular activities); and (3) submitting the first draft or only a slightly edited draft of a written assignment (and as a result not meeting a college instructor's expectations). These strategies may have worked to keep students' heads above water when they were in high school, but many students who continue to do what they did in the past (and who expect the same result) soon find that they are sinking beneath the surface in college.

## • • • • • • • • •
# Recommended Readings

Problem solving is probably the most written about topic in the general area of thinking skills. In fact, as Polya (1971) points out, prescriptions for effective problem solving are found in the wisdom of proverbs that have been passed down for many centuries. Arthur Whimbey and Jack Lochhead (1986) present many useful exercises to help develop problem-solving skills in *Problem Solving and Comprehension.* Also at an introductory level, and also with many exercises, are easily digested books by Martin Levine (1988), *Effective Problem Solving,* and by John D. Bransford and Barry Stein (1984), *The IDEAL Problem Solver.* More sophisticated introductions to the study of cognitive processes involved in problem-solving activities can be found in any of the major textbooks in the field of cognitive psychology. A particularly good one in this regard is Arnold Glass and Keith Holyoak's (1986) *Cognition.* Finally, for those of you who believe that effective problem solving and creative thinking are accomplished only by the supersmart people among us, we recommend Robert W. Weisberg's (1986) *Creativity: Genius and Other Myths.*

# Decision Making

• • • • • • • • • • • • • • • • • • • • • • • • • • • • • • • • • • • • • • • • • • • • •

**Next to good judgment, diamonds and pearls are the rarest things in the world.**

Jean de La Bruyère
(17th-century French moral satirist)

●●●●●●●●●●●●●●●●●●●●●●●●●●●●●●●●●●●●●●●●●●●●●●●●●●●●●●●●●●

Just as we are constantly confronted with problems to solve, so we are constantly faced with decisions to make. And it is the solutions we arrive at and the choices we make that provide the ultimate test of our ability to think critically. The effective critical thinker is one who adapts well to the demands made by the environment, and our problem-solving abilities and decision-making skills are the tools we use to make these adaptations. Just as there are easy and difficult problems, so there are simple and complex decisions. You will see in this chapter that simple decisions can be reached by relatively simple means, such as satisficing (selecting any alternative that satisfies certain minimal criteria). On the other hand, complex decisions are complex because high-quality choices are best arrived at only through the careful and systematic evaluation of large amounts of information. It is the information-management issues of complex problems that often force people to take refuge in quick but poorly thought-out choices, choices that they will surely regret as time goes on. In this chapter you will be introduced to a model of decision making that guides you to consider and manage effectively all of the relevant information involved in a complex decision, and consequently to make wise and adaptive choices.

· · · · · · · · · ·
# Introduction

LIGHTS

Carol's grandmother has had significant hearing loss and is now so deaf that she can no longer hear her doorbell. Carol, a bit of an electronics whiz, wants to help Grandma out, and she has installed a number of bells and buzzers, but she has yet to find one that Grandma can hear reliably. How might Carol solve this problem? Try to think of a solution or two.

Tim has recently changed schools so he can attend college with his girlfriend. At his previous college he had not yet decided on a major but was making excellent grades in a general studies program. He is now a biology major and has just received his grades for the first semester at the new school. He has done so poorly that his chances of qualifying for medical school will rapidly deteriorate from slim to none should he not show marked improvement the next semester. What should Tim do? What might be some possible solutions to Tim's plight?

Now let's contrast some solutions to the two problems. The doorbell problem is a well-defined problem. Some solutions that our students have generated include hooking the doorbell up to lights in various parts of the house so they would flash when the bell was rung, fitting Grandma with a wrist radio receiver that would vibrate when a transmitter attached to the doorbell was activated, and buying Grandma a nervous dog that would go berserk when the doorbell was rung. Maybe you generated these or similar solutions. In general, our experience has been that once a student arrived at a solution for the doorbell problem, he or she was pretty confident it would work. Did you have that sense of confidence about your solution? We hope so.

How about Tim's academic problems? Maybe he could study more, change his major, transfer back to his old college, forget about med school, quit seeing so much of his girlfriend, any of the above, or all of the above. But which solution or combination of solutions is the *best* one? We don't know. Which solution may be the most workable one? We don't know that either. In other words, we don't have the same level of confidence about our solutions to Tim's ill-defined problem as we do for those to Carol's problem.

Many of the problems we must face in life don't lead to certain solutions; that feeling of "Aha, I've got the answer!" just doesn't happen. Rather, we're left with the less reassuring feeling of "I think it'll work, I hope it'll work, omygosh, what if it doesn't work?" That is, we're confronted with uncertainty as to what is the best course of action. We have to decide which course of action to select. In this chapter we will focus on making good decisions in the face of uncertainty.

Because we're constantly confronted with uncertainty, one would think that simply by practice one would become a better decision maker over time. Unfortunately, we don't; people continue to make the same old errors in decision making over and over (Brehmer, 1980). One of the biggest errors that people make is that they don't approach complex decisions systematically. Most people, when confronted with a complex problem, will think about it in an almost

It is easy to recognize good solutions to well-defined problems, which is not the case with ill-defined problems.

random fashion, exploring this alternative or that alternative without considering the full range of alternatives. At best, they conjure up a few benefits or drawbacks without systematically examining the consequences, put off the final decision as long as possible, and then make a hasty decision when time runs out. Their solution is frequently based on those aspects of the problem situation that are most salient or obvious at the time. As an example of this type of decision making, consider an acquaintance of ours (we'll call her Meg) who put off her college selection until the evening before she had to make her final decision. Her "strategy" was to read over all of the descriptive materials of the several colleges she was considering and hope that some judgment would simply leap out at her from this mass of information. As the evening wore on, Meg realized that she couldn't possibly read and digest all of the material in the time available, nor could she keep straight what she had read (Was it Hope or Wooster that was the conference field hockey champ? Was it Hamline or Loyola that had the campus in Rome? Was it Reed, Cornell, or UCLA that had the wilderness experience option during freshman orientation?). Finally, at the midnight hour, Meg closed all of the brochures and catalogs, stared bleakly at them, and, inspiration of inspirations, chose the college with the prettiest catalog! The sadder but wiser sequel is that Meg was terribly unhappy her freshman year; she enjoyed dating and the urban life, yet her rash choice was of a woman's college in the middle of nowhere and 50 miles from the closest men's school. At the end of her first year, Meg transferred to a more carefully chosen school.

Why did Meg, an intelligent young woman, make such a poor choice? If we look at Meg's decision, we can see that it involved multidimensional comparisons; that is, she had several alternatives to consider and many dimensions on which to compare those alternatives. Multidimensional comparisons involve so much information that they commonly exceed the information-processing capacities of the individual (remember Meg's confusion) unless the information is managed efficiently (Halpern, 1989; Slovic, 1972). In this chapter we introduce you to a technique to manage efficiently the information involved in complex decisions so that you can avoid the kinds of errors committed by Meg and other people who approach complex problems in an unsystematic fashion. You will recognize some components of this technique as elaborations of principles introduced in Chapter 7. Other components will probably be new to you.

# • • • • • • • • •
# A Systematic Model for Managing the Information Needed to Make Good Decisions

First of all, the model we are about to present may not be appropriate for many of the decisions you make. That is, this model involves a lot of hard and careful work and it may not be necessary to go to all this work for every decision. For example, many decisions can be reached by the technique of satisficing (Simon, 1953). Basically, *satisficing* (the word is formed from "satisfying" and "sufficing") involves selecting any alternative that meets the minimum requirements of your decision. When you select a movie to see, for example, any entertaining movie may satisfice. Consequently, our model may be unnecessarily cumbersome for such relatively inconsequential decisions as which movie to see, which restaurant to eat at, or which shirt to buy. On the other hand, when you are confronted with decisions that have important consequences for you, this model will help you make the best choice possible with the information available. In the majority of cases, the work that you put into your important decisions will pay off for you in the long run. Conversely, we can all think of important decisions that we took lightly and for which we subsequently paid a heavy price. When you approach an important decision, think of the simple axiom "Pay now, play later; play now, pay later."

• A second word of warning is that our model won't always work; no model is completely foolproof. In decision making we are always dealing with uncertainty, and under such conditions there are no absolute right or wrong answers. What we can tell you, however, is that there is ample evidence (Dawes, 1979, 1988; Dawes & Corrigan, 1974; Janis & Mann, 1977) that you will make many more optimal decisions (that is, the best possible decisions given the information available) by using a systematic approach to decision making than you will by using the informal, intuitive approach that most people rely on.

Before we present the systematic model, we want to acknowledg
some modification, it is a model that was developed by Irving Ja
colleagues through years of research and application (Janis, 1982; Ja
1977; Wheeler & Janis, 1980). In our judgment, this model incorporates all or
the best features of the many systematic models available in the literature (see
Bransford & Stein, 1984; Easton, 1976; Halpern, 1989; Neimark, 1987) and adds
important features of its own. And now, on to the model. The steps in this
model are as follows:

*Step 1.* Acknowledge that a problem exists.
*Step 2.* Refine and elaborate your definition of the problem.
*Step 3.* Clarify your goals.
*Step 4.* Generate alternative solutions.
*Step 5.* Narrow your alternatives.
*Step 6.* Evaluate your alternatives.
*Step 7.* Decide on an alternative.
*Step 8.* Give your chosen alternative a chance.

## Step 1. Acknowledge that a Problem Exists

There are many ways to define a problem. For example, as we indicated in
Chapter 7, a problem exists when something we desire is at least temporarily
unobtainable. We can expand on this definition and say that a problem exists
when we experience a significant deviation from either a standard of performance or a quality of life that is desirable. The deviation may be from an objective standard, as when the dean tells you you're on academic probation because
your GPA is too low, when your physician tells you your blood pressure is too
high, or when your banker tells you your checking account is overdrawn for
the umpteenth time. The deviation may also be from a subjective standard, as
when you're not as wealthy, happy, free of stress, or good at conversation as
you would like to be. Whenever there is a discrepancy between the way things
are and the way they should be or the way we would very much like them
to be, this discrepancy is likely to create discomfort for us. The more intense
our discomfort, the more likely we are to feel a need for change. At the very
least, we must decide either to do nothing or to do something. When the
discrepancies are serious, even this simple choice should be analyzed systematically. Unfortunately, many people endure failure, personal distress, poor health,
and so on with nothing more as a decisional strategy than "That's life" or "My
luck is bound to change" or "This, too, shall pass." Maybe serious problems
will pass, but often when they are ignored, they accelerate into more serious
ones (dentists make a lot of money from problem ignorers!).

So the first step is to acknowledge that a problem exists. Why would one
not ordinarily do so? People frequently avoid acknowledging problems because
they feel that they cannot do much about them anyway. Irving Janis and Leon
Mann (1977) call this defeatist thinking "defensive avoidance." Unfortunately,

not having carefully explored alternatives, these people remain ignorant as to courses of action that may alleviate their failure, discomfort, or dissatisfaction. We hope that you will heed this message and courageously confront your problems rather than defensively avoid them.

**THINK about It**

**8.1**   All of the "Think about Its" in this chapter will be concerned with applying the systematic model to a problem of your choice. What we would like you to do is to select some problem that is of personal relevance to you and that you would like to work on. We make two requests: (1) Select a problem for which there is no definite right solution. (2) Select a problem that you are willing to discuss with other people should the opportunity arise (some of you may be discussing this problem as part of a classroom exercise). If you can't come up with a real problem that fits these criteria, you may use a hypothetical one, but try to choose a hypothetical problem that might be relevant to a future decision you may have to make (such as a career choice, a decision about living arrangements, family planning, or how to spend an inheritance). At this point, just jot down the problem that you want to work on. Don't worry about carefully spelling out the details of the problem; we'll get to that in the next step.

_____

_____

_____

_____

## Step 2. Refine and Elaborate Your Definition of the Problem

Now we want you to do two things. First, define the problem as precisely as you can. Precise definitions of problems are more useful than vague definitions in generating workable alternative solutions. A helpful technique for developing a more precise definition of your problem is to ask the following questions:

1. Are there more specific or accurate words that I can use to describe my problem (*what* is my problem)?
2. Are there certain times *when* the problem occurs or seems to be particularly pressing?
3. Are there certain environments *where* the problem occurs or is particularly apparent?

4. *How*, specifically, is this problem manifested in my behavior?
5. *Why* might this problem occur?

When you answer these questions, you are looking at the basic what, when, where, why, and how of your problem. Not all of these five questions are applicable to all problems, but most will be. Let's look at an example. Recently a student (we'll call her Tina) came into the office of one of your authors with the vague statement that she was unhappy with her college experience and was thinking of quitting school. After a few minutes of general discussion, your author decided to apply the "what, when, where, how, and why" technique, with the following results: Tina, a communications major, feels like an academic failure (what) in her communications classes (where) whenever she has to give oral presentations (when) because she becomes terribly self-conscious and anxious (why) and, as a consequence, becomes tongue-tied and stumbles over her words (how). This formulation provides one with a much better sense of what could be done to reduce Tina's discomfort than does her initial vague complaint of unhappiness.

**THINK
about It**

**8.2**  Apply the what, when, where, why, and how technique to your problem. Refer back to the text for definitions of these five questions.

What? _____

_____

When? _____

_____

Where? _____

_____

Why? _____

_____

How? _____

_____

Now that you have written down specific answers for what, when, where, why, and how, restate your problem incorporating information gleaned from this technique.

_____

_____

_____

_____

_____

_____

_____

_____

• • • • • • • • • • • • • • • • • • • • • • • • • • • • • • • • • • • • • • • • • • • • •

A second part of step 2 involves defining your problem in as many different ways as you can. The reason we do this is that different definitions may lead to different alternative solutions (Bransford & Stein, 1984). Remember Carol, our electronics whiz? As long as she conceived of her problem as coming up with a doorbell or buzzer that Grandma could hear, she was unsuccessful. However, when her problem was recast as a way to devise a signal that Grandma could perceive through some sense other than hearing, several alternative solutions became evident.

• • • • • • • • • • • • • • • • • • • • • • • • • • • • • • • • • • • • • • • • • • • • • •

**THINK
about It**

**8.3**    Are there any other ways in which you can define your problem? List as many as you can think of. You may want to list some alternative statements of your problem now, and then return to this TAI as additional definitions occur to you.

_____

_____

_____

_____

_____

_____

_____

_____

_____

_____

• • • • • • • • • • • • • • • • • • • • • • • • • • • • • • • • • • • • • • • • • • • • • •

## ● Step 3. Clarify Your Goals

Now that you've defined your problem specifically, and we hope in several ways, you can start generating alternative solutions. An important starting point of your search for alternatives is to clarify your goals (Wheeler & Janis, 1980).

That is, a very general goal is simply resolution of the existing problem. However, a definition of what one would consider to be a satisfactory resolution often sets the boundaries of one's search for alternatives. Remember Tina, our tongue-tied communications major? If she accepted only the goal of being a happy and successful communications major, we would have available to us a more limited set of alternative solutions than we would if she accepted the goal of being a happy and successful college student. Goal clarification is a double-edged sword: on the one hand, if you set too narrow a goal, you may exclude alternatives that might turn out to be excellent solutions to your problem; on the other hand, if you define your goal very broadly and vaguely, you are likely to provide little direction for your search for alternative solutions and consequently end up with several alternatives to which you have little or no commitment. In general, it's better initially to define your goal a bit too broadly than to define it too narrowly, because later you can eliminate alternatives that are unacceptable to you.

An important first step in goal clarification is simply to determine what is important to you regardless of the current problem you are attempting to resolve. Most of us have a vague sense of what's important to us, but we rarely reflect on this question. John Crystal and Richard Bolles (1974, p. 46) propose that as a starting point, one write a brief philosophy of one's life. Specifically, they instruct people trying to reach some career decision to "write a brief character study of yourself, emphasizing your philosophy of life, your views on business, social and public ethics, and your opinion of such matters as the rule of law in daily activities, the importance of goals in life, etc." We would add the importance of interpersonal relationships.

Now, this may seem to be a very cumbersome task, but you won't have to write a philosophy of life for every problem that you confront. Write it, put it away, and read it from time to time to refresh your memory and to see if it needs updating or revision. Finally, write it for yourself; don't let others see it. You will want to put down on paper only your very own thoughts about what's important to you, and you don't want to be influenced by any pressure to write a document that would be socially desirable or acceptable to others.

**THINK about It**

**8.4**   Sidney Simon, Leland Howe, and Howard Kirschenbaum, in their book *Values Clarification*, propose a relatively simple technique for determining what our general goals in life are or should be.[1] Daniel Wheeler and Irving Janis (1980) also endorse this technique. Let's try it. First of all, to the right of the numbers below list 20 things in life (big or small) that you love to do.

_____   1. _____

_____      _____

[1]Adapted from *Values Clarification: A Handbook of Practical Strategies for Teachers and Students*, by S. B. Simon et al. Copyright 1972 Dodd, Mead and Co. Reprinted by permission of Breslow and Walker, New York.

2. _____

_____

3. _____

_____

4. _____

_____

5. _____

_____

6. _____

_____

7. _____

_____

8. _____

_____

9. _____

_____

10. _____

_____

11. _____

_____

12. _____

_____

13. _____

_____

14. _____

_____

15. _____

_____

16. _____

_____

_____ 17. _____

_____    _____

_____ 18. _____

_____    _____

_____ 19. _____

_____    _____

_____ 20. _____

_____    _____

Next, we are going to ask you to do some coding to the left of each choice.

1. Describe each activity with a one-word general category (art, socializing, learning, athletics, whatever). Use the category label that first comes to mind.
2. Put *A* to the left of any activity that is normally done alone, *P* next to those activities that are normally done with other people, *AP* next to those activities that can be done either alone or with other people, and *S* next to those activities that are normally done only with a special person in your life.
3. Put *$* next to any activity that is relatively expensive.
4. Put *PL* next to any activity that requires planning.
5. Put *R* next to any activity that involves an element of risk.
6. Put *I* next to activities that involve intimacy.
7. Put *MT* next to items that you would like to devote more time to.
8. Choose three activities you would like to become better at and put *B* next to them.
9. Place, in order of preference, the numbers 1 through 5 beside the five best-loved activities.
10. Finally, indicate as accurately as possible when you last engaged in each of the five best-loved activities.

When you have finished the coding, go back over the list, reading the activities as well as the codes. Write down what this list tells you about yourself. Specifically, answer the following questions:

1. What characteristics are shared by the things that I really like to do?

_____

_____

_____

2. Am I doing my favorite things as much as I would like to?

_____

_____

3. Are there important activities and sources of fulfillment that I may be neglecting? If so, what are they?

_____

_____

_____

4. Are there identifiable obstacles that are getting in the way of doing those things I really enjoy? If so, what are they?

_____

_____

_____

_____

5. What does this exercise tell me about general goals that I might want to set for myself regardless of any given problem situation?

_____

_____

_____

_____

_____

So far, we have spoken about general goal clarification. One can and should also clarify goals in relation to a specific problem. We will show you a technique to do this also, but you will need to generate a list of alternative solutions to your problem to do so. We do hope that by now we have convinced you that goal clarification is a very important yet commonly neglected component of decision making. We have given you a few exercises to start this process. Many people are poor decision makers because they have poorly defined goals; conversely, one cannot be a consistently good decision maker until one can define what one hopes to get out of any decision.

## ● Step 4. Generate Alternative Solutions

A technique by which one can generate alternative solutions to a problem while at the same time achieving some goal clarification is the why-and-how technique (Wheeler & Janis, 1980). This technique works best if it follows completion of the goal-clarification techniques described in step 3. The why-and-how technique starts with stating what you think to be the ideal solution to the problem at hand. The next step is to probe this solution by asking a series of "why" questions about the stated solution. Keep on asking why until you can no longer answer. The point at which the why questions dead-end is likely to be a very fundamental goal for you. Let's go back to a slightly edited dialogue with Tina, our communications major, to illustrate this technique.

**Q.** Tina, what do you think would be the ideal solution to your problem?
**A.** To be able to speak clearly and coherently in my communications classes.
**Q.** Why would this be an ideal solution?
**A.** Because then I could do well in my major.
**Q.** Why do you want to do well in your major?
**A.** So I can get good grades and get a good job in TV.
**Q.** Why do you want a good job in TV?
**A.** So I can become a TV anchorwoman.
**Q.** Why do you want to be a TV anchorwoman?
**A.** So I can make good money in a male-dominated field.
**Q.** Why do you want to make good money?
**A.** So I can live comfortably.
**Q.** Any other reasons?
**A.** No.
**Q.** Why do you want to work in a male-dominated field?
**A.** It's about time women had access to these jobs.
**Q.** Why?
**A.** We're not second-class citizens; it's only fair and just that we have equal access to jobs.
**Q.** Why else?
**A.** That's all.
**Q.** Is there anything else about being a TV anchorwoman that attracts you?
**A.** I like the glamour of the field.
**Q.** Why?
**A.** It sounds exciting
**Q.** Why?
**A.** It just does.

Through this dialogue we've established three fundamental goals that have influenced Tina's academic choices and will probably influence her career choices as well: (1) provision of a comfortable standard of living; (2) the opportunity to further the rights of women; (3) excitement.

The next step in the why-and-how technique is to turn to the "hows" questions. At this point, one is asked (or asks oneself), "How might these goals be achieved?" Like the "whys," the "hows" continue until no further answers can be generated. When answering the "'hows" questions one need not be concerned about the practicality or possibility of generated alternatives; we can weed out the unreasonable ones later. Let's go back to our dialogue to illustrate this technique.

The why-and-how technique helps us effectively generate alternative solutions for our problems.

**Q.** OK, Tina, we've learned that you want a job with good pay, excitement, and the opportunity to further women's rights. How could you satisfy these goals other than by being a TV anchorwoman?

**A.** I could be a TV producer.

**Q.** How else?

**A.** I could be a newspaper reporter.

**Q.** How else?

**A.** I could be an engineer.

**Q.** How else?

**A.** I could be a scientific researcher.

**Q.** How else?

**A.** I could be a lawyer.

**Q.** How else?

**A.** I could be an FBI or CIA agent.

**Q.** How else?

**A.** I could be a spy.

**Q.** How else?

**A.** I could be an advertising executive.

**Q.** How else?

**A.** That's about all I can think of right now.

**THINK about It**

? 

**8.5**

1. Apply the why-and-how technique to your own problem. Write down the fundamental goal or goals identified by your "whys":

_____

_____

_____

Now, write down the alternative solutions generated by your hows:

_____

_____

_____

_____

_____

_____

## Step 5. Narrow Your Alternatives

As we indicated in Chapter 7, one's information-processing capacity is not unlimited (Miller, 1956), and, as we said earlier, a fundamental goal of the systematic model of decision making is to help one manage the large amount of information involved in any complex decision. It may seem to you that we defeated this goal in step 4 when we generated a long list of alternative solutions. Not really, because now we're going to pare that list back down to manageable proportions. One common paring technique is known as *elimination by aspects*. As Amos Tversky (1972) originally formulated this technique, one identified the most important characteristic (aspect) one wanted to be present in the final choice and then eliminated all alternatives that did not have this characteristic. Then one eliminated further alternatives on the basis of the second most important characteristic, the third most important characteristic, and so on until only one alternative remained. One problem with this technique is that as we work down the list, quite workable alternatives are often eliminated on the basis of the absence of relatively unimportant characteristics. The result is that this technique, as it was originally formulated, often becomes a rather sophisticated form of satisficing. That is, it leads to satisfactory choices but not necessarily to the best choices. Consider the Chicago-area high school student who limited his college choices by eliminating alternatives according to the following three aspects: (1) the college had to have a civil engineering program; (2) the yearly costs could be no more than $15,000; (3) the college had to be within one and a-half hours of his home by car. While aspects 1 and 2 may be critical, our friend could triple his list of alternatives by adding two more hours to his driving time, and one of those additional choices might have turned out to be the best one for him.

Because the danger of satisficing is inherent in the original formulation of the elimination by aspects technique, we are going to modify the technique slightly. That is, in applying this technique, we want you to identify the absolutely essential characteristics that *must* be present in your final choice (or absent from it in the case of negative characteristics). If you are having trouble identifying essential characteristics, it will be helpful to review your alternatives, find those that you would reject without a second thought, and then identify the characteristic or characteristics that led to the rejection (was the alternative too expensive, morally reprehensible, very dangerous, harmful to others, something else?). Next, review other alternatives to see if they share the identified characteristic and either keep or reject them accordingly.

**THINK about It**

**8.6**

1. Write down the absolutely minimum essential characteristics that must be present in or absent from the final choice that you make. Keep in mind that this list should be relatively short. If your list gets too long, you may be listing characteristics that are desirable but not essential.

_____

_____

_____

_____

_____

2. Review your list, again asking yourself whether each characteristic is essential or only desirable. Cross off any characteristics which aren't essential.
3. Review your list of alternatives, eliminating any that do not contain all of your essential characteristics.
4. Write down all of those alternatives that have *not* been eliminated by this method.

_____

_____

_____

_____

If, using our modified form of elimination by aspects, you have eliminated all but one choice, your decision is made. However, it is likely that you still have a few viable alternatives. Now you can start evaluating your choices in terms of what would be most desirable and not simply absolutely essential. Sometimes, after application of the elimination by aspects technique, you will find yourself still left with a large number of alternatives. If this is the case, you are still likely to be hampered in your decision making by information overload. Consequently, if you have more than five alternatives left, simply choose for further evaluation those that impress you as the five best alternatives. Don't throw the others out, however, as you may want to bring them back into the evaluation process should further evaluation of your top five produce no satisfactory final choice.

## ● Step 6. Evaluate Your Alternatives

There is good evidence (see Dawes, 1988; Dawes & Corrigan, 1974; Halpern, 1989) that use of decision grids or decision worksheets considerably improves the quality of complex decisions above that of intuitive decisions (that is, choices based on global impressions). Consequently, in this section we will focus on constructing and using decision worksheets to reach high-quality decisions.

You probably have seen some kind of decision grid or worksheet or another, and maybe you have constructed a few of your own. If you've ever shopped seriously for a car, for example, you may have picked up a car buyer's guide that compared various models on such factors as safety, drivability, economy, styling, and reliability. You may also have made a pros-and-cons list for some choice that you have had to make. Most of these decision grids are limited in their applicability by one very significant flaw: they overlook an important dimension that is central to many major life decisions—your personal values.

Many decision grids focus only on utilitarian (tangible, material) gains and losses in a decision. Such a focus may be appropriate when you buy a car or a major appliance, but many life decisions involve a consideration of questions of morality, social responsibility, and self-esteem as well. Self-approval is an essential source of satisfaction in a decision. If you do not consider your personal values in making a decision, but focus only on material gains and losses, then you are very likely to feel alienated from or uncommitted to your choice. Therefore, you will lack the follow-through to bring your choice to a successful conclusion (Sloan, 1986).

Now, you may say that buying a car is not a moral issue, and you may be right (although the morality of your choice may be questioned by environmentalists or unemployed auto workers). However, the really thorny decisions we must face frequently are thorny just because they involve questions of personal values as well as utilitarian gains. We're interested in teaching you a technique to resolve those complex problems that do require a consideration of personal values. You can satisfy purely utilitarian considerations with this model by simply ignoring the values considerations portion of it. As an alternative to generating your own utilitarian grid, you can let others do the work for you. That is, just about any major choice that can be rated on purely utilitarian considerations already has been so rated, and by experts. You can find utilitarian decision grids on thousands of choices, from cars through insect repellents to livable cities, at any library.

Let's now move to the specifics of the decision grid (Janis & Mann, 1977; Wheeler & Janis, 1980). Because our decision grid doesn't have the nice neat format of orderly columns and rows that you might see in a *Consumer Reports* rating of microwave ovens, we prefer to refer to our grids as worksheets. They may not look neat, but they do the job! Janis and his colleagues suggest that you use the worksheets to evaluate those alternatives that are still left after step 5 (narrowing your alternatives). The alternatives are to be evaluated in terms of four major categories of considerations:

*Utilitarian considerations I:* material or tangible gains or losses for oneself.

*Utilitarian considerations II:* material or tangible gains or losses for others (family, friends, colleagues on whom your decision may have a significant impact).

*Personal values considerations I:* considerations pertaining to self-approval or -disapproval (considerations involved in the decision for which you might like yourself more or less).

*Personal values considerations II:* considerations pertaining to whether others will approve or disapprove of you.

Before we examine a sample set of worksheets and develop our own, a consideration of a special kind of cost is important. One of your authors once asked a highly successful friend the secret of his success. The man replied: "There are people in my field who are smarter than I am and who work harder than I do, but are much less successful than I am. My knack is that whenever I see a goal I want to achieve, I always visualize the path I must take to that goal, and then I try to imagine each step on that path. If, after all this imagining, the goal still seems worthwhile, I move down that path one step at a time." There is an important message in this man's description of his success. That is, in considering any major decision, we need to consider not only what we want to achieve but also how we are going to go about achieving it. More specifically, in evaluating any alternative, we should carefully and in detail develop a plan for actually implementing this alternative. In other words, we should spell out the important steps that we must take to reach a desired goal. Each step is likely to have a cost attached to it. Some of these costs may be so minor as to be negligible. Others may be of major significance in the evaluation of the alternative. A careful plan of implementation will tell us which is which and, when we finally decide on an alternative, will give us an action plan for actually carrying out our chosen alternative.

Now let's take a look at a sample set of worksheets. Remember Tim, our struggling pre-med student? Let's say that he's been moving along with us as we progress through the steps in the systematic model of decision making. He's not willing, at this point, to give up his dream of medical school, nor is it financially feasible for him to transfer back to his old college. He recognizes that the alternative of studying more incorporates the alternative of seeing less of his girlfriend, Jenny. Consequently, Tim has narrowed his alternatives to two: (1) studying more by seeing less of his girlfriend; (2) changing majors. Tim next takes out several sheets of paper and prepares a worksheet for each alternative:

Alternative 1. Study more and see Jenny less

*Utilitarian gains for myself*

Get better grades.

Be more knowledgeable about medically relevant areas of study.

Be eligible for Honor Society.

Graduate with honors.

Get into medical school.

*Utilitarian gains for others*

Jenny may get better grades.

Jenny may get into Honor Society.

Jenny may graduate with honors.

Parents won't have to pay for a fifth year or summer school.

*Utilitarian losses for myself*

Less time to pursue other interests.

This will really be a grind.

*Utilitarian losses for others*

This will restrict Jenny's social life.

*Gains in self-approval*

I will be proud of my academic achievements.

I will ultimately be able to serve others.

I will have a high-status career.

*Gains in the approval of others*

Jenny will be proud of me.

My parents will be proud of me.

I will be able to give my future family what they want in life.

*Losses in self-approval*

I will be lonely—missing our time together.

I'll miss the good times I share with other friends.

*Losses in the approval of others*

Jenny will be lonely and unhappy with my decision.

My intramural teammates will be mad at me for quitting the Buzzards.

Alternative 2. Change majors

*Utilitarian gains for myself*

I'll have better fall-back career options if I don't get into med school.

Get better grades.

Be in a more interesting major.

Be eligible for Honor Society.

Graduate with honors.

Get into medical school.

Broaden my development in college (more time for other activities).

*Utilitarian gains for others*
I can be in Jenny's major; maybe we can help each other.
*Utilitarian losses for myself*
I'll have to do some catch-up work in summer school to complete a new major on time.
I'll be less well prepared for the science courses I'll have to take in med school.
I'll be competing in upper-division science classes with science majors.
*Utilitarian losses for others*
I may have to ask my parents to pay summer school tuition.
*Gains in self-approval*
I will have a high-status career.
I ultimately will be able to serve others.
*Gains in approval of others*
Jenny will be happy about my choice.
My parents will be proud of me.
I will be able to give my future family what they want in life.
*Losses in self-approval*
I may feel like a quitter.
*Losses in the approval of others*
My parents may think I'm a quitter.
My adviser may be disappointed.

**THINK about It**

**8.7**   Following Tim's model, take several sheets of paper and make a worksheet for each of your alternatives. Before you proceed, however, let us share an experience and a tip. Our experience has been that people have little trouble generating utilitarian considerations but have more trouble coming up with personal concerns. We recommend that in addition to simply asking yourself, "Will I or others approve or disapprove of my choice?" ask yourself the following three questions (Ruggiero, 1984):

1. Am I violating my obligations to others, and if so, do I have a good reason for doing so?
2. Am I violating certain ideals that make for a better world and that help people meet their responsibilities to others (such ideals as honesty, compassion, fairness, loyalty)?
3. Will the consequences of my actions benefit or harm people?

Now on to your worksheets. For each alternative, try to list specific consequences that you expect to come about for each of the following major categories of considerations. We will refer to these expected consequences as *anticipations*.

1. Utilitarian gains for myself.
2. Utilitarian gains for significant others.
3. Utilitarian losses for myself.

4. Utilitarian losses for significant others.
5. Gains in self-approval.
6. Gains in the approval of significant others.
7. Losses in self approval.
8. Losses in approval of significant others.

In completing this step, try specifically to describe the nature of each gain or loss (see Tim's worksheet, starting on page 231, for an example).

## Step 7. Decide on an Alternative

At this point you may simply be able to look at your worksheet and see that one alternative clearly loads up on many important positive anticipations while the other alternatives have little to recommend them, but do have a host of negative anticipations that dictate their rejection. If such is the case, your selection of the most desirable alternative is easy. In that case, however, your best choice would quite likely have been obvious from the start and you would not have needed to go through this complex decision-making procedure.

When you get to this step in this systematic model of decision making, you are likely to feel a sense of accomplishment for very carefully having considered many important questions that are central to high-quality decision making. You are also likely to feel confused, however, because as you look at the worksheet you may see a multitude of considerations, with no one choice clearly surpassing the others in the ratio of positive to negative anticipations. In other words, our systematic information-management model of decision making has produced information overload! Have you been led astray? Not really; we expect information overload to occur at this point. How, then, is this model superior to those unsystematic, everyday models of decision making in which people avoid information overload by ignoring possible alternatives and important considerations? It is superior because you are *ultimately* able to manage effectively all of the important information without ignoring any. Let us show you how.

First of all, Daniel Wheeler and Irving Janis (1980) recommend that you limit the anticipations in each of the eight categories on your worksheet to no more than five. Their experience is that once you get beyond the five most important anticipations, you are likely to be dealing with fairly trivial issues. Keep in mind that this is a general suggestion and not a hard-and-fast rule. That is, if your sixth, seventh, and eighth anticipations still strike you as truly important, keep them on your list.

Next, examine your worksheet to see if any of the anticipations is listed under all of the alternatives. Eliminate (cross out, erase) such anticipations from further analysis. For example, let's say you're considering career alternatives and the anticipation "allows me to work honestly and ethically with others" is represented under the heading "Personal values I. Positive anticipations" for every alternative career that you are exploring. Just eliminate this anticipation from the list for each alternative choice. Does this mean that you're going to ignore being ethical? Not at all; it simply means that this anticipation is represented in each alternative, so no alternative has a clear advantage over another so far as ethical considerations are concerned.

At this point, you may have sufficiently reduced the information on your worksheet that counting and comparing the number of positive and negative anticipations for your alternatives may indicate the best choice for you (Wheeler & Janis, 1980). If, however, in the process of counting you start to feel uneasy because some of your anticipations are really important, some are kind of important, and still others are only sort of kind of important, then you should develop weights for your anticipations before you reach a final decision.

Developing weights for anticipations is frequently an intimidating process, and people commonly explain their sense of intimidation in one of two ways: (1) "I'm not a mathematician; I don't know how to develop weights," or (2) "How do I know my weights will be the right ones?" Fear not! First of all, while there are fairly technical procedures for developing weights in complex decision making (Edwards & Newman, 1982), we can teach you a simple and workable method in a few minutes. Second, when people are assigning weights, they are working with numbers, and we have been well trained to believe that in working with numbers we must be extremely accurate. Robin Dawes, through his own research as well as through extensive examination of the research of others, has determined that extreme accuracy is not critical in developing weights (Dawes, 1979, 1988; Dawes & Corrigan, 1974). Rather, reasonable guesses by everyday folks enable these people to come quite close to that optimal level of decision making achieved by scientists using complex mathematical procedures. More important, Dawes has conclusively demonstrated that people who break down or "decompose" their decisions into important considerations and anticipations, as we have done here, and then weight these anticipations, will consistently reach higher-quality decisions than will those people who just make global judgments about the adequacy or inadequacy of any given choice.

**THINK about It**

**8.8**   Let us now tell you about our method for assigning weights to anticipations. Earlier in step 7 we asked you to eliminate trivial anticipations from your worksheet. Now read over all of the anticipations that remain on your worksheet just to get a feel for the total contents of your worksheet. Once you have reread the worksheet, go back through it and find all anticipations that meet this description: "In comparison with other anticipations on my worksheet, this particular anticipation is of very minor importance." Place a 1 to the left of any anticipation that meets that description. Now find all anticipations that meet the following description and place a 7 to the left of them: "In comparison with other anticipations on my worksheet, this particular anticipation is of very major importance." Using your ratings of 1 and 7 as anchor points (points of reference), go through your whole list of anticipations and place a weight to the left of each anticipation according to the descriptions given below. Remember, each weight is to be determined in relation to other anticipations remaining on your worksheet. That is, in the process of eliminating unimportant anticipations, you may have left yourself with a list of anticipations all of which are of some importance to you. Now your task is to sort all the anticipations that have not been eliminated into categories that indicate the importance of these anticipations *only in relation to the remaining anticipations on the worksheet.* It is essential that you keep this distinction in mind as you assign your weights. Now, we will give you the descriptions of all the weights on the scale.

1. In comparison with the other anticipations on my worksheet, this anticipation is of very minor importance.
2. In comparison with the other anticipations on my worksheet, this anticipation is of minor importance.
3. In comparison with the other anticipations on my worksheet, this anticipation is slightly below average in importance.
4. In comparison with the other anticipations on my worksheet, this anticipation is average in importance.
5. In comparison with the other anticipations on my worksheet, this anticipation is slightly above average in importance.
6. In comparison with the other anticipations on my worksheet, this anticipation is of major importance.
7. In comparison with the other anticipations on my worksheet, this anticipation is of very major importance.

Go ahead and use this method to assign *relative* weights to all of the considerations that you have remaining on your worksheet. We have assigned weights to the anticipations on Tim's worksheet to provide you with a model. You will also note that Tim crossed out certain anticipations because they were listed under all alternatives.

• • • • • • • • • • • • • • • • • • • • • • • • • • • • • • • • • • • • • • • • • • • • • • • •

Alternative 1. Study more and see Jenny less
*Utilitarian gains for myself*
~~Get better grades.~~
(3) Be more knowledgeable about medically relevant areas of study.
~~Be eligible for Honor Society.~~
~~Graduate with honors.~~
~~Get into medical school.~~
*Utilitarian gains for others*
(2) Jenny may get better grades.
(2) Jenny may get into Honor Society.
(2) Jenny may graduate with honors.
(5) Parents won't have to pay for a fifth year or summer school.

*Utilitarian losses for myself*
   (4) Less time to pursue other interests.
   (5) This will really be a grind.
*Utilitarian losses for others*
   (4) This will restrict Jenny's social life.
*Gains in self-approval*
   (3) I will be proud of my academic achievements.
   ~~I will ultimately be able to serve others.~~
   ~~I will have a high-status career.~~
*Gains in the approval of others*
   (4) Jenny will be proud of me.
   ~~My parents will be proud of me.~~
   ~~I will be able to give my future family what they want in life.~~
*Losses in self-approval*
   (4) I will be lonely—missing our time together.
   (3) I'll miss the good times I share with other friends.
*Losses in the approval of others*
   (5) Jenny will be lonely and unhappy with my decision.
   (1) My intramural teammates will be mad at me for quitting the Buzzards.
Alternative 2. Change majors
*Utilitarian gains for myself*
   (7) I'll have better fall-back career options if I don't get into med school.
   ~~Get better grades.~~
   (4) Be in a more interesting major.
   ~~Be eligible for Honor Society.~~
   ~~Graduate with honors.~~
   ~~Get into medical school.~~
   (4) Broaden my development in college (more time for other activities).
*Utilitarian gains for others*
   (2) I can be in Jenny's major; maybe we can help each other.
*Utilitarian losses for myself*
   (2) I'll have to do some catch-up work in summer school to complete a new major on time.
   (2) I'll be less well prepared for the science courses I'll have to take in med school.
   (2) I'll be competing in upper-division science classes with science majors.
*Utilitarian losses for others*
   (4) I may have to ask my parents to pay summer school tuition.
*Gains in self-approval*
   ~~I will have a high-status career.~~
   ~~I ultimately will be able to serve others.~~
*Gains in approval of others*
   (5) Jenny will be happy about my choice.
   ~~My parents will be proud of me.~~
   ~~I will be able to give my future family what they want in life.~~

*Losses in self-approval*
   (2) I may feel like a quitter.
*Losses in the approval of others*
   (3) My parents may think I'm a quitter.
   (1) My adviser may be disappointed.

What do you do with all of these weights once you've assigned them? At this point, you're still probably suffering from information overload. We did promise you, however, that an important feature of this decision-making process is that it enables you to manage efficiently the myriad of information that goes into a high-quality complex decision. We intend to keep that promise. In the following TAI we will show you how.

**THINK about It**

**8.9**

1. Add up the weights for all of the positive anticipations for your first alternative.
2. Add up the weights for all of the negative anticipations for your first alternative.
3. Obtain the total weight for the first alternative by subtracting the sum of weights for the negative anticipations from the sum of the weights for the positive anticipations (that is, subtract the value obtained in step 2 from the value obtained in step 1).
4. Check all of your additions and subtractions (you don't want all of the work that you have put in thus far to go to waste because of a simple mathematical error).
5. Repeat steps 1 through 4 for each of the remaining alternatives.
6. Compare the total weights (step 3) of all your alternatives. That alternative with the highest positive total weight is your best choice. What is your best choice?

As a model for you to follow, we have carried out this process with Tim's weighted anticipations (see Table 8.1).

**TABLE 8-1**  Tim's decision table

| Alternative | Step 1 sum (gains) | Step 2 sum (losses) | Total weight |
|---|---|---|---|
| Study more | 3 + 2 + 2 + 2 + 5 + 3 + 4 = 21 | 4 + 5 + 4 + 4 + 3 + 5 + 1 = 26 | 21 − 26 = − 5 |
| Change majors | 7 + 4 + 4 + 3 + 5 = 23 | 2 + 2 + 2 + 4 + 2 + 3 + 1 = 16 | 23−16= +7 |

*Note:* It is very important to retain the algebraic sign of plus or minus for your total weight.

When we have introduced this decision-making model to our students, some, but certainly not all, have been skeptical that a complex array of thoughts, values, and judgments can be reduced to a single number and still have any meaning. If you think about it for a moment, however, you can see that many of life's complexities are reduced to numbers, and that these numbers are quite influential in decision making. When you applied to college, for example, you probably took the ACT or SAT. The few numbers generated by these tests reflect a lifetime of cultural and educational experiences. By the time you graduate from college, your GPA will summarize your performance in 30 or more courses covering many and diverse subjects. When you enter the job market, the salary offered you represents a complex judgment concerning, at the very least, your worth to your employer, the number of competitors for your job, and the salary range within which your employer must make decisions. So you see, the complexities of life often boil down to numbers, particularly when decisions must be made regarding those complexities.

We recognize that these numbers are imperfect, but they are still much better than unsystematic and biased judgments. What tells you more about a student's academic performance—the fact that he has a 2.2 GPA or his self-report that he does "great" in school? We can and do trust numbers, and in view of all the careful and systematic work we put into generating them, we can be particularly trusting of the numbers we arrive at by managing decisional information in such a systematic manner.

## Step 8. Give Your Chosen Alternative a Chance

Once you come up with a favored alternative, you have a game plan, so to speak, but the best game plan in the world is worthless unless it is played out properly. At this point, you must convert your well-thought-out choice into action. This is easier said than done. Robert Sternberg (1986b) raises the question as to why intelligent individuals sometimes fail. He identifies procrastination, or the failure to initiate a course of action, as a prime culprit.

After you've worked so diligently to arrive at a high-quality decision, why in the world would you sit on your hands and not translate your decision into action? This question has at least two answers. First of all, you may be experiencing resistance to change from others who are involved in or affected by the decision. Such resistance "is something that a decision maker should expect and consider in the decision making process" (Easton, 1976, p. 22). The resistance to change exerted by others is often a compelling pressure because it is immediate, whereas the gains to be achieved through the change are somewhere out there in the future.

The second answer to this question has to do with the fact that in many complex decisions we are never sure that our choice is the very best one. As we noted earlier, the systematic model of decision making is specifically designed to reach decisions whose goodness cannot be definitively confirmed. We have to implement our decision, and then decide about the adequacy of our decision on the basis of its consequences. Such uncertainty is frequently a source of stress, and people may escape from this stress by clinging to the familiar but unfulfilling status quo rather than venturing into the uncertainties associated with change.

How, then, might you deal with these common pressures to procrastinate that may prevent you from taking that all-important first step to implement your chosen alternative? We have some good news for you. If you have carefully applied the steps in the systematic model of decision making thus far, you have gone a long way toward dealing with these two pressures. First of all, in evaluating your alternatives, you have considered how your decision is likely to affect significant people in your life, both positively and negatively. Knowing that, and knowing also why your decision is not an inconsiderate one, you are better prepared to resist the pressures from others. Second, researchers have demonstrated that people who use a systematic decision model are less likely to experience high levels of stress associated with the uncertainties of a choice and are more likely to carry an implementation plan to completion than are those who approach their decisions unsystematically (Hoyt & Janis, 1975; Mann, 1972).

Just as we must take the first step along the path of implementing our choice and thereby achieving our goal, so must we continue to walk along that path until we reach our goal. Sometimes the path is long and seemingly all uphill, and the walking becomes trudging, and the trudging, slogging. Under such conditions, how can we maintain momentum to full implementation of our chosen alternative? As we have just mentioned, people who have used a systematic decision model find it easier to remain committed to a chosen course of action than do those who make their decisions unsystematically. So, as a careful and systematic decision maker, you will have an easier go of it. You can also make your walk easier if you consider each step in the implementation process as a subgoal and focus your attention on attaining the most immediate subgoal rather than the final goal. When you achieve each subgoal, acknowledge your success. You can do so through something as simple as self-praise or something as complex as a regular series of material rewards.

The important point is that you should develop some way of acknowledging your successes that is meaningful to you. For example, one of your authors had a therapy client who was seriously overweight. His physician instructed him to lose 60 pounds and prescribed a diet. The client felt that attaining this goal could have significant payoffs for him, but he had no hope of achieving it. So we restructured the goals and the payoffs. Your author started out by having his client make a list of things that he really enjoyed but rarely experienced. Several elegant restaurants and expensive foods were on the list, but the client also indicated that he loved the theater but rarely went. We then worked out a series of subgoals, each subgoal consisting of a weight loss of 10 percent of the remaining weight to be lost (6 of the 60 pounds, then 5.4 of the remaining 54 pounds, and so on). The client then rewarded himself by going to a play each time he achieved a subgoal. Though it took the better part of a year, the client did lose the 60 pounds.

One other helpful hint in maintaining momentum toward your goal may be gleaned from your author's experience with his overweight client. That is, the client fell off the diet wagon and went on eating binges occasionally. The first few times he did so, he considered himself an abject failure, much the way a totally abstinent alcoholic might feel once he or she takes that first drink. Research indicates that total abstinence and, by analogy, total commitment to a goal may be unrealistic for many people because it creates a situation in which they consider themselves complete failures after a single instance of backsliding, a deviation from commitment to the goal (Marlatt, 1983). Rather than pass such a judgment on oneself, it is more adaptive to view an instance of backsliding as simply a minor but certainly not insurmountable detour off the desired path, and to get back on the path as quickly as possible. Once the overweight client appreciated this point of view, he could get back on his diet after an eating binge rather than consider himself hopeless and give up his diet altogether.

**THINK about It**

**8.10** If the alternative you have chosen as your best decision requires an implementation plan involving several steps and/or commitment over an extended period of time, break the implementation down into a series of subgoals and list these subgoals:

_____

_____

_____

_____

_____

Now jot down some rewards that you can administer to yourself for each subgoal that you attain. Remember, a good rule for generating meaningful rewards is to select something that you really enjoy but don't commonly receive or experience under normal circumstances. You may want to go back to the exercise on clarification of values (TAI 8.4) to help you identify some meaningful rewards. In self-administering these rewards, you don't have to stick to any one kind of reward; you may want to use a variety of rewards as you progress toward your goal. The rewards:

_____

_____

_____

_____

_____

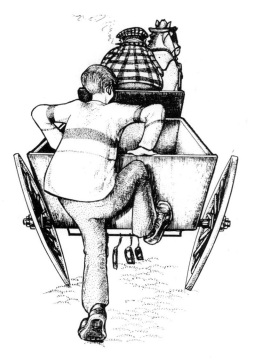

The best remedy for falling off the wagon is climbing right back on.

# When Decisions Fail

As we indicated, when we use the systematic model of decision making we are commonly dealing with problems for which there is no clear-cut right or wrong answer. Consequently, we cannot check out the adequacy of a chosen solution as soon as we reach it, as we might check the solution to a math problem. With problems such as we deal with in this chapter, we may never know whether we made the very best decision, and sometimes it may become apparent that we have made the wrong decision only after we have tried to implement it. How do we make the best of those situations in which, despite our careful attention to the decision-making process, we have apparently made the wrong decisions? We may profit from decisions that have gone awry by carefully monitoring our solutions. You have already been introduced to the idea of solution monitoring in Chapter 7. Now let's look at some of the activities involved in monitoring the solutions to complex decisions.

Good decision makers generally have backup alternatives or contingency plans in case their chosen alternative turns out to be unfeasible. The unfeasibility of a chosen alternative frequently becomes apparent as we start to implement the alternative and unanticipated costs or as problems emerge. When this happens, we can go back to steps 6 (evaluating your alternatives) and 7 (deciding on an alternative), add the newly discovered costs or problems to the decision, and reevaluate our choice. A decided advantage of this systematic model of decision making is that you have carefully considered other alternatives as well as your chosen one, and if unanticipated costs should significantly reduce the merit of your choosen alternative, you have other alternatives as fallback plans. Thus you may still be able to reach a desired outcome by simply using the fallback plan that looks best in light of the added costs that have emerged as you have implemented your original choice.

Sometimes you cannot bail yourself out so easily. You may already have fully implemented your plan, or you may find yourself in a situation (such as a job change) in which you must commit yourself to a choice before it is apparent to you that you have made a mistake. In those cases, you can clearly see that your decision has failed. One thing you should not do in this situation is chastise yourself by saying, "I should have known better," or uncritically accept the words of those who tell you, "I knew this would happen." In other words, we are asking you to be cautious of what researchers have identified as _hindsight bias_ (Fischhoff, 1975, 1977; Fischhoff & Beyth, 1975; Leary, 1981, 1982; Slovic & Fischhoff, 1977). It is well documented that when people know the outcome of an event, they feel quite confident that they would have predicted such an outcome. Yet when the same people are asked to predict an unknown outcome given certain conditions, their predictions are not particularly accurate. Let us illustrate with a few examples.

Bernard Fischhoff (1975) asked research subjects to read an account of an obscure historical event (a hypothetical battle between the British and the Gurkas) and rate the probability of each of the following four outcomes: (1) a victory for the British forces; (2) a victory for the Gurkas; (3) a military stalemate with no peace settlement; (4) a military stalemate with a peace settlement. Half of the subjects were told the "true" outcome (that is, each of these subjects was told that one of the outcomes was the real one, but they were not all told the same outcome). The other half of the subjects were given no information about the outcome. The subjects who had been given information about the outcome were far more likely than subjects who had received no such information to assign a high probability of occurrence to the outcome they had been told was the "true" one.

In another study (Leary, 1981) one group of subjects predicted the score of an actual football game before it was played. After the game was over and the score was known, a second group of subjects was asked to indicate the score they would have predicted if they had been asked _before_ the game was played. As you might guess, the predictions made by the second group were much more accurate than the predictions made by the first group. Hindsight bias, then, gives us the illusion that we would have expected a particular outcome when in fact we would have been unlikely to expect the outcome given the information available to us at the time.

The reason we want to caution you about hindsight bias is that it frequently prevents you from learning from your mistakes. That is, saying, "Oh, I should have known this would happen" in response to a negative outcome may cause

you to assume a defeatist attitude. This attitude may prevent y
ing your decision to see what went wrong, and may cause
faith in your ability to make a good decision in any situatior
rather you recognize that people do make mistakes in decisioii
mistakes are rarely as predictable as hindsight leads us to believe, sysii.
decision makers make fewer mistakes than nonsystematic decision makers, and,
over the long haul, those systematic decision makers who try to learn from their
mistakes make the fewest mistakes of all.

How, then, might one learn from decisions that fail? When you perform
a postmortem on a poor decision, you often can see where you made unwarranted assumptions or where you overlooked important information. Of course,
it is of value to know what those assumptions or missing pieces of information
are, but it is even more important to identify the sources of those errors and
omissions so that they can be avoided in the future. Although many errors are
peculiar to a given decision, some kinds of errors are quite common when
people make complex decisions (Janis & Mann, 1977). These common errors
are summarized in the following questions you can ask yourself as you review
a decision that has had an unfavorable outcome:

1. Did I put off making the decision until my time was so limited that I couldn't
   carefully and thoroughly explore all alternatives?
2. Did I for some reason (shyness, laziness, lack of time) avoid seeking the input of others, such as those affected by my decision or experts (including
   those on library shelves) who might have had valuable input?
3. Did I minimize the costs associated with maintaining the status quo (those
   costs that would follow if I simply chose not to make any changes in my life)?
4. Did I minimize the costs associated with change?
5. Did my decision fail not because it was a poor choice but because I didn't
   have a well-thought-out plan for implementation?

This list of errors is not exhaustive, but it will be useful as a starting point
in identifying the sources of your failed decisions. Once you have identified
those sources, you can be cautious of them in future decisions and work to
overcome them. If you do so, you are very likely to raise your batting average
as an effective decision maker.

# Critical Principles for Effective Decision Making: A Summary

1. Keep in mind that complex decisions are complex because there is no clear-
   cut right or wrong answer to them and they involve the processing of a great
   deal of information.
2. Also remember that people frequently make poor decisions because they
   cannot adequately process or manage all of the information that they should
   to reach a high-quality decision.

3. The necessary steps in making high-quality complex decisions are as follows:

    a. Acknowledge that a problem exists.

    b. Refine and elaborate your definition of the problem.

    c. Clarify your goals.

    d. Generate alternative solutions.

    e. Narrow your alternatives.

    f. Evaluate your alternatives in terms of both utilitarian and personal gains and losses.

    g. Decide on an alternative.

    h. Give your chosen alternative a chance.

4. Avoid hindsight bias in evaluating decisions that have failed.

5. Try to improve your decision making by looking for particular errors that consistently appear in your poorly made decisions, and try to avoid those errors in the future.

6. Remember that people inevitably make mistakes when they are confronted with complex decisions. However, application of a systematic approach to decision making will raise your batting average as a decision maker.

# Think about It: Discussion of Answers

As you have surely noticed, the TAIs in this chapter are different from those in other chapters. That is, in other chapters, the TAIs were used to illustrate or amplify specific points being made in the text. Even within a chapter, these points may have been relatively independent of each other. Further, many of the TAIs needed to be explained or checked against a standard (provided at the end of each chapter) for accuracy. In this chapter, however, each TAI asks you actually to carry out a step in our model of decision making. Each TAI can be understood within the context of the model and does not need to be explained further.

Still, we have some general comments to make about these TAIs. First of all, they were designed in this way because it is essential that you actually carry out the steps in this decision-making model rather than simply read about them if you are to develop a full appreciation of the model. Second, active practice is essential to mastery of the model. By the way, you will find that as you become skilled in the use of this model, it will become less and less time-consuming to use it. Finally, as you become conversant with the model, you will see that other models of decision making are built into this one. For example, if you narrow your alternatives to only one choice in TAI 8.6, you have made your decision by the elimination by aspects model. If you go one step further to TAI 8.7, and are able to reach your decision simply by noting that one alternative really loads up on positive anticipations while the others do not, then you have used the equivalent of a simple balance sheet model. The simple balance sheet model asks you only to list all of the pros and cons of given alternatives and then to base a choice on frequency counts of the pros versus the cons. You are not asked to develop weights with the simple balance sheet model.

It is certainly acceptable to stop your decision-making activities at any step in this model where you have reached a clear picture of your best choice; if your choice is clarified by elimination by aspects, for example, there is no reason to proceed any further. Should you need to proceed further, however, the model presented in this chapter gives you the opportunity to do so. We hope we have presented you with a model that will allow you to attack your complex decisions in a flexible, comprehensive, and effective manner.

# • • • • • • • • •
# Recommended Readings

The decision-making model that served as the core of this chapter is described in greater detail in two books. *Decision Making: A Psychological Analysis of Conflict, Choice, and Commitment,* by Irving Janis and Leon Mann (1977), is written at a fairly high but readable level, and presents the model, the empirical support for it, and a theoretical and empirical analysis of impediments to high-quality decision making (such as conflict and stress). *A Practical Guide for Making Decisions,* by David Wheeler and Irving Janis (1980) is, as the name implies, a presentation of the model for the general public. It is short on citation of research but long on vivid examples, guidelines, and exercises for each step of the model. This book provides a very useful elaboration of the model presented in this chapter. Robyn Dawes's (1988) *Rational Choice in an Uncertain World* is a source of helpful information concerning the detection and avoidance of common errors in decision making, and also helps convince nonbelievers that one need not be a rocket scientist to develop and use weights as meaningful and effective aids to decision making. Though Edith Neimark (1987) develops no particular decision-making model in detail, she does give the reader an informative overview of a number of simple aids to decision making in Chapter 11 ("Decision and Choice") of her book *Adventures in Thinking.* Finally, Hal Arkes and Kenneth Hammond (1986) bring together a number of important articles on decision making in their edited book, *Judgment and Decision Making: An Interdisciplinary Reader.* In addition to providing a theoretical overview of decision making, this book includes consideration of specific areas of application, such as social policy making, economics, law, interpersonal conflict, medicine, and mental health. This book is written at an advanced level and some of the chapters are quite technical; most are fairly readable, however.

# Arguments: Good and Bad

**Loyalty to petrified opinion never yet broke a chain or freed a human soul.**

Mark Twain
(19th-century American author and humorist)

• • • • • • • • • • • • • • • • • • • • • • • • • • • • • • • • • • • • • • • • • • • • • • • • • • • • • •

**As we solve problems and make decisions, we may encounter people who hope to convince us that our proposed solutions are wrong and our choices are not the best. Once we have arrived at a well-worked-out solution to a problem or a carefully made decision, we may need to influence others to accept our choices. Thus the process of critical thinking involves the ability to evaluate arguments advanced by others as well as to present our own point of view in a logical and convincing manner. In this chapter we will examine two common forms of argumentation, deductive and inductive, and the criteria to be used in evaluating the adequacy or validity of these arguments. We will also examine some of the more common kinds of fallacious arguments that people at times fall victim to.**

## Introduction

There will be times when you have to go public with your well-thought-out decisions and solutions to problems. That is, you will have to seek commitments from family, friends, co-workers, and others to your chosen course of action, because that course of action affects them as well as you. Some of the time the appropriateness of a given course of action will be readily apparent. For example, one needn't call a family council to decide that someone should run upstairs and turn off the overflowing bathtub before the effects of water, weight, and gravity relocate the bathroom to the first floor. Frequently, however, complex problems are complex because they can be solved in a variety of ways, none of which is the perfect solution. In Chapters 7 and 8 you have studied ways of coming up with high-quality, if still imperfect, solutions. We hope this study will give you an edge in reaching sound, workable solutions to problems. Unfortunately, many of those other folks who are going to be affected by your decision may have their own solutions, and many of those solutions probably won't be as well thought out as yours. The conditions, then, are ripe for argument. Your job is to convince others that your solution is best; otherwise all of your skill in problem solving and decision making may be wasted. Conversely, your friends, family members, co-workers, whoever is affected by your decision, may be trying to show you the brilliance of their solutions or decisions. If all of your hard work in problem solving and decision making is not to be wasted, you must be able to differentiate between strong and weak counterarguments, and you must also be able to present your conclusions in a convincing way. That is, your arguments must be strong, logical, and well supported. If you can't muster such arguments, then perhaps you should rethink your position. In this chapter we will examine the characteristics of effective and ineffective argumentation.

## Definition of ''Argument''

Let's start by examining what we mean by the word "argument." C. A. Missimer (1986) suggests that "argument" can be defined loosely or strictly. In the loose sense, one simply claims or asserts that something is correct, true, or appropriate. In the strict sense, one makes such a claim or assertion and then backs it up with solid reasons. For example, your friend may assert that Paul Newman is one of America's greatest actors. If you ask your friend why he makes this statement and he answers, "Just because," your friend is arguing in the loose sense. If, on the other hand, your friend replies, "Because Newman has won numerous prestigious awards for his acting and has mastered a variety of roles from the dramatic to the comedic and from the classic hero to the all-purpose sleaze," your friend is arguing in the strict sense. Obviously, good arguments are arguments in the strict sense. That is, good arguments consist of statements or reasons that strongly support a final conclusive statement. In the jargon of

Sometimes we don't have to convince other people that our decisions are good; sometimes we do.

the logician (a person who studies the logic or adequacy of arguments), the supporting statements or reasons are called *premises*, while the statement that is supported is called the *conclusion*.

## Two Common Kinds of Argument: An Overview

Logicians differentiate between two major classes of (strict-sense) arguments, the deductive argument and the inductive argument. A *deductive argument* is an argument in which a person reasons from premises or statements that he or she holds to be true to a conclusion that is logically demanded by those premises. Deductive arguments can be particularly compelling because, if the premises are true and one follows the principles of formal logic to reach the conclusion, then the conclusion is a logically necessary consequence of the premises. In other words, the conclusion *has to be* true (Walton, 1989). Here is an example of a deductive argument:

*Premise:* All living humans need oxygen.
*Premise:* John is a living human.
*Conclusion:* John needs oxygen.

An *inductive argument,* on the other hand, is an argument in which the premises provide support for the conclusion, but the conclusion is not a logically necessary consequence of the premises. In inductive argumentation, we can conclude only with greater or lesser probability (but not certainty) that a conclusion is supported. Perhaps an example of an inductive argument will help illustrate this point.

*Premise 1:* Dave eats a well-balanced, nutritious diet.
*Premise 2:* Dave engages in one hour of aerobic exercise a day.
*Premise 3:* Dave is 26 years old.
*Premise 4:* Dave is of an ideal weight for his height and frame.
*Premise 5:* Dave neither smokes nor drinks.
*Conclusion:* Dave is in good health.

How certain are you of this conclusion? Probably not as certain as you are of the conclusion that John needs oxygen. Your lack of certainty can be attributed to the fact that inductive arguments never unequivocally prove anything; they only make a conclusion seem more or less plausible or probable depending on the quantity and quality of the evidence presented to support the conclusion. In fact, the Dave in this example is based on an acquaintance of one of your authors. Dave died of a heart attack at the age of 27. An autopsy revealed a congenital heart abnormality and an (apparently genetically determined) extremely elevated cholesterol level.

Inductive arguments fail to provide us with unequivocal proofs for a couple of reasons. First of all, inductive reasoning involves looking for patterns or resemblances (Kahane, 1984). What we are saying in inductive arguments, taking the above argument as an example, is that this kind of pattern (exercise, diet, weight control, and so on) has been associated with health in our past experiences, so this pattern should be associated with present instances of good health and should also enable us to predict future instances of good health (if we encourage our children to exercise and eat well, for example, they will be healthy). It is quite possible that in looking for patterns we may ignore or be unaware of some important component of the pattern. For example, Dave's father died of a heart attack in his early 40s. Further, the everyday instances that we try to match up with the patterns are rarely faithful reproductions of the patterns. Dave seemed to be a very nervous individual who responded poorly to job stress. So while he conformed behaviorally to much of the pattern that one would associate with good health, his psychological characteristics suggest that he would be prone to stress-related physical disorders.

Another reason that inductive arguments do not provide us with the same level of certainty that we find in deductive arguments is that the conclusion of an inductive argument goes beyond the evidence provided in the premises (Damer, 1987). A deductive argument simply organizes the existing evidence in the premises in such a way as to enable us to reach a logically valid conclusion. Contrast the following arguments:

*Deductive Argument*
*Premise:* Carlos has a 3.5 GPA.
*Premise:* HiTech U accepts all students with a 3.5 GPA.
*Conclusion:* Carlos will get into HiTech U if he applies.
*Inductive Argument*
*Premise:* Ann has a 3.2 GPA.
*Premise:* Ann was editor of the school newspaper.
*Premise:* Ann was captain of the tennis team.
*Premise:* Ann was senior class president.
*Premise:* Ann is an accomplished musician.
*Premise:* Ann has strong letters of recommendation.
*Conclusion:* Ann will get into HiTech U if she applies.

In the deductive argument one need not make any additional assumptions beyond the stated premises to reach the conclusion. In the inductive argument one goes beyond the provided evidence in making an assumption that HiTech U is looking for well-rounded students as opposed to simply those students with the highest GPAs. If in going beyond the existing evidence we are in error, then our conclusion may be in error. (Our conclusion may also turn out to be right for the wrong reasons. That is, maybe HiTech U is selecting students solely on GPA, but they've gotten only seven applicants this year with GPAs of 3.0 or better.)

**THINK about It**

**9.1**   You've probably heard the following statement many times: "A chain is only as strong as its weakest link." Do you think that this statement is more applicable to deductive or inductive arguments? Explain your answer.

_____

_____

_____

_____

Compare your explanation with the one at the end of the chapter.

## Criteria for Evaluating Deductive Arguments

As we have indicated, the ultimate truth of a deductive argument depends on two criteria: (1) the premises from which the conclusion is drawn must be true, and (2) those premises must be organized according to the principles of formal logic to reach the conclusion (that is, the form of the argument must be valid). Thus, in evaluating a deductive argument, we must consider the truthfulness of the supporting premises as well as the form of the argument used. If any of the supporting premises is false, or if the form of the argument is invalid, the argument is worthless. On the other hand, if all of the premises are true and the deductive argument follows a logically valid form, then the conclusion has to be true.

## Evaluating the Form of a Deductive Argument

Let's first examine the forms of some deductive arguments. While logically valid arguments may take many different forms, we will focus our attention on a restricted class of deductive arguments, the conditional argument. The conditional argument is a very common form of deductive argument when people argue either in support of or in opposition to a decision that has been made but not yet implemented.

*Conditional arguments* are basically "if–then" kinds of arguments. The components of a conditional argument are seen in Table 9.1. These arguments are very common in complex decision making because of the uncertainties involved in such decision making. In Chapter 8, we said that complex decisions commonly have no clear-cut right or wrong resolution. Rather, we have to make our best guess on the basis of available information and evidence as to what the (future) outcome of our choice will be: If I change jobs will I be happy? If I study harder will I do better on my next biology test? If I ask the stranger next to me in the cafeteria line, "What's your favorite broccoli dish," will the stranger talk to me or call a security guard? Conditional deductive arguments are a way of applying logical rules to this prediction of the future.

**TABLE 9-1.**  The components of a conditional deductive argument

*The form of the argument*

|  | Antecedent | | Consequent |
| --- | --- | --- | --- |
| *Premise 1* | If *A*, | | then *C*. |
| *Premise 2* | | *A* | |
| *Conclusion* | | Therefore *C*. | |

A Sample Argument

|  | Antecedent | Consequent |
| --- | --- | --- |
| *Premise 1* | If Brad meets Yolanda, | he will like her. |
| *Premise 2* | Brad is going to meet Yolanda. | |
| *Conclusion* | Therefore, Brad will like her. | |

Let's look at two valid forms of conditional argument. One valid form that a conditional argument can take is known as *asserting the antecedent*. The form of this argument is as follows:

A given antecedent event or condition (*A*) is followed by a given consequent event or condition (*C*).

The antecedent (*A*) has occurred or will occur.
Therefore, the consequent (C) has followed or will follow.

Let's translate this abstract formulation into a concrete example:

If I pay my library fine, I'll be allowed to graduate.
I'm going to pay my library fine.
Therefore, I'll be allowed to graduate.

Another valid but slightly more complicated form of the conditional deductive argument is called *denying the consequent* and can be expressed as follows:

A given antecedent is followed by a given consequent.
The consequent has not occurred (or will not occur).
Therefore, the antecedent has not occurred.

Again, a concrete example:

If I get accepted to Darrow U's law school, I will get a fat envelope in the mail
   from them.
I didn't get the fat envelope (I got the skinny one).
Therefore, I didn't get accepted to Darrow U's law school.

There are two common invalid forms of the conditional deductive argument. The first one, *denying the antecedent,* is as follows:

A given antecedent is followed by a given consequent.
The antecedent has not occurred or will not occur.
Therefore, the consequent has not occurred or will not occur.

Let's concretize this description with an example:

If I go to medical school I will be able to help others.
I'm not going to get into medical school.
Therefore, I won't be able to help others.

This is an invalid argument because the consequent of helping others could be brought about by other antecedents (by becoming a teacher, say, or a member of the clergy, or a social worker) as well as by the specified one of going to medical school.

Finally, another common but invalid form of the conditional deductive argument is known as *asserting the consequent:*

A given antecedent is followed by a given consequent.
The consequent has occurred.
Therefore, the antecedent must have occurred.

For example:

If my study habits are good, I will get good grades.
I'm getting good grades.
Therefore, my study habits are good.

Basically, asserting the consequent is invalid for the same reason that denying the antecedent is. That is, the consequent could have been caused by any number of antecedents. For example, one may be getting good grades because of very high intelligence or an easy schedule of courses, despite relatively poor study habits.

Of course, not everybody talks like a logician; in fact, very few people do. What you're certain to find in everyday conversation and argumentation is that deductive reasoning comes in disguised forms; premises and/or conclusions are omitted and only implied. The four conditional arguments presented above are likely to show up in everyday language like this:

1. I'd better pay my library fine so I can graduate
2. Darn it! Darrow U's skinny envelope!
3. With my grades, I won't get into med school, so I won't be able to help people.
4. What's wrong with my study habits? I'm getting good grades, aren't I?

When conditional deductive arguments do appear in such disguised forms, you may have to map them onto the known forms of deductive arguments. That is, you have to translate the everyday conditional deductive argument so that it conforms to a known formal deductive argument (the valid form of asserting the antecedent or denying the consequent or the invalid form of denying the antecedent or asserting the consequent). As an aid to mapping everyday deductive arguments, you may look for certain words that provide cues that one is stating either a premise or a conclusion (Copi, 1986). Common premise indicators include such terms as "since," "because," "for," "as," "inasmuch as," and "in view of the fact that." Conclusions are frequently preceded by such terms as "therefore," "hence," "so," "thus," "in consequence," "consequently," "in conclusion," "it stands to reason that," "it follows that," "which shows that," and "we may infer." This list is not exhaustive, nor will every premise or conclusion that occurs in everyday deductive arguments be preceded by a cue word or phrase. Finally, in everyday deductive arguments a premise or conclusion often has to be supplied by the audience; the originators of the argument may only imply a given premise or conclusion, perhaps considering it too obvious to state. If it's obvious, however, it's also pretty easy for you to reconstruct in the process of mapping the argument. Finally, if you are uncertain of given premises or conclusions, you can always ask the originator of the argument to clarify or to comment on the accuracy of your mapping by simply presenting your formally mapped version of the argument back to him or her and inquiring if the argument, as now formulated, accurately captures his or her point.

**THINK about It**

**9.2**    With some practice, people can become adept at formally mapping arguments. They must, of course, know the map; that is, they must be very familiar with the form of the deductive argument into which they will retranslate everyday deductive arguments. We've given you only four forms of conditional deductive arguments to master: asserting the antecedent, denying the consequent, denying the antecedent, and asserting the consequent. These arguments are shown schematically in Table 9.2. We have chosen these four forms because we feel that they are the most common forms used in the process of decision making, particularly after a decision is made but before it is fully implemented.

**TABLE 9-2.** Two valid and two invalid conditional deductive arguments

| Valid Arguments | Invalid Arguments |
|---|---|
| *Asserting the antecedent* | *Denying the antecedent* |
| If *A*, then *C*. | If *A*, then *C*. |
| *A*. | Not *A*. |
| Therefore, *C*. | Therefore, not *C*. |
| *Denying the consequent* | *Asserting the consequent* |
| If *A*, then *C*. | If *A*, then *C*. |
| Not *C*. | *C*. |
| Therefore, not *A*. | Therefore, *A*. |

After thoroughly familiarizing yourself with the four forms, try mapping the following everyday arguments. (*Hint:* These are all conditional arguments, so premise 1 follows the "if–then" format).

Argument *A:* "I deserved to have my license suspended; I was driving while drunk."

*Premise 1:* _____

*Premise 2:* _____

*Conclusion:* _____

Which of the four kinds of conditional arguments is this?

_____

Is this a formally valid or a formally invalid argument?

_____

Argument *B:* "I know that smokers get lung cancer, but I'm safe; I don't smoke."

*Premise 1:* _____

*Premise 2:* _____

_____

*Conclusion:* _____

_____

Which kind of conditional argument is this? _____

_____

Is this argument formally valid or invalid? _____

Argument *C:* "Since you won't go to Europe with me this summer, I don't think you love me."

*Premise 1:* _____

*Premise 2:* _____

*Conclusion:* _____

Which kind of conditional argument is this? _____

_____

Is this argument formally valid or invalid? _____

"You do love me! You're going to Europe with me!"

*Premise 1:* _____

*Premise 2:* _____

*Conclusion:* _____

Which kind of conditional argument is this? _____

_____

Is this argument formally valid or invalid? _____

Answers for this exercise are at the end of the chapter.

## Evaluating the Truthfulness of Premises

Keep in mind the very simple rule that if any premise in a deductive argument is false the argument is invalid. (Also keep in mind that this rule does *not* apply to inductive arguments.) Sometimes false premises are very easy to detect; sometimes they're not. Let's look at two of the more clever disguises false premises may wear.

One disguise involves dressing up an assertion of permission as though it were an assertion of obligation. An assertion of obligation indicates that the occurrence of certain conditions or situations creates an obligation to perform certain actions (Cheng, Holyoak, Nisbett, & Oliver, 1986). On the other hand, an assertion of permission indicates that the preconditions for a given action have been satisfied and that one may, but need not, take this action (Cheng & Holyoak, 1985). Consider the following examples:

*Obligation assertion:* If you want to remain in college, then you *must* maintain a satisfactory grade point average.

*Permission assertion:* If you have a 3.5 grade point average, you *may* join the honors program.

Fundamentally, the difference between permission assertions and obligation assertions boils down to the difference between the mays and the musts—that is, between those things you may do or are entitled to do if you choose to do them and those things you should do, must do, or are required to do whether you like it or not.

A common source of untruthfulness or deceit (intended or unintended) in conditional deductive arguments is that the "if–then" premise will be stated as an assertion of obligation when in fact it should be only an assertion of permission. For example, the director of the honors program may argue as follows:

Really good students should all join the honors program.
You haven't joined the honors program.
Therefore, you're not a really good student.

While this argument follows the logically valid form of denying the consequent, our hypothetical honors director has stated an assertion of permission ("Really good students may all join the honors program") as an assertion of obligation. As a result of our ability to detect the difference between assertions of obligation and assertions of permission, we are able to point out the error of our honors director's ways, demonstrating to her that she has presented us with an untruthful premise, and so is left with an unsound conclusion.

Another rather clever way of disguising an untruthful premise is to dress up a necessary *but not sufficient* cause as though it were either a sufficient cause or a necessary and sufficient cause. You may have some recollection of these three kinds of causes from Chapter 2, but let us freshen that recollection a bit. A necessary cause is one without which the effect cannot occur. For example, you cannot expect to master a foreign language without some exposure to that language. Thus exposure to a language is a necessary cause of mastery. However, unless you have a photographic memory, mere exposure isn't sufficient; you also have to practice. So, if one or more of the necessary causes of an effect are missing, that effect cannot occur. A sufficient cause, on the other hand, is any cause whose presence is adequate to bring about the effect. For example, there are lots of ways you can hurt your toe: you can stub it, drop an iron on it, slam it in the door, and so on. Any one of these causes will be quite enough to cause pain. But what if those nerves that transmit pain sensations are not working in your toe? Then a necessary cause would be missing and you wouldn't experience the effect of pain. Finally, a necessary and sufficient cause is a cause that must be present for an effect to occur, and its presence, in and of itself, is sufficient for an effect to occur. For example, transmission of pain impulses from the toe to your brain is a necessary and sufficient cause for you to experience pain in your toe. It really doesn't make any difference what causes the transmission, be it a trauma, a change in your body chemistry, electrical stimulation, whatever. The fact that the transmission occurs is a necessary and sufficient cause of the effect of pain.

Why is it important to distinguish among necessary, sufficient, and necessary and sufficient assertions of causality in conditional arguments? It's important because if we start our argument with an assertion of sufficient causality, we can validly reason to a conclusion by means of asserting the antecedent or denying the consequent. We can also do this with necessary and sufficient assertions but not with necessary but not sufficient assertions. In other words, assertions that include sufficient causality allow us to reason to a valid conclusion by asserting the antecedent or denying the consequent. Assertions that include necessary causality without also including sufficient causality do not allow us to reason to a valid conclusion by asserting the antecedent or denying the consequent. Let's look at a few examples.

If I send Brenda a dozen roses, she'll call and thank me.
I've sent her a dozen roses.
She'll call and thank me.

In this example we've asserted the antecedent, stating an assertion of sufficient causality. Other causes, such as sending Brenda candy, tickets to a play, or a Porsche might also have brought about the thank-you phone call.

If I turn in my homework, I'll get an A in math.
I've turned in my homework.
I'll get an A.

You probably won't get an A if your teacher also requires good performances on exams for a grade of A. Thus you have met a necessary but not necessary *and* sufficient requirement for the desired effect.

Before moving on to a consideration of inductive arguments, let us briefly summarize the principles for evaluating conditional deductive arguments. First of all, determine whether or not any or all of the premises are false. In making this determination, watch out for assertions of permission masquerading as assertions of obligation, and necessary causes masquerading as sufficient or necessary *and* sufficient causes. If the deductive argument under consideration passes this first test, then determine whether or not the argument is of a logically valid form. If any of the premises is false, or if the form of the argument is not valid, reject the argument as worthless. If all premises are true and the form of the argument is logically valid, accept the argument as true.

- - - - - - - - - - - - - - - - - - - - - - - - - - - - - - - - - - - - - - - - - - - - -

**THINK
about It**

**9.3**    Following are seven causal relationships. We want you to judge whether each of these relationships typically would be considered necessary, sufficient, or necessary and sufficient. Indicate your reasoning for each judgment. Compare your answers with those at the end of the chapter.

1. Eating more calories than one burns as a cause of gaining weight.
   What kind of relationship is this? Explain your answer.

   _____

   _____

   _____

2. Throwing a rock at a window as a cause of breaking the window.
   What kind of relationship is this? Explain your answer.

   _____

   _____

   _____

3. Registering for a course as a cause of passing that course.
   What kind of relationship is this? Explain your answer.

   _____

   _____

   _____

4. Obtaining a lottery ticket as a cause of winning the lottery.
   What kind of relationship is this? Explain your answer.

   _____

   _____

   _____

5. Driving under the influence of alcohol as a cause of losing one's driver's license.
   What kind of relationship is this? Explain your answer.

   _____

   _____

   _____

6. Maintaining the required grade point average as a cause of maintaining one's academic eligibility to compete on an intercollegiate sport team.
   What kind of relationship is this? Explain your answer.

   _____

   _____

   _____

7. Turning the knob on the drinking fountain as a cause of starting the water to flow.
   What kind of relationship is this? Explain your answer.

   _____

   _____

   _____

## •••••••••
# Criteria for Evaluating Inductive Arguments

OK, the good news is that if your deductive argument is composed of truthful premises organized in a logically valid form flowing to a conclusion, you've got your hands on the living, breathing *Truth*! The bad news is that most everyday arguments are not deductive arguments. Most everyday arguments are that second kind, inductive arguments. While a good inductive argument may provide lots of support for its conclusion, the conclusion is not a logically necessary consequence of its premises. Rather, the premises (if they are good) add to the probability that our conclusion is right. Think back to Dave, the young man who died of a heart attack. His characteristics, as described in the premises, suggested that the probability was quite high that Dave was in good health. Probabilities are not certainties, however, and in Dave's case the probabilities did not help us to predict his fate. Thus we have no criteria for establishing our conclusions in inductive arguments with complete certainty. We can only increase the probability that our conclusions may be right by formulating good inductive arguments.

Even if we can't set criteria for determining absolute certainty in inductive arguments, we can provide you with some criteria for evaluating how good or plausible an inductive argument is. T. Edward Damer (1987, p. 6) proposes that a good inductive argument "must have premises that are true or *acceptable* (A), premises that are *relevant* (R) to the truth of the conclusion, and premises that together constitute good or adequate *grounds* (G) for the truth of the conclusion." Damer also provides us with the memory aid "ARGument" to help us remember these three criteria. Let's examine further what Damer and others have to say about ARG.

## Acceptability of Premises

In general, *acceptable* (A) premises are true premises. But frequently our premises represent value judgments. When such is the case, the absolute truth of these premises cannot be determined. Consequently, we must focus on presenting premises that are either currently acceptable or potentially acceptable to a rational person (and we hope the person we're trying to convince is rational). After all, it is by acceptance of the premises of an argument that one's opponent can be led to a logical acceptance of the conclusion.

To be considered acceptable, premises should conform to one or more of the following standards (Damer, 1987, pp. 7–8):

1. A premise that is a matter of common knowledge or is well supported by evidence.
2. A premise "that is adequately defended (established, proven, supported) in the same discussion or at least capable of being adequately defended upon request or further inquiry."
3. A premise that is "a conclusion of another good argument."

By the way, the argument whose conclusion becomes a premise can be either inductive or deductive. If it's deductive, we can examine the argument according to the criteria presented for deductive arguments to determine if it leads to a logically necessary truth.

With respect to the second and third standards of acceptable arguments, we urge you to be explicit in stating the support for your premises. Otherwise, your opponent may not see the acceptability of these premises in the same way you do. That is, he or she may not have access to all of the supporting information that leads you to accept the premise yourself. Your opponent needs to be convinced. He or she is not going to fill in the missing links in your reasoning for you. Therefore, you must be thorough in supporting your premises. Let's now turn to the next standard of acceptability.

4. A premise that is based on eyewitness testimony.

Concerning this criterion, social psychologists have demonstrated eyewitness testimony to be very susceptible to bias and distortion (Loftus, 1979). Consequently this kind of premise can be weak. Its acceptability may be strengthened, however, if the eyewitness is the very person you're trying to convince or someone whom your opponent considers to be credible.

5. A premise that derives from the *relevant* knowledge of one who is expert in the field *under consideration*.

We italicized certain words in this sentence to differentiate this standard from a form of fallacious argument, the appeal to authority (we will consider fallacious or faulty forms of argumentation in more detail later in this chapter). An argument that appeals to authority depends for support on a statement by someone who has achieved high status in some endeavor but who gives an opinion on something connected with another field of endeavor. For example, basketball stars tell us what cars to buy, and U.S. presidents are asked to predict Superbowl winners. Though these people are experts at something, their expertise does not extend to the subject they are discussing.

● ● ● ● ● ● ● ● ● ● ● ● ● ● ● ● ● ● ● ● ● ● ● ● ● ● ● ● ● ● ● ● ● ● ● ● ● ● ● ● ● ● ● ● ● ● ● ● ● ● ● ●

**THINK about It**

**9.4**   While it's clear that athletic stars may not be qualified as automotive experts, a more subtle kind of appeal to authority involves using people who probably do have relevant knowledge concerning high-performance machines. In one commercial, for example, the president of a major automobile manufacturer endorses his cars, while in another commercial a famous test pilot endorses another make of car. What factor or factors do you think might limit the credibility of these commercials?

Describe the most credible appeal to authority that you can recall ever having seen in some form of advertisement. Why was it so credible? Do you see any limits to its credibility?

The appeal to authority is a faulty but very common kind of argument.

_____

_____

_____

_____

_____

An example from your authors' experience is at the end of this chapter.

There are also standards that indicate that there is a strong probability that a given premise is unacceptable:

1. The premise is in direct contradiction to available evidence on the matter.
2. The premise is in conflict with information provided by a credible source.

3. The premise is "a questionable claim that is not adequately defended in the context of the discussion or in some other accessible source" (Damer, 1987, p. 8).

Again, the proponent (supporter) of any given argument is urged to support these claims adequately or at least to make supporting sources highly accessible to the opponent. Don't expect your opponents to break their necks trying to gain access to *supposedly* accessible sources of information that support *your* argument. In other words, your opponents are very unlikely to troop to the library to find some possibly vague references that you cite in support of your premise. However, they might be willing to review photocopies of these references if you should provide them.

4. The premise is in conflict with or contradictory to other premises in the same argument.

For example, the person who argues in favor of capital punishment by saying "I place the utmost value on human life" and later argues that "one who takes a life must forfeit his or her life" is being inconsistent. The opponent of the argument should at least ask the proponent to resolve this contradiction.

5. A premise is expressed in vague, unclear, or incomprehensible language.

This premise may be made acceptable if the opponent asks for clarification and the proponent provides such clarification. It is good practice, by the way, for the proponent of an argument occasionally to ask the opponent if he or she understands the points being made as the argument proceeds. If not, the proponent can attempt clarification and possibly turn an unacceptable premise into an acceptable one.

To review, then, what we've said about the A criterion: to be acceptable, any given premise must meet at least one of the five standards for acceptability and none of the five standards for unacceptability.

## Relevance of Premises

The second major criterion of a good inductive argument is *relevance* (the R in ARG). This criterion demands that every premise of an argument be relevant to the conclusion if the argument is to be considered sound. A relevant premise is one that provides support for or confirms the truth of the conclusion. Obviously, the more strongly a premise supports a conclusion, the better that premise is. An irrelevant premise is one that has no bearing on the truth or falsity of a conclusion. Consider the father who can't find any loopholes in the logic of his adolescent daughter's arguments. Rather than concede the argument, however, he counterargues: "What do you know about life? You're only seventeen." This kind of argument, known as an ad hominem argument, really has nothing to do with the soundness of the daughter's evidence and logic. As such, it's a copout and constitutes an unacceptable or fallacious form of argumentation.

## Sufficient Grounds for Conclusion

We may have acceptable and relevant premises for our conclusion and still not have strong support for the conclusion: we may not have provided sufficient *grounds* (G) for the conclusion. Consider the following simple argument: Kim shouldn't fly her private plane at 20,000 feet because there is not sufficient atmospheric oxygen at that altitude. The premise is true; she is very likely to suffer from lack of oxygen at that altitude. The premise is relevant; if she loses consciousness or if her judgment is impaired, she is likely to have an accident, and airplane accidents are almost always serious. The premise is not sufficient, however, because it hasn't been established that Kim doesn't carry her own oxygen supply when she flies. If she does, then the argument is of no particular value. If, however, we can add the premise that Kim has to rely on atmospheric oxygen when she flies, then our argument meets all three criteria of acceptability, relevance, and sufficient grounds, and is a good inductive argument.

A very common kind of inductive argument is known as the empirical generalization (Chaffee, 1988). This argument involves reaching some general conclusion about an entire group on the basis of observation of only some members of that group. For example, you might have concluded that "the staff and students at this college are really friendly" after having contact with a few of them during High School Visitation Day at the college. So your conclusion about the group is based on a sampling (observation of a small portion) of the group.

In deciding whether such a sampling provides us with sufficient grounds to reach a general conclusion about the whole group, we need to ask three key questions: "(1) Is the sample known? (2) Is the sample sufficient? (3) Is the sample representative?" (Chaffee, 1988, p. 416). Maybe you've gotten into an argument like the following with a friend at one time or another:

You: Who says?
Friend: Everybody.
You: Who's everybody?
Friend: Well . . . most people.
You: Who's most people?
Friend: Well, . . . my mother . . . my uncle Fred . . . and my brother!

As you can see, the argument starts out with a vaguely defined but impressive-sounding sample. As you ask for further clarification, the sample becomes known, but limited to the point of absurdity. There are two points to be made here. First of all, for an argument to be persuasive, the sample should be clearly and explicitly described. Second, people with weak arguments often hide behind the smokescreen of a vague but impressive-sounding sample.

The second key question, "Is the sample sufficient?" has to do with the size of the sample one's generalization is based upon. Statisticians have developed technical procedures to answer this question, but we can't give you hard-and-fast rules for determining sufficient sample size without teaching you a course or at least major portions of a course in statistics. We aren't going to do that, but while we're digressing, let us mention that some experts in the study of thinking (Nisbett & Ross, 1980) suggest that coursework in statistics and probability theory can enhance one's skills in inductive reasoning. To return to the question "How many?" let us simply say that the larger the sample size, the greater the probability that the empirical generalization will be accurate. How so? Let's say that you are in a math class with 11 other people and you want to determine how smart, on the average, the class is. So you choose two members of the class, give them IQ tests, and find their IQs to be 140 and 115. You average these two scores and find that the average class IQ is 127.5. Since your IQ is 120, you find this a bit deflating, so you decide to sample every member of the class and you find the following IQ scores: 110, 115, 105, 118, 108, 140, 120 (that's you), 115, 125, 113, 122, and 90. If you average these scores you will get a class IQ of 115. That's better; you're smarter than your average classmate. But what happened with our first estimate? You'll notice that when we picked only two people, one of those people had the highest IQ in the class. Extreme scores have an undue and distorting influence on the averages of very small samples. The larger the sample, the less influential is any given extreme score.

● ● ● ● ● ● ● ● ● ● ● ● ● ● ● ● ● ● ● ● ● ● ● ● ● ● ● ● ● ● ● ● ● ● ● ● ● ● ● ● ● ● ● ● ● ●

**THINK about It**

**9.5**   Let's play with the idea of sample size a bit.

A. Write the following 12 scores on separate, equal-sized bits of paper: 110, 115, 105, 118, 108, 140, 120, 115, 125, 113, 122, 90. Now turn the papers face down, mix them up, close your eyes, and pull out any two numbers. Calculate the average for the remaining 10 scores. How much has this average changed from 115?

_____

B. Return the two numbers to the pile and repeat step A. How much has the average changed from 115 this time?

_____

C. Repeat step B. How much has the average changed from 115 this time?

_____

D. Now randomly select any four scores and calculate the average? How much has this average changed from 115?

_____

E. From the eight scores that weren't used in step D, randomly select four more scores and calculate the average for these scores. How much has this average changed from 115?

_____

F. Calculate the average for the remaining four scores. How much has this average changed from 115?

_____

Now, rank-order your averages in terms of how much they changed from 115. Just put the letter designating the step (A through F) next to the rank number.

Greatest change  1. ____

                  2. ____

                  3. ____

                  4. ____

                  5. ____

Least change     6. ____

Now, in a sentence or two, state a conclusion about the effect of sample size on your rankings.

_____

_____

_____

_____

A more general conclusion concerning the effects of sample size on group averages is at the end of the chapter.

• • • • • • • • • • • • • • • • • • • • • • • • • • • • • • • • • • • • • • • • • • • • • • • • •

The third key question in evaluating an empirical generalization asks: "Is the sample representative?" A sample is representative of the group from which it is drawn if the sample and the larger group are proportionately very similar in important characteristics (that is, characteristics that may be relevant to the conclusion). For example, if we want to determine a town's attitudes toward building low-income housing in that town by asking 100 of the townspeople their attitudes, and assuming that we know these attitudes are influenced by political preference, and that we also know that the town is 40 percent Democratic and 60 percent Republican, then a truly representative sample would have approximately 40 Democrats and 60 Republicans in it.

The more representative one's sample is of the larger group, the higher is the probability that conclusions based on that sample will be accurate for the group as a whole. Some time ago a chewing gum company mounted an advertising campaign that went something like this: "Four out of five dentists who recommend that their patients chew gum recommend Bent-Dent Gum as an important component of good dental hygiene." However, is a sample of "dentists who recommend that their patients chew gum" representative of dentists in general? The next time you visit your dentist ask him or her if many dentists specifically recommend gum chewing to their patients. We think you'll find such recommendations to be very uncommon and therefore unrepresentative. If the recommendation is based on an unrepresentative sample, then we can't conclude that it ranks right up there with frequent brushing and flossing (common recommendations of dentists) for keeping your teeth in tiptop shape.

**THINK about It**

**9.6**    1. Many high school students visit colleges before they make their final college choice. These visits are intended to give students an opportunity to sample what college students, teachers, administrators, and college life in general are really like. Describe what limits there might be to the representativeness of this sampling of the college experience.

_____

_____

_____

_____

_____

2. Some politicians used to refer to the "silent majority" as a source of support for their various positions. Basically, the "silent majority" argument suggests that those people who are in opposition to a given politician's position are likely to be very vocal in their opposition, whereas those people who aren't actively vocalizing opposition are assumed to be in support of the position. This argument was common during the Vietnam war. It was proposed by our government's officials that only those people who were highly visible in such activities as burning draft cards, going to peace rallies, and taking part in protest marches were in opposition to the war. Those people who were not so involved were assumed by these officials to be in support of U.S. involvement in Vietnam. In general, what do you think of the "silent majority" argument? Specifically, which one of the three criteria for a good inductive argument is violated in this example?

_____

_____

_____

_____

We analyze these problems at the end of the chapter.

Samples are sometimes not representative because the person who is doing the sampling intentionally or unintentionally introduces a bias into the selection of the sample. A sample is biased if certain important characteristics exist in significantly different proportions in the sample than they do in the group as a whole. For example, if you're trying to determine how students *in general* at your college feel about building a new science center on campus and you survey everybody in an introductory biology class, your sample is likely to be biased in favor of science majors; that is, the sample has a higher proportion of science majors than does the college as a whole. Consequently, you might conclude that students *in general* are more in favor of the new science center than they really are.

**THINK about It**

**9.7**   Let's say you were actually going to do the science center survey and you could administer this survey to any three classes offered on your campus. What classes would you choose? Why?

_____

_____

_____

_____

We offer some suggestions at the end of the chapter.

One way you can guard against bias is to select your sample at random. A randomly selected sample is one in which any member of the total group under study has the same chance of being selected for the sample as any other member of the group. For example, if you write 20 names on equal-sized pieces of paper, fold each piece of paper identically, put them all in a shopping bag, shake them up, and then blindly pull ten names out of the bag, you have randomly selected those ten names.

This procedure may sound simple and straightforward, but subtle biases can be introduced into supposedly random samples in many ways, and the biases make them nonrandom. Suppose you work for a research firm that is surveying the residents of a community concerning their attitudes toward a change in local government. You start work at 9 A.M. and for eight hours you randomly select numbers from the local phone book, dial them, and ask your questions of the person who answers. Do you have a random sample? No, you don't. This sample deviates from randomness in at least two ways: (1) Your sample includes only people who own phones and have published phone numbers. (2) Your sample includes only people who are at home during the day, so you're going to have a disproportionately large number of homemakers, unemployed people, retirees, and possibly even sick children in your sample. As you can see, it's not as easy as it may seem to obtain a completely random sample. If you try random selection as a means of developing a representative sample, you are urged to exercise extreme care in examining your means of sample selection for possible biases. While complete randomness in sample selection is frequently impossible, the closer one approaches random selection, the more likely becomes the validity of one's empirical generalization from the sample to the group as a whole. The ultimate goal of random selection of a sample is to construct a sample that is representative of the population under study.

**THINK about It**

**9.8**    You work for an advertising firm that has been contracted by a major candy company to determine the best packaging for its new candy bar. Your artists have just completed several alternative label designs and you have to evaluate the customer appeal of each design. Therefore, you prepare a questionnaire on which the subject examines each design and then responds to a number of questions about the designs by checking the appropriate choices on the questionnaire (much like a multiple-choice exam). In this way, a large amount of information can be gathered in a relatively short time. In addition, the subject selection seems to be very efficient. Your ad agency is located in a medium-sized town and you are able to get the names of every man, woman, and child living in the town from the county clerk. You randomly select 1000 names from this list and contact all 1000 of these people, requesting that they take part in your study. If they agree, you drop your questionnaire off at their home and make arrangements to pick it up one week later. People who complete the questionnaire are given a free selection of the candy company's products for their participation.

Will the final sample in this research be random? In what ways might the sample deviate from randomness?

_____

_____

_____

_____

We discuss the likely composition of this sample at the end of the chapter.

In summary, inductive arguments do not provide us with the same certainty about our conclusions that deductive arguments might. Nevertheless, there are three basic criteria (remember ARG?) that one should attend to in developing and/or evaluating an inductive argument. First of all, the premises should be acceptable. That is, their truth should be established, or if a premise is a value judgment, it is best supported if it is consistent with expert opinion in the field. Second, the premises should be relevant to the conclusion. That is, any premise should have a direct and logical relation to the conclusion. For example, if a licensed nutritionist, hired by you, tells you that eating Oat Bran Crunchies will be good for you, the (unstated) premise that the nutritionist is an expert in the field is relevant to the conclusion that Oat Bran Crunchies are good for you. On the other hand, if the endorser of Oat Bran Crunchies has established his or her credentials in show business or athletics, then his or her fame in no way provides a relevant supportive premise for the conclusion that Oat Bran Crunchies are healthful. In fact, some athletes and show business celebrities have notoriously poor nutritional habits. The third criterion for a sound inductive argument is that its premises must provide sufficient grounds for the conclusion. Sufficiency basically asks two questions: (1) Have all of the premises that are necessary to reach a valid conclusion been presented? (2) If the conclusion is an empirical generalization (that is, based upon sampling), is the sample known, of adequate size, and representative?

**THINK about It**

**9.9**    Following is a hypothetical situation that led to an inductive argument. Read the description and all the premises and conclusions. Next, evaluate the premises of this argument as to whether they are acceptable and/or relevant. Then evaluate the subconclusions and the final conclusion as to whether sufficient grounds have been provided to support these conclusions.

About seven years ago a con man defrauded more than 30 elderly people of their life savings. Most but not all of these people were of very limited means. The consequences for several of these people were dire, and included loss of home, loss of needed medical care, and loss of any financial security. The confidence game was finally detected, and the con man was tried and convicted. None of the money was ever recovered, however, and one of the victims suffered a fatal heart attack during the trial. The con man served his term and was released from prison. Soon after his release, he started receiving threats on his life both over the phone and through the mail. The contents of the threats suggested that they were all from one person, either one of the victims or someone who was well acquainted with a victim. The con man has now demanded police protection.

This case prompted a caller to a radio talk show to make the following arguments. As we have indicated, we want you to evaluate the premises and conclusions of these arguments on the basis of the ARG criteria.

Argument A:
*Premise A1:* People would not have fallen prey to this con if they were not poor.

Evaluation of acceptability and relevance: _____

_____

_____

_____

*Premise A2:* The man who had the heart attack will never see all of his grand-children grow to adulthood.

Evaluation of acceptability and relevance: _____

_____

_____

_____

*Premise A3:* This is a very heartless crime.

Evaluation of acceptability and relevance: _____

_____

_____

_____

*Premise A4:* These kinds of crimes are frequently committed by sociopaths, and sociopaths are very difficult to rehabilitate (assume that this statement is acceptable).

Evaluation of relevance: _____

_____

_____

_____

*Conclusion A:* Anyone who would commit such a heartless crime probably couldn't be rehabilitated.

Evaluation of sufficiency of grounds for this conclusion:

_____

_____

_____

_____

_____

Argument B:

*Premise B1:* Some of the victims now have to receive additional support from the government either through public aid or through victim assistance programs (assume that this premise is acceptable).

Evaluation of relevance: _____

_____

_____

_____

*Premise B2:* It has cost the government approximately $36,000 a year to imprison the con man (assume that this premise is acceptable).

Evaluation of relevance: _____

_____

_____

_____

*Premise B3:* It will cost the government several million dollars a year to provide protection for the con man.

Evaluation of acceptability and relevance: _____

_____

_____

_____

*Premise B4:* The government is required to guarantee the safety of all former prisoners.

Evaluation of acceptability and relevance: _____

_____

_____

_____

*Conclusion B:* The con man has cost and will continue to cost the government considerable amounts of money.

Evaluation of sufficiency of grounds for this conclusion: _____

_____

_____

_____

*Final Conclusion:* Since it costs the government a lot of money to keep the con man alive, and since he is beyond rehabilitation anyway, he should be put to death for his crimes.

Evaluation of sufficiency of grounds for this conclusion: _____

_____

_____

_____

_____

We analyze these arguments at the end of the chapter.

# Fallacious Arguments

As you can see, good arguments are frequently not all that easy to construct. Nonetheless, if you follow the guidelines we've given you, you can construct solid and logical arguments that should be convincing to rational people. Unfortunately, not all people are rational or logical when they develop their arguments. If you can recognize (and perhaps tactfully point out) logical inconsistencies and irrationalities in the arguments of others, two positive results may occur: (1) You may be able to sway your opponents by your more logical counterarguments; (2) You are less likely to be convinced by their fallacious but persuasive arguments. Let's take a look at some of the more common kinds of fallacious but persuasive arguments that people use. Try to identify which of the three criteria of inductive logic the fallacious arguments violate. Remember that many of these arguments may violate more than one criterion.

A very common type of fallacious argument is the *ad hominem argument*. The term "ad hominem" literally means "to the person," and this translation basically describes the strategy of this argument. That is, the person who resorts to an ad hominem strategy commonly is arguing with a person who is presenting a solid argument. Not being able to find loopholes in the logic of his or her opponent, the ad hominem arguer attacks not the argument but the opponent, casting aspersions on his or her intelligence, character, experience, ancestry, and integrity. The insinuation in an ad hominem argument is, of course, that someone who is so stupid, inexperienced, inferior, immoral (some of the above; all of the above) would not be capable of reaching any well-thought-out and reasonable conclusion.

**THINK about It**

**9.10** We see an example of the ad hominem argument in the father–daughter conflict discussed earlier in this chapter. Criticize this argument in terms of the ARG criteria. Specifically, which one of the three criteria (acceptability, relevance, and sufficient grounds for the conclusion) seems most likely to be violated in this argument? Explain your choice.

_____

_____

_____

_____

_____

_____

Do you agree with the choice indicated at the end of this chapter?

• • • • • • • • • • • • • • • • • • • • • • • • • • • • • • • • • • • • • • • • • • • • •

Another common kind of fallacious argument, similar to the ad hominem argument, is known as *poisoning the well*. The arguer who uses this method "attempts to forestall disagreement altogether by making it uncomfortable or embarrassing to disagree" (Neimark, 1987, p. 179). That is, one prevents counter-arguments before they occur by including in one's arguments such statements as "It would be foolish [morally depraved, stupid, un-American, uncool . . . you fill in your favorite perjorative term] to disagree with my conclusion that . . ."

The *false dilemma* is a form of argumentation that proposes that there are only two possible conclusions or choices, the one that the arguer supports and a quite unacceptable one. The implication, of course, is that if you can't accept the latter alternative, then you must accept the former alternative (Cederblom & Paulsen, 1986).

• • • • • • • • • • • • • • • • • • • • • • • • • • • • • • • • • • • • • • • • • • • • •

**THINK about It**

**9.11** Apply the ARG criteria to the following false dilemma:

A young faculty member found fault with some of the procedures in her academic department. An older faculty member suggested the following alternative to her: "If you don't like the way things are done here, you should seek employment elsewhere."

Which one of the three ARG criteria is most seriously violated in this example? Explain your answer.

_____

_____

_____

_____

_____

Check your explanation against the one provided at the end of the chapter.

• • • • • • • • • • • • • • • • • • • • • • • • • • • • • • • • • • • • • • • • • • • • •

Once identified, the straw man argument is easy to knock down.

The *slippery slope argument* (who names these arguments, anyway?) proposes a kind of snowballing effect in which one undesirable action will lead to a more undesirable action, which in turn will lead to an even more undesirable action, until catastrophe is inevitable (Walton, 1989). One of your authors was once called upon to do a psychological evaluation of a father who had severely beaten his 15-year-old daughter for wearing lipstick. The father's reasoning was classic slippery slope: "If she starts wearing lipstick, she'll attract boys. If she attracts boys, she'll start dating. If she starts dating, she'll start having sex. If she starts having sex, she'll want it all the time. If she wants it all the time, she'll become a prostitute. Therefore, if my daughter wears lipstick, she'll become a prostitute." Occasionally the slippery slope argument is valid (it truly is hard to eat just one potato chip). However, when a person seems to be making a mountain out of a molehill, there is very likely a slippery slope somewhere on that mountain.

The *straw man argument* is a technique through which you make "your own position appear strong by making the opposing position appear weaker than it actually is" (Cederblom & Paulsen, 1986, p. 104). There are two relatively common ways of constructing a straw man, which can then be very easily knocked down. First of all, you may restate your opponent's position in a way more extreme than your opponent intended; extreme positions often seem unreasonable in their extremeness. To illustrate, the elderly faculty member of TAI 9.11 may say to the younger faculty member, "You don't seem to think we know how to do anything right in this department," and then knock down that straw man by talking about the things that have been done well. Second, you may take a relatively minor point or feature of your opponent's argument and focus on it as though it were the whole argument. For example, a political candidate who is criticized by his older opponent for lack of experience may counterargue that the opponent obviously is against young people. The basic issue that the older opponent brought up was experience and not age per se. The younger candidate could more appropriately have responded that young people can also have relevant experience, and older people may be quite inexperienced in issues of relevance to the particular tasks at hand.

The *appeal to ignorance* is yet another deceptively convincing form of argumentation. In such an appeal we are asked to accept a conclusion because we cannot disprove it. We may scratch and search for a valid disproof and continually come up empty. We must remember, however, that failure to disprove, in and of itself, does not constitute proof. The fact that I can't disprove that there are higher life forms on other planets, for example, does not confirm their existence. We can reasonably say at this point only that we don't know if such life forms exist. In a similar vein, the person who is using an appeal to ignorance does not affirm the certainty of his or her position by your failure to disprove it. All we can conclude from a failure to disprove is that a position *may be* tenable. However, the proponent of the position must be able to add substantial proof to the failure to disprove if the position is finally to be acceptable.

There are many more kinds of fallacious arguments, but we'll mention just one more, the *appeal to emotion*. This argument involves an attempt to motivate people to reach conclusions on the basis of emotional states that the arguer elicits from the audience rather than on the basis of an evaluation of the logical support offered by the proponent. Two emotions frequently played upon in the appeal to emotion are pity and fear (Chaffee, 1988). For example, lawyers may try to defend the coldblooded premeditated acts of their client-murderers by describing the unhappy childhoods of these clients. An employer may send subtle (and sometimes not-too-subtle) cues to the employees that adverse consequences await anyone who fails to agree with the boss at any time.

**THINK about It**

**9.12** Let's check out your understanding of the fallacious arguments with a short matching test. Below you will find brief descriptions of several kinds of fallacious arguments. Match each description with its appropriate name by placing the number of the description to the right of the name of the argument.

ad hominem ＿＿＿

poisoning the well ＿＿＿

slippery slope ＿＿＿

straw man ____

appeal to ignorance ____

appeal to emotion ____

false dilemma ____

1. Bill breaks his brother Ed's bicycle. Mother tries to talk Ed out of pulverizing Bill by saying, "You shouldn't be angry with Bill; he's your brother."

2. A political candidate has difficulty answering the very good points his opponent is making in a debate with him. In frustration, he suggests, "After all, my charming opponent shouldn't be troubling her pretty head with these weighty political issues."

3. A hypochondriac has visited many doctors, complaining of vague ailments that he believes to be life-threatening. The doctors never find anything physically wrong with him. Their failure leads him to argue that he obviously has a very rare disease that medical science has not yet confronted.

4. Your friend frequently drives at speeds in excess of 85 miles an hour on the expressways. Fearful for your own life, you suggest to him that driving that fast is illegal and dangerous, and besides, it wastes gas. He argues that time is money, so you shouldn't worry about the gas.

5. Critics of U.S. foreign policy are sometimes confronted with the bumper-sticker argument: "America, love it or leave it."

6. A debater bolsters a particularly weak point by telling her opponent, "If you can't see the logic of my position, you ought to have your head examined."

7. A teenager stays out 15 minutes after a parent-imposed curfew. When he comes home he is confronted by the irate parent. The teenager questions why the parent is making such a big deal about 15 minutes. The parent says that 15 minutes is not the issue. Rather, the parent argues that "disobeying a parent is the first step on the long road to hell."

You'll find the scoring key for this test at the end of the chapter.

## Critical Principles for Effective Argumentation: A Summary

1. Keep in mind that there are two valid conditional deductive arguments: asserting the antecedent and denying the consequent.

2. Also remember that there are two invalid conditional deductive arguments: denying the antecedent and asserting the consequent.

3. Differentiate between assertions of permission and assertions of obligation; a common tactic in argumentation is to state an assertion of permission as though it were an assertion of obligation.

4. In examining assertions of causality, differentiate between necessary causes, sufficient causes, and necessary and sufficient causes; a common tactic in argumentation is to present a necessary *but not sufficient* cause as though it were a sufficient cause or a necessary and sufficient cause.

5. For a deductive argument to be a sound one, it must be formally valid and every premise must be truthful. If either of these conditions is violated, the argument is worthless. It provides no support for the conclusion even if the conclusion itself is truthful.

6. Inductive arguments do not provide one with the same certainty that a truthful and valid deductive argument does. Rather, inductive arguments make a conclusion more or less probable or plausible in accordance with the quality and quantity of evidence that is presented to support the conclusion.

7. In evaluating an inductive argument, determine whether each premise or supporting reason is true or *acceptable,* whether each premise or supporting reason is *relevant* to the conclusion, and whether all of the premises or supporting reasons, taken together, provide sufficient *grounds* for the conclusion (ARG).

8. Be on the lookout for the common kinds of fallacious arguments: the ad hominem argument, poisoning the well, the slippery slope argument, the straw man argument, the false dilemma, the appeal to ignorance, and the appeal to emotion.

# Think about It: Discussion of Answers

**9.1**    The statement "A chain is only as strong as its weakest link" is more clearly applicable to deductive arguments than to inductive arguments, because deductive arguments can have no weak links. That is, for a deductive argument to be valid, all of its premises must be true and it must follow an acceptable logical form. Any violation of these requirements makes the argument worthless. On the other hand, an inductive argument consists of presenting a number of premises, each of which supports the conclusion. Some of these premises may be stronger than others, but the weaker premises do not disqualify the stronger ones.

**9.2**    The everyday argument "I deserved to have my license suspended; I was driving while drunk" may be mapped as follows:

*Premise 1*: If one drives while drunk, then one deserves to have one's license suspended.
*Premise 2*: I was driving while drunk.
*Conclusion*: I deserve to have my license suspended.

You will recognize this argument as following a valid form, asserting the antecedent.

The argument that "I know that smokers get lung cancer, but I'm safe; I don't smoke" maps like this:

*Premise 1*: If one smokes, then one may get lung cancer.
*Premise 2*: I don't smoke.
*Conclusion*: Therefore, I won't get lung cancer.

The form of this argument is denying the antecedent and is an invalid form (in this case there may be other causes of lung cancer in addition to smoking).

We can map the everyday argument "Since you won't go to Europe with me this summer, I don't think you love me" in this way:

*Premise 1*: If you love me, then you will go to Europe with me.
*Premise 2*: You won't go to Europe with me.
*Conclusion*: Therefore, you don't love me.

The form of this argument, denying the consequent, is valid. While the form is valid, you should keep in mind that the conclusion may not be truthful because premise 1 may not be truthful.

"You love me! You're going to Europe with me!" can be mapped as follows:

*Premise 1*: If you love me, then you will go to Europe with me.
*Premise 2*: You're going to Europe with me.
*Conclusion*: Therefore, you love me.

This argument is an example of asserting the consequent, and is an invalid form. That is, the person may be accompanying our logician to Europe for reasons that have nothing to do with love.

**9.3**   Under normal circumstances, eating more calories than one burns would be considered a necessary and sufficient cause of weight gain. That is, this is all one needs to do to gain weight, and, excluding unusual conditions (such as abnormal fluid retention), taking in more calories than one uses up is the only way to gain weight. Turning the knob on the drinking fountain is also a necessary and sufficient cause of starting the water to flow in a functioning drinking fountain. It is what you have to do, all that you have to do, and all that you can do to get a drink from the fountain.

Throwing a rock at a window and driving under the influence of alcohol are sufficient causes of breaking a window and losing your license, respectively. Each is sufficient to produce the specified effect, but the effects can be produced by other causes as well (such as, hitting the window with a hammer and reckless driving).

Registering for a course is a necessary cause of getting a good grade in a course in that it is something, but not the only thing, that must be done to get that grade. Obtaining a lottery ticket is also a necessary cause of winning the lottery. It is not sufficient, however, in that you must also pick the winning number and present your ticket to the lottery officials to win the prize. Maintaining the required grade point average is a necessary cause for maintaining academic eligiblility in athletics. It is not a necessary and sufficient cause, however, because athletes must also complete a specified number of academic units (courses, semester hours, or quarter hours) per year to maintain eligibility. Thus maintaining a 3.5 average while completing only four courses per year would not be sufficient to maintain academic eligibility.

**9.4**    While the president of the company and the test pilot may have relevant knowledge, they, like the athlete, are making a solicited endorsement. That is, they are being paid to work as actors in a playlet that has been written by an advertising firm. Thus, whether or not these people are giving testimony on the basis of their expertise is in question.

More credible ads are those that cite unsolicited endorsements from experts in support of their products. For example, if a car is selected as *Motor Trend's* car of the year, this selection is an unsolicited endorsement by a group of experts; that is, the experts are not in the employ of the car company or its advertising firm. Limitations on these ads are sometimes seen in the fine print of the ad. You have all probably seen one of those ads on TV during which a very brief message flashes across the screen. The almost undetectable message may read something like this: "This award was for cars in this class, subcompact coupes missing one fender." Another limitation on the credibility of unsolicited endorsements is that some products, such as movies, are evaluated by many people, and a few of them may find something to like about even an inferior product. These people, then, are the ones who are likely to be cited in the advertisement. They clearly would not represent the majority opinion concerning this product, however.

**9.5**    In general, the means based on ten scores should be closer to the mean of 115 than the means based on four scores. The fewer scores any given mean is based on, the more vulnerable is that mean to influence by extreme scores. So the majority of times this TAI is carried out, means based on four scores will fall toward the "greatest change" end of the distribution while means based on ten scores will fall toward the "least change" end of the distribution.

**9.6**    **1.** High school visitation days rarely provide students with a completely representative sample of campus life. Rather, the people who coordinate these programs do their utmost to present the college in the best possible light. Thus they recruit the most interesting teachers, the most intelligent, attractive, and articulate students, and the most socially skilled administrators to take part in these programs. Visitation days are one way a college advertises, and like other advertisements, this one is designed to put together an extremely appealing (but not necessarily completely realistic) picture of the product being marketed.

**2.** The silent majority argument presents us with a sample that is not truly known. The assumption underlying this argument, that everyone who is not in vocal opposition to the war is in support of it, is not a valid one. Some people who were personally opposed to the Vietnam war never went public in their opposition. Thus they were just as much a part of this silent majority as some people who supported the war. As we cannot distinguish silent opposers from silent supporters, we cannot conclude that we have knowledge of the sample (that is, the sample is not known).

**9.7**    The choices made will vary from college to college, but most of your choices will probably come from general education or core requirements rather than major requirements. Everyone has to take core requirements, so you are unlikely to find any one major overrepresented in your sample. Some schools allow a fair amount of latitude in satisfying core requirements, however, and your sample may be biased if you select the wrong courses under these conditions. Let's illustrate with an example. Suppose that students can satisfy science core requirements by taking anything from biochemistry to Physics for Poets. If you select the biochemistry course, you will probably have almost all science majors; if you select Physics for Poets, it is unlikely that you will have any science majors in your sample. Another bias that you should be aware of if you choose your courses from core requirements is that most core courses are taken early in a student's collegiate career. Therefore, you should be careful to choose courses that allow for adequate representation of students at all points of their collegiate careers.

**9.8**    We can reasonably assume that the candy company wants to market the product nationally. If such is the case, then the sample is unrepresentative in that it hasn't been drawn from various regions of the country, and doesn't include people from a large city, a small town, and the countryside. In addition, one has to question whether the ethnic diversity of our nation is represented in a sample drawn from one medium-sized town. The format of the survey requires a certain level of literacy and may exclude people (including young children—a significant candy-consuming group) because they cannot read or comprehend the survey. Finally, while our sample was randomly drawn, not everybody will complete the questionnaire. The problem of missing cases, discussed in Chapter 2, looms large here. This problem may be compounded by the fact that candy was offered as a reward for completing the survey. That is, such an incentive might have overloaded the sample with candy lovers, the very people who might already be disposed to use this company's products. On the other hand, people who don't ordinarily buy candy may be underrepresented in the sample, and these people are a market that the candy company would most definitely want to attract to increase sales.

**9.9**    Premise A1 is neither acceptable nor relevant: (1) it is not true (some of the people who did fall prey to the con were not poor); (2) it has no relevance to the conclusion in that the conclusion has to do with the con man's potential for rehabilitation.

Premise A2, while true and therefore acceptable, is not relevant in that it has no relation to the question of rehabilitation.

Premise A3 seems to be quite acceptable. One must have some idea of the criminal's motives to be certain of this, however. If the criminal was suffering from the psychotic delusion that he had to get money from evil elderly agents of the devil to feed starving children, would this crime still be heartless? Since we don't have direct evidence of the con man's motives, we have to infer what his motives might be. We would assume that since his cons involved careful planning and execution to be successful, he was not suffering from a psychotic disorder. We use this argument to support the contention that premise A3 is probably acceptable. The premise may have some relevance to the conclusion also, in that a person who commits premeditated and heartless crimes is likely to be harder to rehabilitate than one who commits an isolated crime of passion.

As we have indicated, premise A4 is acceptable. It also bears direct relevance to the conclusion in that both the premise and the conclusion deal with the question of rehabilitation.

Conclusion A is not sufficiently supported. We say this for two reasons: (1) the acceptable premises have established that certain kinds of criminals as well as some people who have committed certain kinds of crimes are difficult to rehabilitate, but the premises did not establish that they couldn't be rehabilitated; (2) it was not established that the con man is a sociopath.

Premises B1 and B2 not only are acceptable but also are relevant to the question of cost indicated in conclusion B.

Premise B3 is not acceptable in that it is not clearly established. For example, the authorities could protect the con man by catching the person who is threatening him. This premise, if acceptable, would be relevant to the question of cost, but since it is not acceptable, its relevance cannot be considered to support the conclusion.

Premise B4 is not acceptable in that the government is not required to guarantee the safety of all former prisoners. Being unacceptable, it cannot be considered relevant to the conclusion.

Conclusion B actually has two parts to it. The first part indicates that the con man has cost the government considerable money, and this conclusion is sufficiently supported by premises B1 and B2. The second part of conclusion B indicates that the con man will continue to cost the government considerable amounts of money. The premises relevant to this conclusion are B1, B3, and B4, and, of these, only B1 is acceptable. Thus the support for the second part of conclusion B is less strong than the support for the first part. This second part is a weakly supported conclusion.

The final conclusion lacks sufficiency of support for two reasons. First of all, it is based on conclusion A, that the con man can't be rehabilitated. As you will recall, we rejected this conclusion because it has not been sufficiently supported. Second, the final conclusion also derives from the second part of conclusion B, that the con man will continue to cost the government considerable amounts of money. We saw that this conclusion was only weakly supported. Further, what support was available for this conclusion was derived from premise B1. This premise had to do with the payments to the con man's victims, and those payments would continue whether or not the con man was put to death for his crimes. Thus, in the final analysis, even this premise loses its relevance to the conclusion.

**9.10**    The ad hominem argument most clearly violates the criterion of relevance. The father in this example does not provide relevant counterarguments to his daughter's arguments. Rather, he deflects the argument to an issue that has nothing to do with the validity of the daughter's arguments, her age and supposed immaturity. If the daughter's immaturity has in fact led her to present weak arguments, a relevant counterargument would point to the specific weaknesses in her argument rather than to her immaturity. In this example, however, it appears that the daughter's arguments are strong enough to have dear old dad running for cover in the form of a fallacious argument. Should you find yourself the target of an ad hominem argument, simply ask your opponent to point out the weaknesses in your argument rather than the weaknesses in your character.

**9.11** This example of the false dilemma violates the criterion of acceptability because the argument implies that the young faculty member doesn't like the way *anything* is done here. She may, in fact, like many things about her department and may only seek to improve those things that she sees as needing improvement. Such a colleague is to be valued rather than censured. One could also make a case for the proposition that the criterion of representativeness is violated in that the older faculty member is making a sweeping generalization that the younger faculty member doesn't like the way anything is done on the basis of his observation of only a few criticisms voiced by her.

**9.12**  ad hominem: 2, the sexist politician.
poisoning the well: 6, the weak-pointed debater.
slippery slope: 7, the irate parent.
straw man: 4, the speeding friend.
appeal to ignorance: 3, the undiagnosed hypochondriac.
appeal to emotion: 1, the peacemaking mother.
false dilemma: 5, "America, love it or leave it."

# • • • • • • • • •
# Recommended Readings

In this chapter, we have focused primarily on evaluating inductive arguments. If you feel shortchanged and would like to read further about the evaluation of deductive arguments, we recommend that you consider *Thinking Straight*, by Anthony Flew (1977). Flew, a former Royal Air Force officer (Flew flew!—Sorry about that!), has written a clear, concise, and slightly irreverent consideration of deductive logic. His book is relatively free of those pseudo-mathematical symbols and diagrams that permeate many logic texts and that cause logic shock in some students. Rather, he gives such practical advice as "Don't be snowed" and "Sort fact from bunk." Further, Flew effectively shows the reader how to follow his advice. Much of Raymond Nickerson's (1986) *Reflections on Reasoning* deals with argumentation. He provides guidelines for evaluating both deductive and inductive arguments and describes an extensive list of fallacious arguments. If reading about fallacious forms of argumentation interests you, then you should find Nicholas Capaldi's (1979) book, *The Art of Deception*, fascinating. He describes just about every dirty trick possible in argumentation.

Ralph Johnson and J. Anthony Blair (1977) come to the rescue by helping readers protect themselves against these dirty tricks. Their book, *Logical Self-defense,* is a very readable and nontechnical exposition of the use of both deductive and inductive reasoning to defend oneself against the onslaughts of everyday persuasive rhetoric. Particular emphasis is given to self-defense against media bombardment, and lots of practical, real-life examples and good exercises are provided. Finally, Robert Cialdini (1988), in *Influence: Science and Practice,* goes beyond the consideration of argumentation per se to examine additional strategies of social persuasion that people may use to influence the decisions of others. He not only describes these strategies, he also proposes specific defenses against them.

# CONCLUSION

# Epilogue

**Passivity is the opposite of thought.**

John Dewey
(American philosopher and educator, 1859–1952)

# •••••••••
# Reflecting on Thinking and Thinking Reflectively

The philosopher and educator John Dewey (1933, p. 4) told an amusing anecdote to illustrate what effective or critical thinking is *not*. It seems that a New Englander whom everyone knew to be of only marginal intelligence was seeking election to public office in his community. Stung by the criticism he heard, he decided to tackle it boldly in his next campaign speech. "I hear you don't believe I know enough to hold office," he said to the assembled voters. "I wish you to understand that I am thinking about something or other most of the time."

Dewey's story makes the point that everyone, or should we say *anyone*, thinks. We can assume that everyone thinks about something most of the time. It is obvious that what we think about is not always important or significant. We are all given to uncontrolled and unregulated thoughts, which often seem to come to us at random as we go about our daily business. As Dewey (1933) notes, "More of our waking life than most of us would care to admit is whiled away in this inconsequential trifling with mental pictures, random recollections, pleasant but unfounded hopes, flitting half-developed impressions" (p. 4).

The inconsequential mental activity in which we engage may have a purpose. The best-built car on the road is not capable of cruising endlessly at high speed; it needs pit stops for fueling and to let the engine cool, as well as to give the driver a chance to relax. During these frequent and necessary stops the engine is put in neutral and allowed to rest. Periods of inconsequential mental activity may be necessary to prevent the mental fatigue and burnout that can be the consequence of prolonged high-performance mental activity. There is no doubt that we often get some pleasure from these periods of uncontrolled thinking. Who among us wants to give up the opportunity to daydream or to think "crazy thoughts"? During these times thinking typically does not have direction; it is usually not organized, nor is it likely to be systematic. The mind is in neutral.

There are times, of course, when we need to move out of neutral in order to get up to speed. The starting signal, according to Dewey (1933), is a state of doubt, perplexity, mental difficulty, or confusion. Once encountered, this state of perplexity may lead to the formation of some tentative plan or theory that will resolve the perplexity or provide a solution for a problem. This kind of thinking, which Dewey called *reflective thinking,* is often considered the same as what we and others have called critical thinking. "Critical thinking has to do with whether individuals think reflectively, rather than simply accepting statements and carrying out procedures without significant understanding and evaluation" (Greeno, 1989, p. 139). We think reflectively when we consider in a thoughtful and perceptive manner the problems that come within the range of our everyday experience (Glaser, 1985). Many people also agree with Dewey's suggestion that teaching reflective thinking should be a major goal of education (Baron, 1981). Certainly we do, as we hope this book has made clear.

It was Dewey, you may remember from Chapter 1, who argued that if he had to choose between the personal traits that contribute to the *readiness* to consider thoughtfully the subjects that come within one's range of experience and the knowledge of principles of reasoning (as well as the skills necessary to use these principles), he would opt for the former. Not everyone who experiences a difficult problem, a perplexing situation, or a state of doubt responds in in a reflective manner. Not everyone, in other words, is sufficiently critical, is willing to endure the trouble of searching or a protracted period of doubt (Dewey, 1933). Without the disposition to engage in reflective thinking, we do not seek solutions to our problems, we remain perplexed by situations in which we find ourselves, and our doubts go unresolved.

## Critical Thinking: A Call to Action

Reflective thinking is, most important, *active* thinking. It *requires* action. Once begun, reflective thinking is carried along, according to Dewey, by the demand for a solution or resolution. It requires, as you saw in Chapter 1, many personal traits that lead to the thinker's active participation in the process: intellectual curiosity, objectivity, open-mindedness, flexibility, intellectual skepticism, intellectual honesty, being systematic, persistence, decisiveness, and respect for other viewpoins (D'Angelo, 1971). The active nature of reflective or critical thinking is seen in the ways Dewey (1933) described this kind of thinking. Reflective thinking

. . . consists in *turning a subject over* in the mind and giving it serious and consecutive consideration (p. 3).
. . . *aims* at a conclusion (p. 5).
. . . *impels* to inquiry (p. 7).
. . . *impels belief* on evidence (p. 11).

Only if we are ready and willing *actively* to engage in a thoughtful way the problems and subjects that come within our range of experience can we become critical thinkers.

In this book we have attempted to convince you that everyday thinking can be given direction by appropriate principles (strategies, guidelines, tactics, and other prescriptions) for effective thinking. We have introduced many examples of such principles. When we reflect on those principles that are relevant to a particular subject or problem that comes within our everyday experience, we are beginning to think critically. Whether the problem or subject is associated with determining causation, understanding our own or another's behavior, analyzing beliefs, deciding about what we know, solving problems, making decisions, or some other everyday experience, serious consideration of what principle or principles of effective thinking might apply in this situation moves our mind out of neutral. By expending the effort required to search actively for effective principles that are relevant to a particular everyday domain we can get up to speed.

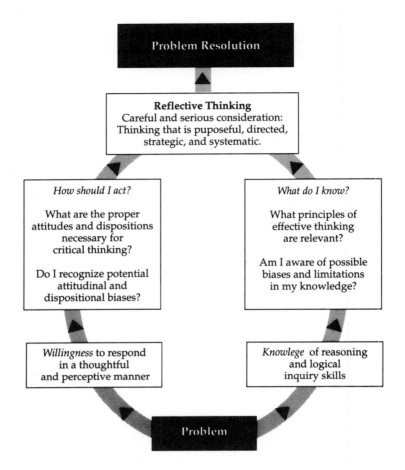

**Figure 10.1**    A Model of Critical Thinking

The *process* of thinking critically that you have practiced should now be clear. It is summarized in Figure 10.1. A problem (a difficult question, a state of doubt, a perplexing set of circumstances) comes within the range of your experience. In order to think critically, you must possess two complementary sets of characteristics. First, the proper attitudes or dispositions must be present. A critical thinker must be disposed to act in certain ways: to keep an open mind, to be intellectually honest, to avoid jumping to conclusions, and so forth. The critical thinker is *set* to respond in a thoughtful and perceptive manner. Second, a critical thinker is willing to search actively for and give careful consideration to knowledge that is relevant to the problem at hand. As part of this act of reflective thinking, the critical thinker will ask: "What do I know about this problem? What do I still need to know? What principles (strategies, tactics, etc.) am I familiar with? How should my thinking be directed?"

By applying principles of effective and adaptive thinking and by working to incorporate the right attitudes you can continue to develop the critical thinking skills to which you have been introduced in this book. You will be able to monitor your progress by observing the number of everyday problems that you have resolved successfully. However, because life continually throws us into new situations and introduces us to new problems, you may need to modify and refine the principles that you have learned. When you encounter problems in specialized domains, such as mathematics, history, and the sciences, you will find it necessary to learn and apply new principles and strategies of effective thinking. Developing an ability to think critically is a lifelong endeavor.

# References

Abramson, L. Y. (Ed.) (1988). *Social cognition and clinical psychology: A synthesis.* New York: Guilford Press.

Abramson, L. Y., Seligman, M. E. P., & Teasdale, J. D. (1978). Learned helplessness in humans: Critique and reformulation. *Journal of Abnormal Psychology, 87,* 49–74.

Alloy, L. B., & Abramson, L. Y. (1979). Judgment of contingency in depressed and nondepressed students: Sadder but wiser? *Journal of Experimental Psychology: General, 108,* 441–485.

Anderson, N. H. (1974). Cognitive algebra: Integration theory applied to social attribution. In L. Berkowitz (Ed.), *Advances in experimental social psychology,* Vol. 7 (pp. 1–101). New York: Academic Press.

Arkes, H. R. (1981). Impediments to accurate clinical judgment and possible ways to minimize their impact. *Journal of Consulting and Clinical Psychology, 49,* 323–330.

Arkes, H. R., Christensen, C., Lai, C., & Blumer, C. (1987). Two methods of reducing overconfidence. *Organizational Behavior and Human Decision Processes, 39,* 133–144.

Arkes, H. R., & Hammond, K. R. (Eds.). (1986). *Judgment and decision making: An interdisciplinary reader.* New York: Cambridge University Press.

Aronson, E. (1984). *The social animal.* New York: W. H. Freeman.

Asch, S. E. (1952). *Social psychology.* Englewood Cliffs, N.J.: Prentice-Hall.

Baron, J. (1981). Reflective thinking as a goal of education. *Intelligence, 5,* 291–309.

Baron, J. B., & Sternberg, R. J. (Eds.) (1987). *Teaching thinking skills: Theory and practice.* New York: W. H. Freeman.

Baron, R. A., & Byrne, D. (1987). *Social psychology: Understanding human interaction.* Boston: Allyn & Bacon.

Baum, A., Fisher, J. D., & Singer, J. E. (1985). *Social psychology.* New York: Random House.

Benassi, V. A., Singer, B., & Reynolds, C. B. (1980). Occult belief: Seeing is believing. *Journal for the Scientific Study of Religion, 19,* 337–349.

Benbow, C. P. (1988). Sex differences in mathematical reasoning ability in intellectually talented preadolescents: Their nature, effects, and possible causes. *Behavioral and Brain Sciences, 11,* 169–232.

Benderson, A. (1984). *Critical thinking.* Princeton, N.J.: Educational Testing Service.

Berglas, S. (1985). Why did this happen to me? *Psychology Today, 19,* 44–48.

Berglas, S., & Jones, E. E. (1978). Drug choice as a self-handicapping strategy in response to noncontingent success. *Journal of Personality and Social Psychology, 36,* 405–417.

Bloom, B. S., Engelhart, M. D., Furst, E. J., Hill, W. H., & Krathwohl, D. R. (1956). *Taxonomy of educational objectives. Handbook I: Cognitive domain.* New York: McKay.

Boring, E. G. (1969). Perspective: Artifact and control. In R. Rosenthal & R. L. Rosnow (Eds.), *Artifact in behavioral research* (pp. 1–11). New York: Academic Press.

Bower, G. H., Black, J. B. & Turner, T. J. (1979). Scripts in memory for text. *Cognitive Psychology, 11,* 177–220.

Bower, G. H., & Morrow, D. G. (1990). Mental models in narrative comprehension. *Science, 247,* 44–48.

Bransford, J. D., & Johnson, M. K. (1972). Contextual prerequisites for understanding: Some investigations of comprehension and recall. *Journal of Verbal Learning and Verbal Behavior, 11,* 717–726.

Bransford, J. D., Sherwood, R., Vye, N., & Rieser, J. (1986). Teaching thinking and problem solving. *American Psychologist, 41,* 1078–1089.

Bransford, J. D., & Stein, B. S. (1984). *The IDEAL problem solver: A guide for improving thinking, learning, and creativity.* New York: W. H. Freeman.

Brehmer, B. (1980). In one word: Not from experience. *Acta Psychologica, 45,* 223–241.

Brigham, J. C. (1986). *Social psychology.* Boston: Little, Brown.

Brown, A. L., & Palincsar, A. S. (1982). Inducing strategic learning from texts by means of informed self-control training. *Topics in Learning and Learning Disabilities, 2,* 1–17.

Burt, M. R. (1980). Cultural myths and supports for rape. *Journal of Personality and Social Psychology, 38,* 217–230.

Campbell, D. T., & Stanley, J. C. (1963). *Experimental and quasi-experimental designs for research.* Chicago: Rand McNally.

Capaldi, N. (1979). *The art of deception.* Buffalo, N.Y.: Prometheus.

Cederblom, J., & Paulsen, D. W. (1986). *Critical reasoning: Understanding and criticizing arguments and theories.* Belmont, Calif.: Wadsworth.

Chaffee, J. (1988). *Thinking critically.* Boston: Houghton Mifflin.

Chapman, L. J. (1967). Illusory correlation in observational report. *Journal of Verbal Learning and Verbal Behavior, 6,* 151–155.

Cheng, P. W., & Holyoak, K. J. (1985). Pragmatic reasoning schemas. *Cognitive Psychology, 17,* 391–416.

Cheng, P. W., Holyoak, K. J., Nisbett, R. E., & Oliver, L. M. (1986). Pragmatic versus syntactic approaches to training deductive reasoning. *Cognitive Psychology, 18,* 293–328.

Cialdini, R. B. (1988). *Influence: Science and practice.* Glenview, Ill: Scott, Foresman.

Clement, J. (1988). Observed methods for generating analogies in scientific problem solving. *Cognitive Science, 12,* 563–586.

Collins, A., & Smith, E. E. (1982). Teaching the process of reading comprehension. In D. K. Detterman & R. J. Sternberg (Eds.), *How and how much can intelligence be increased?* (pp. 173–185). Norwood, N.J.: Ablex.

Copi, I. M. (1986). *Informal logic.* New York: Macmillan.

Cordaro, L., & Ison, J. R. (1963). Observer bias in classical conditioning of the planarian. *Psychological Reports, 13,* 787–789.

Crystal, J. C., & Bolles, R. N . (1974). *Where do I go from here with my life? A very systematic, practical, and effective life/work planning manual for students, instructors, counselors, career seekers, and career changers.* Berkeley, Calif.: Ten Speed Press.

Curt, C. L., & Zechmeister, E. B. (1984). Primacy, recency, and the availability heuristic. *Bulletin of the Psychonomic Society, 22,* 177–179.

Damer, T. E. (1987). *Attacking faulty reasoning.* Belmont, Calif.: Wadsworth.

D'Angelo, E. (1971). *The teaching of critical thinking.* Amsterdam: B. R. Gruner.

Darley, J. M., & Fazio, R. H. (1980). Expectancy confirmation processes arising in the social interaction sequence. *American Psychologist, 35,* 867–881.

Dawes, R. M. (1979). The robust beauty of improper linear models in decision making. *American Psychologist, 34,* 571–582.

Dawes, R. M. (1988). *Rational choice in an uncertain world.* New York: Harcourt Brace Jovanovich.

Dawes, R. M., & Corrigan, B. (1974). Linear models in decision making. *Psychological Bulletin, 81,* 95–106.

Dewey, J. (1933). *How we think.* Lexington, Mass.: D. C. Heath.

Diener, C. T., & Dweck, C. S. (1978). An analysis of learned helplessness: Continuous changes in performance, strategy, and achievement cognitions following failure. *Journal of Personality and Social Psychology, 36,* 451–462.

Duncan, C. P. (1961). Attempts to influence performance on an insight problem. *Psychological Reports, 9,* 35–42.

Duncker, K. (1926). A qualitative (experimental and theoretical) study of productive thinking (solving of comprehensible problems). *Pedagogical Seminary, 33,* 642–708.

Duncker, K. (1945). On problem-solving. *Psychological Monographs, 58* (Whole No. 270).

Dweck, C. S. (1975). The role of expectations and attributions in the alleviation of learned helplessness. *Journal of Personality and Social Psychology, 31,* 674–685.

Easton, A. (1976). *Decision making: A short course for professionals.* New York: Wiley.

Edwards, W., & Newman, J. R. (1982). *Multiattribute evaluation.* Beverly Hills, Calif.: Sage.

Einhorn, H. J., & Hogarth, R. M. (1986). Judging probable cause. *Psychological Bulletin, 99,* 3–19.

Ellis, A. (1962). *Reason and emotion in psychotherapy.* Secaucus, N.J.: Citadel Press.

Ellis, A., & Harper, R. A. (1975). *A new guide to rational living.* North Hollywood, Calif.: Wilshire.

Ennis, R. H. (1987). A taxonomy of critical thinking dispositions and abilities. In J. B. Baron & R. J. Sternberg (Eds.), *Teaching thinking skills: Theory and practice* (pp. 9–26). New York: W. H. Freeman.

Epstein, W., Glenberg, A. M., & Bradley, M. M. (1984). Coactivation and comprehension: Contribution of text variables to the illusion of knowing. *Memory & Cognition, 12,* 355–360.

Fazio, R. H., Effrein, E. A., & Falender, V. J. (1981). Self-perceptions following social interaction. *Journal of Personality and Social Psychology, 41,* 232–242.

Festinger, L., Riecken, H., & Schachter, S. (1956). *When prophecy fails.* Minneapolis: University of Minnesota Press.

Fischhoff, B. (1975). Hindsight ≠ foresight: The effect of outcome knowledge on judgment under uncertainty. *Journal of Experimental Psychology: Human Perception and Performance, 1,* 288–299.

Fischhoff, B. (1977). Perceived informativeness of facts. *Journal of Experimental Psychology: Human Perception and Performance, 3,* 349–358.

Fischhoff, B., & Beyth, R. (1975). "I knew it would happen": Remembered probabilities of once-future things. *Organizational Behavior and Human Performance, 13,* 1–16.

Fischhoff, B., Slovic, P., & Lichtenstein, S. (1977). Knowing with certainty: The appropriateness of extreme confidence. *Journal of Experimental Psychology: Human Perception and Performance, 3,* 552–564.

Fiske, S. T., & Taylor, S. E. (1984). *Social cognition.* Reading, Mass.: Addison-Wesley.

Flavell, J. H. (1979). Metacognition and cognitive monitoring: A new area of cognitive-developmental inquiry. *American Psychologist, 34,* 906–911.

Flew, A. (1977). *Thinking straight*. Buffalo, N.Y.: Prometheus.

Forstelling, F. (1985). Attributional retraining: A review. *Psychological Bulletin, 98*, 495–512.

Freedman, J. L., Sears, P. O., & Carlsmith, J. M. (1981). *Social psychology*. Englewood Cliffs, N.J.: Prentice-Hall.

Friedrich-Cofer, L., & Huston, A. C. (1986). Television violence and aggression: The debate continues. *Psychological Bulletin, 100*, 364–371.

Gergen, K. J., & Gergen, M. M. (1981). *Social psychology*. New York: Harcourt Brace Jovanovich.

Gick, M. L., & Holyoak, K. J. (1983). Schema induction and analogical transfer. *Cognitive Psychology, 15*, 1–38.

Glaser, E. M. (1985). Critical thinking: Education for responsible citizenship in a democracy. *National Forum, 65*, 24–27.

Glaser, R. (1984). Education and thinking: The role of knowledge. *American Psychologist, 39*, 93–104.

Glass, A. L., & Holyoak, K. J. (1986). *Cognition* (2nd ed.). New York: Random House.

Glenberg, A. M., Sanocki, T., Epstein, W., & Morris, C. (1987). Enhancing calibration of comprehension. *Journal of Experimental Psychology: General, 116*, 119–136.

Glenberg, A. M., Wilkinson, A. C., & Epstein, W. (1982). The illusion of knowing: Failure in the self-assessment of comprehension. *Memory & Cognition, 10*, 597–602.

Goffman, E. (1959). *The presentation of self in everyday life*. Garden City, N.Y.: Doubleday.

Golin, S., Terrell, F., Weitz, J., & Drost, P. L. (1979). The illusion of control among depressed patients. *Journal of Abnormal Psychology, 88*, 454–457.

Gordon, W. J. (1961). *Synectics*. New York: Harper & Row.

Greeno, J. G. (1989). A perspective on thinking. *American Psychologist, 44*, 134–141.

Halpern, D. F. (1989). *Thought and knowledge: An introduction to critical thinking*. Hillsdale, N.J.: Erlbaum.

Hamilton, D. L., Dugan, P. M., & Trolier, T. K. (1985). The formation of stereotypic beliefs: Further evidence for distinctiveness-based illusory correlations. *Journal of Personality and Social Psychology, 48*, 5–17.

Hammond, E. C., & Auerbach, O. (1971). Effects of cigarette smoking on dogs. *Cancer Journal for Clinicians, 21*, 78–94.

Hasher, L., Goldstein, D., & Toppino, T. (1977). Frequency and the conference of referential validity. *Journal of Verbal Learning and Verbal Behavior, 16*, 107–112.

Hastie, R. (1984). Causes and effects of causal attributions. *Journal of Personality and Social Psychology, 46*, 44–56.

Holland, J. H., Holyoak, K. J., Nisbett, R. E., & Thagard, P. R. (1986). *Induction: Processes of inference, learning, and discovery*. Cambridge, Mass.: MIT Press.

Holyoak, K. J., & Koh, K. (1987). Surface and structural similarity in analogical transfer. *Memory & Cognition, 15*, 332–340.

Howard, J. W., & Rothbart, M. (1980). Social categorization and memory for in-group and out-group behavior. *Journal of Personality and Social Psychology, 38*, 301–310.

Hoyt, M. F., & Janis, I. L. (1975). Increasing adherence to a stressful decision via a motivational balance-sheet procedure: A field experiment. *Journal of Personality and Social Psychology, 31*, 833–839.

Huck, S. W., & Sandler, H. M. (1979). *Rival hypotheses*. New York: Harper & Row.

Hume, D. (1969). *A treatise on human nature*. (E. C. Mossner, Ed.). Oxford: Clarendon. (Original work published 1739.)

Janis, I. L. (1982). Decision making under stress. In L. Goldberger & S. Breznitz (Eds.), *Handbook of stree: Theoretical and clinical aspects* (pp. 69–87). New York: Free Press.

Janis, I. L., & Mann, L. (1977). *Decision making: A psychological analysis of conflict, choice, and commitment.* New York: Free Press.

Janoff-Bulman, R. (1979). Characterological versus behavioral self-blame: Inquiries into depression and rape. *Journal of Personality and Social Psychology, 37,* 1798–1809.

Jenkins, J. R., & Pany, D. (1981). Instructional variables in reading comprehension. In J. T. Guthrie (Ed.), *Comprehension and teaching: Research reviews* (pp. 163–202). Newark, Del.: Instructional Reading Assoc.

Johnson, J. E., Petzel, T. P., Hartney, L. M., & Morgan, R. A. (1983). Recall and importance ratings of completed and uncompleted tasks as a function of depression. *Cognitive Therapy and Research, 7,* 51–56.

Johnson, J. E., Petzel, T. P., & Mascari, C. (1987, May). Recall of criticisms of self or partner as a function of depression. Midwestern Psychological Association Convention, Chicago.

Johnson, J. E., Petzel, T. P., & Munic, D. (1986). An examination of the relative contribution of depression versus global psychopathology to depressive attributional style in a clinical population. *Journal of Social and Clinical Psychology, 4,* 107–113.

Johnson, R. H., & Blair, J. A. (1977). *Logical self-defense.* New York: McGraw-Hill Ryerson.

Jones, E. E., & Berglas, S. (1978). Control of attributions about the self through self-handicapping strategies: The appeal of alcohol and the role of underachievement. *Personality and Social Psychology Bulletin, 4,* 200–206.

Jones, E. E., & Harris, V. A. (1967). The attribution of attitudes. *Journal of Experimental Social Psychology, 3,* 2–24.

Jones, E. E., & Nisbett, R. E. (1971). The actor and the observer: Divergent perceptions of the causes of behavior. In E. E. Jones, D. Kanouse, H. H. Kelley, R. E. Nisbett, S. Valins, & B. Weiner (Eds.), *Attribution: Perceiving the causes of behavior* (pp. 79–94). Morristown, N.J.: General Learning Press.

Kahane, H. (1984). *Logic and contemporary rhetoric: The use of reason in everyday life.* Belmont, Calif.: Wadsworth.

Kahneman, D., & Tversky, A. (1972). Subjective probability: A judgment of representativeness. *Cognitive Psychology, 3,* 430–454.

Kahneman, D., & Tversky, A. (1973). On the psychology of prediction. *Psychological Review, 80,* 237–251.

Kail, R. (1990). *The development of memory in children* (3rd ed.). New York: W. H. Freeman.

Kasarda, J. D. (1976). The use of census data in secondary analysis: The context of ecological discovery. In M. P. Golden (Ed.), *The research experience* (pp. 424–431). Itasca, Ill.: F. E. Peacock.

Kelley, H. H. (1973). The processes of causal attribution. *American Psychologist, 28,* 107–128.

Kidder, L. H., & Judd, C. M. (1986). *Research methods in social relations.* New York: Holt, Rinehart & Winston.

Kimble, G. A. (1978). *How to use (and misuse) statistics.* Englewood Cliffs, N.J.: Prentice-Hall.

King, J. F., Zechmeister, E. B., & Shaughnessy, J. J. (1980). Judgments of knowing: The influence of retrieval practice. *American Journal of Psychology, 93,* 329–343.

Klare, R. (1990). Ghosts make news. *Skeptical Inquirer, 14,* 363–371.

Kolditz, T. A., & Arkin, R. M. (1982). An impression management interpretation of the self-handicapping strategy. *Journal of Personality and Social Psychology, 43,* 492–502.

Koriat, A., Lichtenstein, S., & Fischhoff, B. (1980). Reasons for confidence. *Journal of Experimental Psychology: Human Learning and Memory, 6,* 107–118.

Kuhn, D., Amsel, E., O'Loughlin, M., Schauble, L., Leadbeater, B., & Yotive, W. (1988). *The development of scientific thinking skills.* San Diego: Academic Press.

Kuhn, D., Pennington, N., & Leadbeater, B. (1983). Adult thinking in developmental perspective. In P. B. Baltes & O. G. Brim, Jr. (Eds.), *Life-span development and behavior,* Vol. 5 (pp. 157–195). New York: Academic Press.

Kurfiss, J. G. (1988). *Critical thinking: Theory, research, practice, and possibilities.* ASHE-ERIC Higher Education Report no. 2. Washington, D.C.: Association for the Study of Higher Education.

Langer, E., Blank, A., & Chanowitz, B. (1978). The mindlessness of ostensibly thoughtful action: The role of "placebic" information in interpersonal interaction. *Journal of Personality and Social Psychology, 36,* 635–642.

Langer, E. J. (1989). *Mindfulness.* Reading, Mass.: Addison-Wesley.

Langer, E. J., & Piper, A. I. (1987). The prevention of mindlessness. *Journal of Personality and Social Psychology, 53,* 280–287.

Leary, M., & Miller, R. S. (1986). *Social psychology and dysfunctional behavior: Origins, diagnosis, and treatment.* New York: Springer-Verlag.

Leary, M. R. (1981). The distorted nature of hindsight. *Journal of Social Psychology, 115,* 25–29.

Leary, M. R., & Shepperd, J. A. (1986). Behavioral self-handicaps versus self-reported handicaps: A conceptual note. *Journal of Personality and Social Psychology, 51,* 1265–1268.

Lerner, M. J. (1970). The desire for justice and reactions to victims. In J. R. MaCaulay & L. Berkowitz (Eds.)., *Altruism and helping behavior* (pp. 205–229). New York: Academic Press.

Lerner, M. J., & Miller, D. T. (1978). Just-world research and the attribution process: Looking back and ahead. *Psychological Bulletin, 85,* 1030–1051.

Levine, M. (1988). *Effective problem solving.* Englewood Cliffs, N.J.: Prentice-Hall.

Lichtenstein, S., & Fischhoff, B. (1980). Training for calibration. *Organizational Behavior and Human Performance, 26,* 149–171.

Lichtenstein, S., Fischhoff, B., & Phillips, L. D. (1982). Calibration of probabilities: The state of the art to 1980. In D. Kahneman, P. Slovic, & A. Tversky (Eds.), *Judgment under uncertainty: Heuristics and biases* (pp. 306–334). Cambridge: Cambridge University Press.

Linville, P. W. (1982). The complexity-extremity effect and age-based stereotyping. *Journal of Personality and Social Psychology, 42,* 193–211.

Linville, P. W., & Jones, E. E. (1980). Polarized appraisals of out-group members. *Journal of Personality and Social Psychology, 38,* 689–703.

Lockard, J. S., & Paulhus, D. L. (Eds.) (1988). *Self-deception: An adaptive mechanism?* Englewood Cliffs, N.J.: Prentice-Hall.

Loftus, E. F. (1979). The malleability of human memory. *American Scientist, 67,* 312–320.

Lovelace, E . A. (1984). Metamemory: Monitoring future recallability during study. *Journal of Experimental Psychology: Learning, Memory, and Cognition, 10,* 756–766.

Luchins, A. S., & Luchins, E. H. (1950). New Experimental attempts at preventing mechanization in problem solving. *Journal of General Psychology, 42,* 279–297.

Mackie, J. L. (1974). *The cement of the universe: A study of causation.* Oxford: Clarendon.

Maier, N. R. F. (1931). Reasoning in humans: II. The solution of a problem and its appearance in consciousness. *Journal of Comparative Psychology, 12,* 181–194.

Maier, N. R. F., & Janzen, J. C. (1968). Functional values as aids and distractors in problem solving. *Psychological Reports, 22,* 1021–1034.

Maki, R. H., Foley, J. M., Kajer, W. K., Thompson, R. C., & Willert, M. G. (1990). Increased processing enhances calibration of comprehension. *Journal of Experimental Psychology: Learning, Memory, and Cognition, 16,* 609–616.

Mann, L. (1972). Use of a "balance sheet" procedure to improve the quality of personal decision making: A field experiment with college applicants. *Journal of Vocational Behavior, 2,* 291–300.

Marks, D., & Kammann, R. (1980). *The psychology of the psychic.* Buffalo, N.Y.: Prometheus.

Marlatt, G. A. (1983). The controlled drinking controversy: A commentary. *American Psychologist, 38,* 1097–1110.

Mayer, R. E. (1983). *Thinking, problem solving, cognition.* New York: W. H. Freeman.

Mill, J. S. (1950). *Philosophy of scientific method* (E. Nagel, Ed.). New York: Hafner. (Original work published 1843.)

Miller, G. A. (1956). The magical number seven plus or minus two: Some limits on our capacity for processing information. *Psychological Review, 63,* 81–97.

Miller, J. D. (1986, May). Some new measures of scientific illiteracy. Paper presented at the meeting of the American Association for the Advancement of Science, Philadelphia.

Mischel, W. (1973). Toward a cognitive social learning reconceptualization of personality. *Psychological Review, 80,* 252–283.

Mischel, W. (1986). *Introduction to personality: A new look.* New York: Holt, Rinehart & Winston.

Missimer, C. A. (1986). *Good arguments: An introduction to critical thinking.* Englewood Cliffs, N.J.: Prentice-Hall.

Morris, C. C. (1990). Retrieval processes underlying confidence in comprehension judgments. *Journal of Experimental Psychology: Human Learning, Memory, and Cognition, 16,* 223–232.

Myers, D. (1987). *Social psychology* (2nd ed.) New York: McGraw-Hill.

Neimark, E. D. (1987). *Adventures in thinking.* New York: Harcourt Brace Jovanovich.

Newell, A., & Simon, H. A. (1972). *Human problem solving.* Englewood Cliffs, N.J.: Prentice-Hall.

Nickerson, R. S. (1987). Why teach thinking? In J. B. Baron & R. J. Sternberg (Eds.), *Teaching thinking skills: Theory and practice* (pp. 27–37). New York: W. H. Freeman.

Nickerson, R. S. (1988). *Reflections on reasoning.* Hillsdale, N.J.: Erlbaum.

Nickerson, R. S., Perkins, D. N., & Smith, E. E. (1985). *The teaching of thinking.* Hillsdale, N.J.: Erlbaum.

Nisbett, R., & Ross, L. (1980). *Human inference: Strategies and shortcomings of social judgment.* Englewood Cliffs, N.J.: Prentice-Hall.

Nisbett, R. E., Fong, G. T., Lehman, D. R., & Cheng, P. W. (1987). Teaching reasoning. *Science, 238,* 625–631.

Nyberg, S. E. (1975). Comprehension and long-term retention of prose passages. Ph.D. dissertation, State University of New York at Stony Brook.

Owings, R. A., Petersen, G. A., Bransford, J. D., Morris, C. D., & Stein, B. S. (1980). Spontaneous monitoring and regulation of learning: A comparison of successful and less successful fifth graders. *Journal of Educational Psychology, 72,* 250–256.

Park, B., & Rothbart, M. (1982). Perception of out-group homogeneity and levels of social categorization: Memory for the subordinate attributes of in-group and out-group members. *Journal of Personality and Social Psychology, 42,* 1051–1068.

Paulos, J. A. (1988). *Innumeracy: Mathematical illiteracy and its consequences.* New York: Hill & Wang.

Perkins, D. N. (1986). Thinking frames. *Educational Leadership, 43,* 4–10.

Perkins, D. N. (1987). Thinking frames: An integrative perspective on teaching cognitive skills. In J. B. Baron & R. J. Sternberg (Eds.), *Teaching thinking skills: Theory and practice* (pp. 41–61). New York: W. H. Freeman.

Perry, W. G., Jr. (1968). *Patterns of development in thought and values of students in a liberal arts college: A validation of a scheme.* Cambridge, Mass.: Harvard University (ERIC Document Reproduction Service No. ED 024 315).

Perry, W. G., Jr. (1970). *Forms of intellectual and ethical development in the college years: A scheme.* New York: Holt, Rinehart & Winston.

Peterson, C., & Seligman, M. E. P. (1984). Causal explanations as a risk factor for depression: Theory and evidence. *Psychological Review, 91,* 347–374.

Pettigrew, T. F. (1979). The ultimate attribution error: Extending Allport's cognitive analysis of prejudice. *Personality and Social Psychology Bulletin, 5,* 461–476.

Pittman, T. S., & Heller, J. F. (1987). Social motivation. *Annual Review of Psychology, 38,* 461–489.

Polya, G. (1971). *How to solve it* (2nd ed.). Princeton, N.J.: Princeton University Press.

Pratt, M. W., Luszcz, M. A., MacKenzie-Keating, S., & Manning, A. (1982). Thinking about stories: The story schema in metacognition. *Journal of Verbal Learning and Verbal Behavior, 21,* 493–505.

Randi, J. (1975). *The magic of Uri Geller.* New York: Ballantine.

Randi, J. (1986). *Flim-flam: Psychics, ESP, unicorns, and other delusions.* Buffalo, N.Y.: Prometheus.

Raps, C. S., Peterson, C., Reinhard, K. E., Abramson, L. Y., & Seligman, M. E. P. (1982). Attributional style among depressed patients. *Journal of Abnormal Psychology, 91,* 102–108.

Reeder, G. D. (1985). Implicit relations between dispositions and behaviors: Effects on dispositional attribution. In J. H. Harvey & G. Weary (Eds.), *Attribution: Basic issues and applications* (pp. 87–116). New York: Academic Press.

Rhodewalt, F., Saltzman, A. T., & Wittmer, J. (1984). Self-handicapping among competitive athletes: The role of practice in self-esteem protection. *Basic and Applied Social Psychology, 5,* 197–209.

Rodin, J., & Langer, E. J. (1977). Long-term effects of a control-relevant intervention with the institutionalized aged. *Journal of Personality and Social Psychology, 35,* 897–902.

Rosenthal, R. (1966). *Experimenter effects in behavioral research.* New York: Appleton-Century-Crofts.

Rosenthal, R., & Jacobson, L. F. (1968). *Pygmalion in the classroom.* New York: Holt, Rinehart & Winston.

Ross, L. (1977). The intuitive psychologist and his shortcomings: Distortions in the attribution process. In L. Berkowitz (Ed.), *Advances in experimental social psychology,* Vol. 10 (pp. 173–220). New York: Academic Press.

Rothbart, M., Evans, M., & Fulero, S. (1979). Recall for confirming events: Memory processes and the maintenance of social stereotypes. *Journal of Experimental Social Psychology, 15,* 343–355.

Rotter, J. B. (1966). Generalized expectancies for internal versus external control of reinforcement. *Psychological Monographs, 80* (Whole No. 609).

Ruggerio, V. R. (1984). *The art of thinking: A guide to critical and creative thought.* New York: Harper & Row.

Rusch, K. M. (1984). The effectiveness of study skills training for students of different personality types and achievement levels. Ph.D. dissertation, Loyola University, Chicago.

Ryan, M. P. (1984a). Conceptions of prose coherence: Individual differences in epistemological standards. *Journal of Educational Psychology, 76,* 1226–1238.

Ryan, M. P. (1984b). Monitoring text comprehension: Individual differences in epistemological standards. *Journal of Educational Psychology, 76,* 248–258.

Sagan, C. (1987, February 1). The fine art of baloney. *Parade,* pp. 12–13.

Schneider, D. J. (1973). Implicit personality theory: A review. *Psychological Bulletin, 79,* 294–309.

Schoenfeld, A. H. (1983). Beyond the purely cognitive: Belief systems, social cognitions, and metacognitions as driving forces in intellectual performance. *Cognitive Science, 7,* 329–363.

Shaughnessy, J. J., & Zechmeister, E. B. (1990). *Research methods in psychology* (2nd ed.). New York: McGraw-Hill.

Siegler, R. S. (1989). Mechanisms of cognitive development. *Annual Review of Psychology, 40,* 353–379.

Simon, H. A. (1953). *Models of man.* New York: Wiley.

Simon, H. A. (1973). The structure of ill-structured problems. *Artificial Intelligence, 4,* 181–201.

Simon, H. A. (1978). Information-processing theory of human problem solving. In W. K. Estes (Ed.), *Handbook of learning and cognitive processes,* Vol. 5, *Human information processing* (pp. 271–295). Hillsdale, N.J.: Erlbaum.

Simon, H. A. (1980). Problem solving and education. In D. T. Tuma & F. Reif (Eds.), *Problem solving and education: Issues in teaching and research* (pp. 81–96). Hillsdale, N.J.: Erlbaum.

Simon, H. A. (1981). Studying human intelligence by creating artificial intelligence. *American Scientist, 69,* 300–309.

Simon, S. B., Howe, L. W., & Kirschenbaum, H. (1972). *Values clarification: A handbook of practical strategies for teachers and students.* New York: Dodd, Mead and Co.

Singer, B., & Benassi, V. A. (1981). Occult beliefs. *American Scientist, 69,* 49–55.

Sloan, T. S. (1986). *Deciding: Self-deception in life choices.* New York: Methuen.

Slovic, P. (1972). From Shakespeare to Simon: Speculations—and some evidence—about man's ability to process information. *Oregon Research Institute Monograph, 12* (Whole No. 2).

Slovic, P., & Fischhoff, B. (1977). On the psychology of experimental surprises. *Journal of Experimental Psychology: Human Perception and Performance, 3,* 544–551.

Snyder, M. (1974). Self-monitoring of expressive behavior. *Journal of Personality and Social Psychology, 30,* 526–537.

Snyder, M. (1979). Self-monitoring processes. *Advances in Experimental Social Psychology, 12,* 85–128.

Snyder, M. (1987). *Public appearances/private realities: The theory of self-monitoring.* New York: W. H. Freeman.

Snyder, M., & Gangestad, S. (1986). On the nature of self-monitoring: Matters of assessment, matters of validity. *Journal of Personality and Social Psychology, 51,* 125–139.

Spencer, R. M., & Weisberg, R. W. (1986). Context-dependent effects on analogical transfer. *Memory & Cognition, 14,* 442–449.

Sternberg, R. J. (1977). *Intelligence, information processing, and analogical reasoning: The componential analysis of human abilities.* Hillsdale, N.J.: Erlbaum.

Sternberg, R. J. (1984). Toward a triarchic theory of human intelligence. *Behavioral and Brain Sciences, 7,* 269–315.

Sternberg, R. J. (1986a). Inside intelligence. *American Scientist, 74,* 137–143.

Sternberg, R. J. (1986b). *Intelligence applied.* San Diego: Harcourt Brace Jovanovich.

Sternberg, R. J., & Detterman, D. K. (Eds.) (1986). *What is intelligence? Contemporary viewpoints on its nature and definition.* Norwood, N.J.: Ablex.

Sweeney, P. D., Anderson, K., & Bailey, S. (1986). Attributional style in depression: A meta-analytic review. *Journal of Personality and Social Psychology, 50,* 974–991.

Targ, R., & Puthoff, H. (1974). Information transmission under conditions of sensory shielding. *Nature, 252,* 602–607.

Taylor, R. (1967). Causation. *Encyclopedia of Philosophy,* Vol. 2 (pp. 56–66). New York: Macmillan.

Tedeschi, J. T., Lindskold, S., & Rosenfeld, P. (1985). *Introduction to social psychology.* St. Paul, Minn.: West.

Tversky, A. (1972). Elimination by aspects: A theory of choice. *Psychological Review, 79,* 281–299.

Tversky, A., & Kahneman, D. (1971). Belief in the law of small numbers. *Psychological Bulletin, 2,* 105–110.

Tversky, A., & Kahneman, D. (1973). Availability: A heuristic for judging frequency and probability. *Cognitive Psychology, 5,* 207–232.

Tversky, A., & Kahneman, D. (1980). Causal schemas in judgments under uncertainty. In M. Fishbein (Ed.), *Progress in social psychology,* Vol. 1 (pp. 49–72). Hillsdale, N.J.: Erlbaum.

Walczyk, J. J., & Hall, V. C. (1989). Effects of examples and embedded questions on the accuracy of comprehension self-assessment. *Journal of Educational Psychology, 81,* 435–437.

Walsh, D., & Paul, R. (1986). *The goal of critical thinking: From educational ideal to educational reality.* Washington, D.C.: American Federation of Teachers.

Walton, D. N. (1989). *Informal logic: A handbook for critical argumentation.* Cambridge: Cambridge University Press.

Ward, W. C., & Jenkins, H. M. (1965). The display of information and the judgment of contingency. *Canadian Journal of Psychology, 19,* 231–241.

Weiner, B. (Ed.). (1974). *Achievement motivation and attribution theory.* Morristown, N.J.: General Learning Press.

Weiner, B., Frieze, I., Kukla, A., Reed, L., Rest, S., & Rosenbaum, R. M. (1971). *Perceiving the causes of success and failure.* Morristown, N.J.: Silver Burdett/General Learning Press.

Weisberg, R. W. (1986). *Creativity: Genius and other myths.* New York: W. H. Freeman.

Wheeler, D. D., & Janis, I. L. (1980). *A practical guide for making decisions.* New York: Free Press.

Whimbey, A., & Lochhead, J. (1986). *Problem solving and comprehension.* Hillsdale, N.J.: Erlbaum.

Wickelgren, W. A. (1974). *How to solve problems: Elements of the theory of problems and problem solving.* San Francisco: W. H. Freeman.

Wilson, Jr., E. B. (1952). *An introduction to scientific research.* New York: McGraw-Hill.

Wilson, T. D., & Linville, P. W. (1985). Improving the performance of college freshmen with attributional techniques. *Journal of Personality and Social Psychology, 49,* 287–293.

Wong, P. T., & Weiner, B. (1981). When people ask "why" questions, and the heuristics of attributional search. *Journal of Personality and Social Psychology, 40,* 650–663.

Zechmeister, E. B. (1989). Mnemonics and noetics. *Teaching Thinking and Problem Solving, 11,* 4–7.

Zechmeister, E. B., & Nyberg, S. E. (1982). *Human memory: An introduction to research and theory.* Pacific Grove, Calif.: Brooks/Cole.

Zechmeister, E. B., Rusch, K. M., & Markell, K. A. (1986). Training college students to assess accurately what they know and don't know. *Human Learning, 5,* 3–19.

# Author Index

# Subject Index